# Business Intelligence and Analytics: Concepts, Techniques and Applications

# Business Intelligence and Analytics: Concepts, Techniques and Applications

Samuel Brooks

MURPHY & MOORE
www.murphy-moorepublishing.com

Published by Murphy & Moore Publishing,
1 Rockefeller Plaza,
New York City, NY 10020, USA



ISBN: 978-1-63987-088-2

**Cataloging-in-Publication Data**

Business intelligence and analytics : concepts, techniques and applications / Samuel Brooks.
p. cm.
Includes bibliographical references and index.
ISBN 978-1-63987-088-2
1. Business intelligence. 2. Business requirements analysis. 3. Business analysts. 4. Business.
5. Management science. I. Brooks, Samuel.
HD38.7 .B87 2022
658.472--dc23

For information on all Murphy & Moore Publications
visit our website at www.murphy-moorepublishing.com

MURPHY & MOORE

# Contents

# Preface

Business intelligence and analytics refers to the set of techniques and strategies which are used by enterprises to convert raw data into meaningful information which drive profitable business actions. These techniques can give insights into historical, current and predictive views of business operations. Some common features of business intelligence technologies are analytics, reporting, benchmarking, data mining, business performance management, predictive analytics, complex event processing and prescriptive analytics. Technologies used in business intelligence are capable of handling both structured and unstructured data. While understanding the long-term perspectives of the topics, the book makes an effort in highlighting their impact as a modern tool for the growth of this discipline business intelligence. The topics included herein on business intelligence are of utmost significance and bound to provide incredible insights to readers. Those in search of information to further their knowledge will be greatly assisted by this book.

To facilitate a deeper understanding of the contents of this book a short introduction of every chapter is written below:

Chapter 1- Business intelligence is a set of processes, architectures and techniques that analyze and convert current and historical data with the objective of improving strategies, decision making and providing a competitive advantage. Financial intelligence, accounting intelligence, commercial intelligence, competitive intelligence, market intelligence, retail intelligence, real-time intelligence, organizational intelligence, etc. are some of its aspects. This chapter serves as an introduction to business intelligence.

Chapter 2- Business analytics is the process by which businesses use statistical methods and technologies to analyze past data and predict future states in order to gain new insights and improve strategic decision-making. Business analytics can be sub-divided into prescriptive analytics, predictive analytics, decision analytics, descriptive analytics, pricing analytics, retail analytics, etc. This chapter sheds light on Business Analytics and its related aspects to provide a better understanding of the topic.

Chapter 3- Business intelligence and analytics cannot work without data and it comes in all sorts of shapes and sizes. Data and its related topics like big data, data mining, data warehouse, data presentation architecture, data sampling, data preparation, data visualization, data profiling, data filtering, data clearing, etc. are examined extensively in this chapter for the reader's benefit.

Chapter 4- Operational intelligence is an approach to data analysis that enables decisions and actions in business operations to be based on real-time data as it is generated or collected by companies. Business activity monitoring, complex event processing, business process management, metadata, root cause analysis, etc. are some of its concepts. This chapter closely examines the technical components of operational intelligence to provide an extensive understanding of the subject.

Chapter 5- Business analytics makes use of data and models to expedite decision making processes or solve various kinds of decision problems. Business performance management, customer analytics, diamond model, funnel analytics, uplift modeling, win-loss analytics, etc. are included in its domain. This chapter covers the subject matter in a comprehensive manner.

I owe the completion of this book to the never-ending support of my family, who supported me throughout the project.

**Samuel Brooks**

# 1

# An Introduction to Business Intelligence

Business intelligence is a set of processes, architectures and techniques that analyze and convert current and historical data with the objective of improving strategies, decision making and providing a competitive advantage. Financial intelligence, accounting intelligence, commercial intelligence, competitive intelligence, market intelligence, retail intelligence, real-time intelligence, organizational intelligence, etc. are some of its aspects. This chapter serves as an introduction to business intelligence.

Business intelligence (BI) combines business analytics, data mining, data visualization, data tools and infrastructure, and best practices to help organizations to make more data-driven decisions. In practice, you know you've got modern business intelligence when you have a comprehensive view of your organization's data and use that data to drive change eliminate inefficiencies, and quickly adapt to market or supply changes.

It's important to note that this is a very modern definition of BI—and BI has had a strangled history as a buzzword. Traditional Business Intelligence, capital letters and all, originally emerged in the 1960s as a system of sharing information across organizations. It further developed in the 1980s alongside computer models for decision-making and turning data into insights before becoming specific offering from BI teams with IT-reliant service solutions. Modern BI solutions prioritize flexible self-service analysis, governed data on trusted platforms, empowered business users, and speed to insight.

## Examples of Business Intelligence

Much more than a specific "thing," business intelligence is rather an umbrella term that covers the processes and methods of collecting, storing, and analyzing data from business operations or activities to optimize performance. All of these things come together to create a comprehensive view of a business to help people make better, actionable decisions.

Over the past few years, business intelligence has evolved to include more processes and activities to help improve performance. These processes include:

- Data mining: Using databases, statistics and machine learning to uncover trends in large datasets.
- Reporting: Sharing data analysis to stakeholders so they can draw conclusions and make decisions.
- Performance metrics and benchmarking: Comparing current performance data to historical data to track performance against goals, typically using customized dashboards.
- Descriptive analytics: Using preliminary data analysis to find out what happened.
- Querying: Asking the data specific questions, BI pulling the answers from the datasets.

- Statistical analysis: Taking the results from descriptive analytics and further exploring the data using statistics such as how this trend happened and why.
- Data visualization: Turning data analysis into visual representations such as charts, graphs, and histograms to more easily consume data.
- Visual analysis: Exploring data through visual storytelling to communicate insights on the fly and stay in the flow of analysis.
- Data preparation: Compiling multiple data sources, identifying the dimensions and measurements, preparing it for data analysis.

## Importance of Business Intelligence

Business intelligence can help companies make better decisions by showing present and historical data within their business context. Analysts can leverage BI to provide performance and competitor benchmarks to make the organization run smoother and more efficiently. Analysts can also more easily spot market trends to increase sales or revenue. Used effectively, the right data can help with anything from compliance to hiring efforts.

A few ways that business intelligence can help companies make smarter, data-driven decisions:

- Identify ways to increase profit,
- Analyze customer behavior,
- Compare data with competitors,
- Track performance,
- Optimize operations,
- Predict success,
- Spot market trends,
- Discover issues or problems.

## How Business Intelligence Works

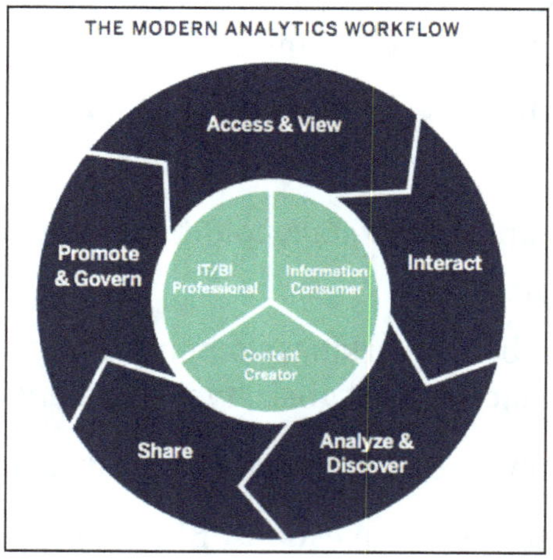

Businesses and organizations have questions and goals. To answer these questions and track performance against these goals, they gather the necessary data, analyze it, and determine which actions to take to reach their goals.

On the technical side, raw data is collected from the business's activity. Data is processed and then stored in data warehouses. Once it's stored, users can then access the data, starting the analysis process to answer business questions.

## How BI, Data Analytics and Business Analytics Work Together

Business intelligence includes data analytics and business analytics, but uses them only as parts of the whole process. BI helps users draw conclusions from data analysis. Data scientists dig into the specifics of data, using advanced statistics and predictive analytics to discover patterns and forecast future patterns. Data analytics asks "Why did this happen and what can happen next?" Business intelligence takes those models and algorithms and breaks the results down into actionable language.

According to Gartner's IT glossary, "business analytics includes data mining, predictive analytics, applied analytics, and statistics." In short, organizations conduct business analytics as part of their larger business intelligence strategy. BI is designed to answer specific queries and provide at-a-glance analysis for decisions or planning. However, companies can use the processes of analytics to continually improve follow-up questions and iteration.

Business analytics shouldn't be a linear process because answering one question will likely lead to follow-up questions and iteration. Rather, think of the process as a cycle of data access, discovery, exploration, and information sharing. This is called the cycle of analytics, a modern term explaining how businesses use analytics to react to changing questions and expectations.

## Difference between Traditional BI and Modern BI

Historically, business intelligence tools were based on a traditional business intelligence model. This was a top-down approach where business intelligence was driven by the IT organization and most, if not all, analytics questions were answered through static reports. This meant that if someone had a follow-up question about the report they received, their request would go to the bottom of the reporting queue and they would have to start the process over again. This led to slow and frustrating reporting cycles and people weren't able to leverage current data to make decisions. Traditional business intelligence is still a common approach for regular reporting and answering static queries.

However, modern business intelligence is interactive and approachable. While IT departments are still an important part of managing access to data, multiple levels of users can customize dashboards and create reports on little notice. With the proper software, users are empowered to visualize data and answer their own questions.

## How Major Industries use Business Intelligence

Many disparate industries have adopted BI ahead of the curve, including healthcare, information technology, and education. All organizations can use data to transform operations.

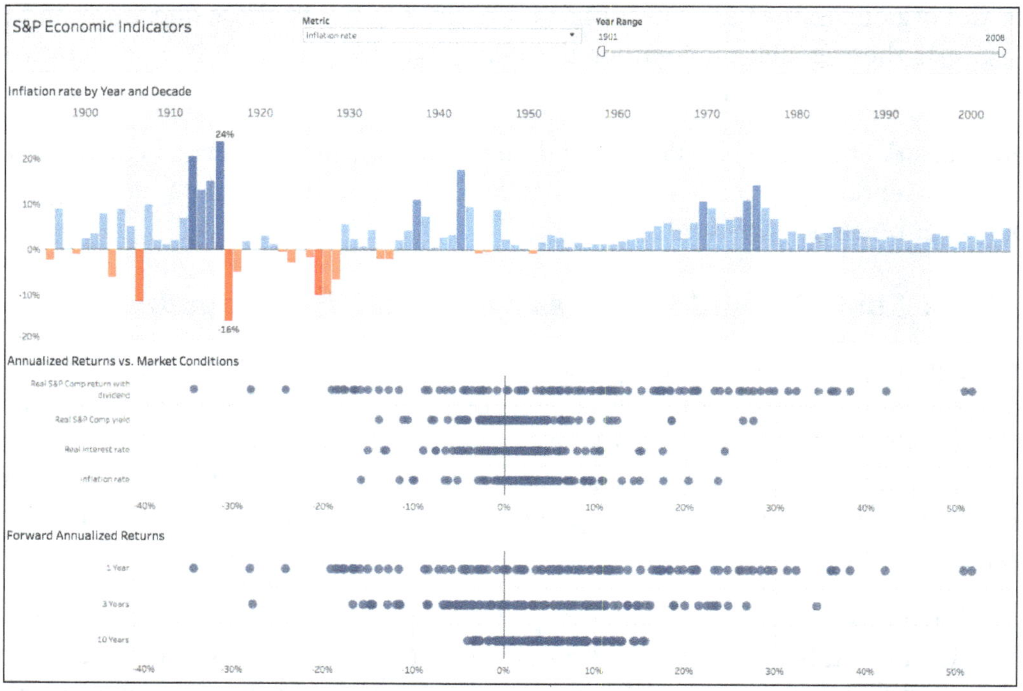


Example of an economic indicators dashboard, showing the long-term drivers of the U.S. economy.

Financial services firms used business intelligence to see a comprehensive view of all of their branches across the United States to understand performance metrics and identify areas of opportunity. Access to a central business intelligence platform allowed Schwab to bring all of their branch data into one view.

Now branch managers can identify clients that may have a change in investment needs. And leadership can track if a region's performance is above or below average and click in to see the branches that are driving that region's performance. This leads to more opportunities for optimization along with better customer service for clients.

## Business Intelligence Tools and Platforms

Many self-service business intelligence tools and platforms streamline the analysis process. This makes it easier for people to see and understand their data without the technical know-how to dig into the data themselves. There are many BI platforms available for ad hoc reporting, data visualization, and creating customized dashboards for multiple levels of users. One of the more common ways to present business intelligence is through data visualization.

## Benefits of Visual Analytics and Data Visualization

One of the more common ways to present business intelligence is through data visualization. Humans are visual creatures and very in tune with patterns or differences in colors. Data visualizations show data in a way that is more accessible and understandable.

Visualizations compiled into dashboards can quickly tell a story and highlight trends or patterns that may not be discovered easily when manually analyzing the raw data. This accessibility also enables more conversations around the data, leading to broader business impact.

## Semantic Business Intelligence

Fierce competition in the digital economy and increasing volume of available data are forcing organizations to find efficient ways to gain valuable information and knowledge to improve the efficiency of their business processes. Business Intelligence (BI) solutions offer the means to transform data to information and derive knowledge through analytical tools in order to support decision making. Analytical tools should support decision makers to find information quickly and enable them to make well-informed decisions.

Despite the importance of analytical tools to organizations, there are challenges that should be tackled in order to leverage the impact of those tools in the decision making process. These challenges include difficulties to extend those tools according to the business requirements, no support to analyze and interpret data and lack of flexibility to customize information presentation according to users' profile.

## The Semantic Business Intelligence Architecture

The SBI architecture comprehends a set of loosely-coupled modules that are illustrated in the figure below. The SBI ontologies comprise business semantics and describe the relationship among such semantics, BI terminology, operational semantics, and data sources.

SBI ontologies are used by the Query Manager to parse analytical tools and data requests, and to execute such requests on heterogeneous data sources, enabling the combination of unstructured and structured data on the very same analysis. The Ontology Manager is the module that provides access to SBI ontologies. Such module relies on a Reasoner to support on-the-fly and batch based inferences over business semantics. These inferences make semantic driven slice and drill based on business rules possible.

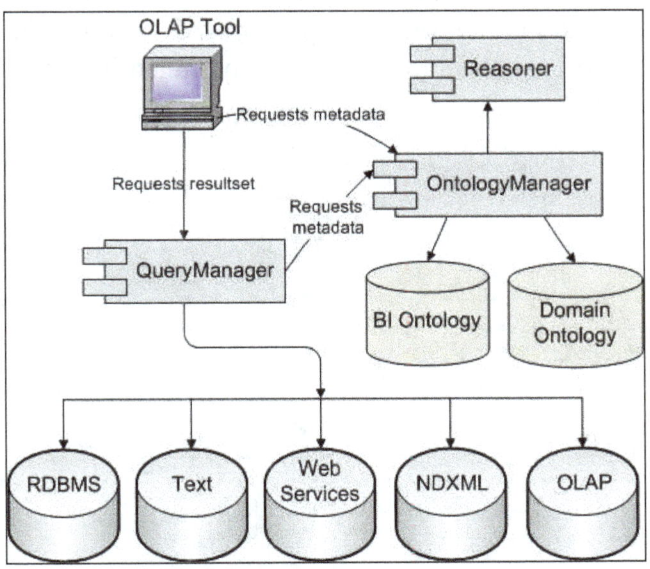


Illustration of SBI main components.

## The SBI Ontologies

In current version, the SBI ontologies have a version modeled in RDF and OWL.

## The Domain Ontology

The domain ontology supplies the business terminology used to enable data sources annotation. Therefore, users will be able to explore information repositories by using business concepts instead of technical descriptions. Also, the relations, rules, and logical expressions described in the domain ontology will support semantic drill and slice, query definition, and extraction of further details from data presented by analytical tools.

All required inferences to extend the analytical functionalities are supported by business rules and expressions represented in the domain ontology. Domain specific relations and rules can be defined to slice and drill OLAP cubes. The Listing below defines the Alumni rule that infers institutions in which students have completed their degree. A new relation called is Alumni between Person class and Institution class is inferred by this business rule.

Person(?p) ∧ Degree(?d) ∧ Institution(?i) ∧
hasDegree(?p, ?d) ∧ hasInstituion(?d, ?i) ∧
isCompleted(?d, 'yes') → isAlumni (?p, ?i)

Listing: The Alumni rule: former student of an institution.

## The BI Ontology

The BI ontology models the concepts used to describe how the data is organized in data sources and to map such data to the concepts described in the domain ontology. These definitions are used to: a) support inferences using the domain ontology to extend query results; b) support the presentation of query results using business terminology; c) provide an abstraction of data sources to guide the interaction of decision maker on the exploration of organizations' information sources. The main concepts related to business intelligence are modeled in the BI ontology. Figure below shows its main constructors.

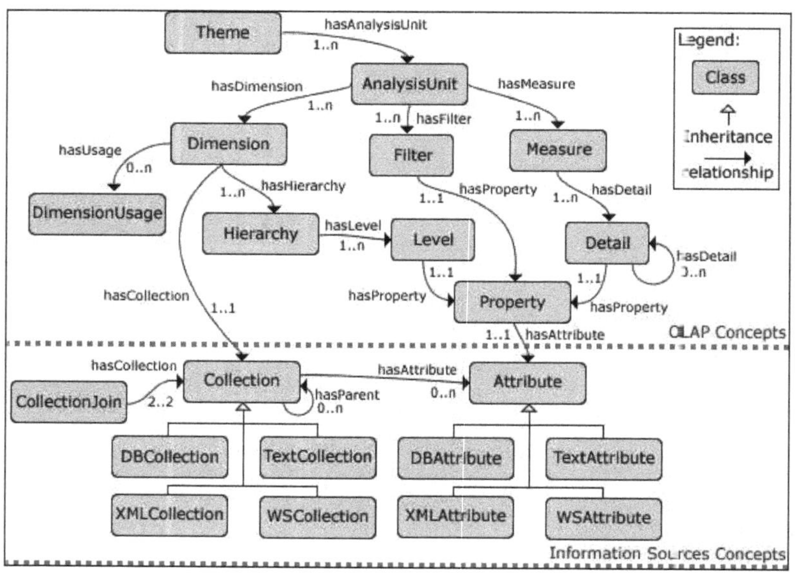


The BI ontology's main constructors.

As depicted in Figure above, the BI ontology maps OLAP concepts used by analytical tools to guide decision makers on analysis definitions and to provide semantic drill and slice operations. The information source concepts are used to represent data source structures and to map those structures to domain concepts represented in the domain ontology. The Table below presents more details about BI ontology concepts.

Table: Description of BI ontology concepts.

| Concept | Description |
|---|---|
| Theme | A Theme represents documents, fact and dimension tables associated with a business process (e.g. *R&D*). |
| Analysis Unit | It defines fact tables and document collections related to a specific subject of a theme. In the R&D theme, for instance, one can find Analysis Units such as *School dropout*. An Analysis Unit may have several dimensions and measures. |
| Measure | This concept is used to represent quantitative values, aggregations or summarizations related to Analysis Unit content (e.g. *Number of students*). |
| Filter | Filters are dimension attributes that could be applied to slice and dice data related to an Analysis Unit (e.g. Students age, gender and so on). |
| Dimension | It describes analysis unit's dimensions. Dimensions can have many Hierarchies and properties (e.g. *State*). |
| Hierarchy | This concept describes dimension hierarchies. Each hierarchy is Composed of one or more levels (e.g. *City, State, and Country*). |
| Level | It represents a hierarchy level that is used on drill-up and drill-Down operations. |
| Detail | It describes how an analysis unit can be detailed or presented in its Atomic level. (E.g. *name, e-mail*). |
| Property | Property identifies the terminology used to present an information unit. It also maps instances of the attribute concept to instances of Detail, filter, level, and measure concepts. |
| Dimension Usage | It describes how data collections are linked to analysis units. |
| Collection | This concept represents a data collection or a data provider and Describes how these data sources relate to the concepts represented in the domain ontology. |
| Collection Join | It describes how a collection can be joined to another collection. It also identifies which properties and operations are used to join two Collections. |
| Attribute | It corresponds to items contained in collections such as table fields, XML elements, entities extracted from documents, or spreadsheet columns. The Attribute concept also associates these elements with slots of concepts represented in the domain ontology. |

## SBI Functional Modules

SBI ontologies are used by functional modules to support analytical tools on the localization and exploration of data sources.

The QueryManager supports analytical tools by providing a transparent access to heterogeneous data sources and data providers based on a XML-based protocol. It enables the combination of query results from structured or non-structured data sources, independently of their localization. The QueryManager hides data sources complexities from analytical tools. Requests of analytical tools are translated by QueryManager in queries that are processed on corresponding data sources. Analysis definitions (i.e. analysis units, filters, measures and so on) from analytical tools are received and translated in an XML message. The Ontology Manager retrieves the information required from the BI ontology.

The OntologyManager component is responsible for manipulating the BI ontology and retrieving the necessary information to support the formulation of data requests. It retrieves details about data collections such as table names, their field definitions and their relationships from concepts defined in the domain ontology.

QueryManager performs intersections or unions between heterogeneous repositories by using common attributes of each result set returned by drivers. For instance, an inverted index structure is used just to find the papers ids produced by students, and these id's are used to join with other information about such students stored in a data mart. In this example, one can summarize the number of students by department that has written papers that mention the term "semantic web."

For each type of data repository or data provider, we create a different driver to handle specific issues of that data source. For instance, in the textual driver, a set of algorithms were used for data indexing and retrieval, while the RDBMS driver uses JDBC driver to access relational data bases.

## Reasoning

Since SBI ontologies are described in formal language that enables the explication of business rules and the definition of axioms for specifying relationships between concepts, Semantic slice and drill are made possible by the architecture ontologies in which relations and rules are applied to filter or expand the results of queries relying on synonyms, hyponyms, and other relations specified in the SBI ontologies.

In order to infer new knowledge or, more precisely, to provide new ways to decision makers explore their data, we have integrated Ontology Manager to Jena and Pellet. All results of inferences are stored in a data mart, more specifically in a star schema called Triple Model. The Triple Model is used as an extension of a dimensional model and its tables can be connected to the remaining tables in data marts. In this strategy, semantic inferences occur in batch as the traditional ETL processing. So, besides the strategic information available in the dimensional model, the OLAP tools can also access the inferred conclusions from business rules processed over the data stored in data marts.

The triple model is composed of an associative table, called Triple Fact, and a dimension, called Inferred Predicate. The triple fact table is responsible for storing inferred information that describes different relationships between two dimensions. The relationships inferred from business rules are stored in the inferred predicate dimension. In the triple model the reference of each dimension represents a subject or an object similarly to RDF statements.

Figure illustrates the Triple Model integrated to a star schema. In this example, the DI_PERSON dimension is a subject and the DI_INSTITUTION dimension is an object of a statement stored in the triple fact table. Such relation has been inferred from business rules such as works in, graduated in and alumnus of described in the domain ontology.

Our approach enables the creation of multiples associations between dimensions based on business rules. For instance, at any time, a knowledge engineer can add new business rules in the domain ontology to define new kinds of relationships between people and institutions.

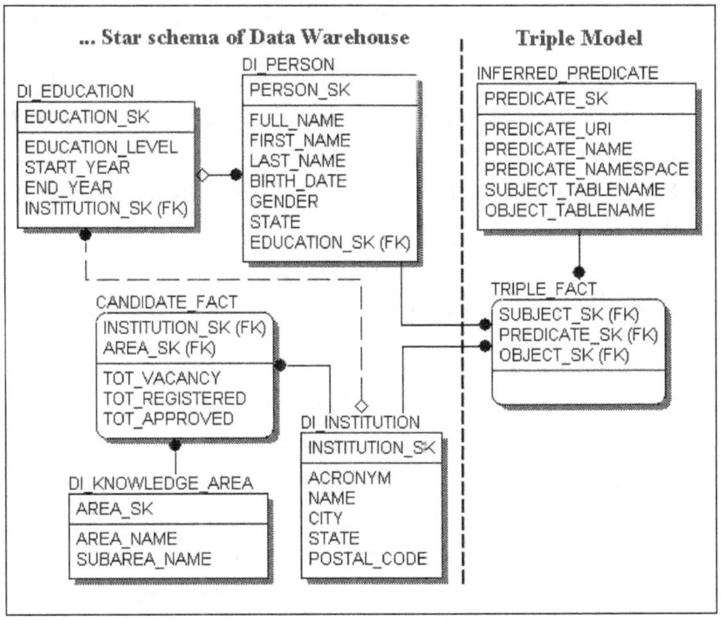


The triple model and its integration with star schema.

The reasoning process is performed by a Reasoner such as Pellet integrated to the Ontology Manager, as follows:

- The Ontology Manager imports the domain ontology model and its business rules. In this step, in the R&D scenario described before all classes, properties, axioms and business rules are brought to the Ontology Manager Work area.
- The Ontology Manager reads all BI ontology instances used to map the domain ontology to data sources. In this step, each concept defined in the R&D domain ontology will be associated to the Collection class' instances. In addition, all domain properties will be associated to instances of Attribute and Collection Join classes.
- The Ontology Manager retrieves the necessary data to create the domain ontology instances. The query is guided by the mapping between business concepts and data sources defined in the BI ontology.
- New instances of domain ontology are created by Ontology Manager based on the information retrieved in the last step.
- Once created the instances, the reasoner is invoked to perform inferences based on business rules defined in the domain ontology. In this step, the Alumni rule shown in the Listing above is applied.
- At last, the Ontology Manager stores inferred concepts from domain ontology into triple model. The new inferred concepts are saved into the inferred predicate dimension and the new relations between two dimensions are stored in the Triple Fact.

The inferred information stored in the Triple Model may be accessed by analytical tools to offer decision makers the possibility to slice, dice and drill over data sources by applying business rules defined in the domain ontology.

## SBI and its Question Answering Approach to Support Decision Making

It is true that the simplicity of current Web search continuously contributes to the growth of its popularity. The ease of use in these search interfaces allows that by informing a few words in free text one can find almost any type of content so fast and ubiquitous. For its intuitive and natural way of providing access to information for people of virtually all ages, the same metaphor of Web search should be considered for the next generation of BI solutions. Such trend for the future of BI takes into account its proximity to resources and services of the Web, both in the use of heterogeneous sources as in the way of finding information.

The combination between the new research on BI and aspirations of the Semantic Web is focus of study that can be addressed further. To meet different stakeholders, it is necessary to the analytical tools rely on strategies for the representation of business knowledge and mechanisms the make it possible the use of that knowledge in the exploration of data sources. Just as the Semantic Web provides agile ways and navigation interfaces based on high semantic expressiveness to locate relevant content on the Internet, BI architectures must also make use of semantic to support the analytical processing. However, BI solutions lack the use of effective methods of exploration of content such as those already used by the billions of current Web users, yet without losing the potential conjectured by the Semantic Web.

Analytical tools usually require long and expensive training sessions due to: a) the potential number of users and time needed to train those users; b) the complexity of the tools; and c) the skills of each user. To reduce these costs, the use of natural language is considered one of the most appropriate and feasible strategy. Therefore, the ability to express information needs through natural language should be introduced in the new BI architectures and is the goal of this work.

In this research, analysis submitted to the organization' data sources, instead of being guided through the conventional OLAP operations, are carried out through the semantic interpretation of a question expressed in natural language. That is, we provide access to OLAP cubes through questions stated by users in their language, in which the concepts and terminology of the business are expressed descriptively and independent of specific formalisms.

Unlike the strategies of searches driven by keywords, we apply an approach based on knowledge engineering methods and Question Answering (QA) techniques. This approach is characterized by adopting more significant use of natural language or questions for returning a data cube that may have the information required by the decision maker.

## Question Answering Support

The processing of natural language questions is performed by the modules of the architecture in three main steps:

- A step associated with the construction and maintenance of the model and knowledge base, which is essential for the subsequent steps.
- A second step related to the interpretation of the question and its formalization in a structure that represents its meaning.
- A third and final step responsible for returning an OLAP cube.

The first step occurs prior to the decision-making process and should be performed regularly according to the evolution of the domain ontology and to the growth and changes in data sources of the organization. It aims at preparing the ontology and knowledge base used both in the process of analysis and interpretation of the question formulated by decision makers. In the second step, the question reported in natural language is analyzed and processed by a set of methods and technologies that rely on the semantic context defined by the organization's domain ontology. Here, some QA tasks are applied to the interpretation of questions aimed at translating the natural language in a formal language. This formal representation of the resulting question has the definition of quantitative measures, descriptive groupings and filters for the execution of OLAP operations (e.g. drill-down, roll-up, slice, dice, etc). Once the query is built and formalized, in the last step the information request is performed on the data sources in order to answer the question.

The following figure shows the arrangement of the complementary elements of the SBI architecture as follows:

- Processes and techniques - Representing the tasks, techniques, procedures and processes performed by functional modules of the architecture.
- Inputs and outputs - Input data and results of the processes and techniques.
- Functional modules - Architecture subsystems or components developed by third parties that have some peculiarities in the roles they play.
- Repositories and data sources - Include repositories of ontologies, models and knowledge base, configuration items and also the data sources.

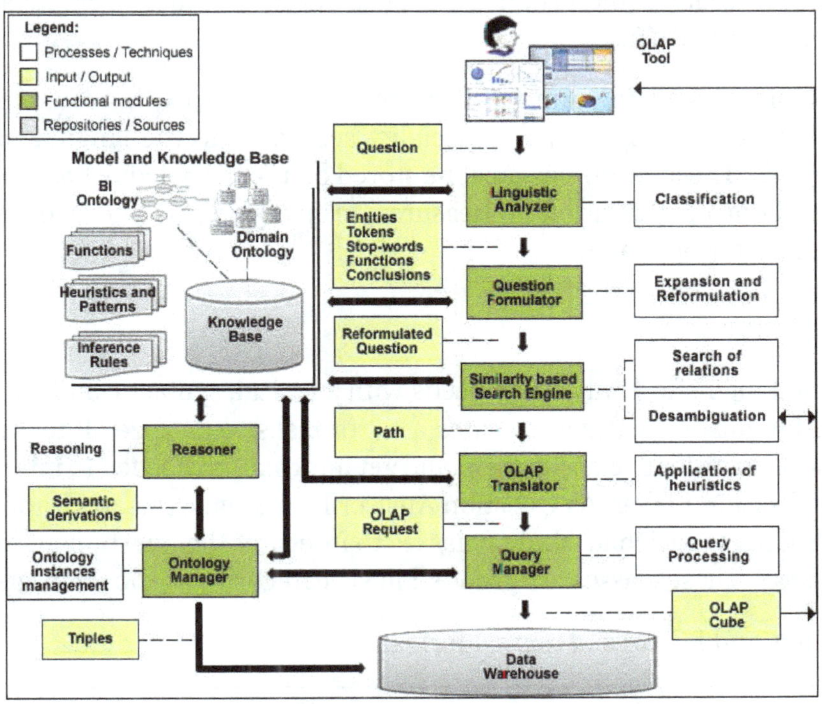


Schematic view of QA modules.

In a nutshell, the question after being informed by the decision maker in the OLAP module is assessed by the Linguistic Analyzer. This module classifies all the elements of the question as specific concepts, such as textual entities, stop-words, functions and other specific classifications reported below. From the classification of the tokens of the question, the module applies query expansion and reformulation techniques to detail and expand the question proposed originally. Based on the reformulated question, the module Similarity Search Engine tries to find relationships between concepts and entities in the question by searching the domain ontology. Once discovered the relationships between concepts in domain ontology, the OLAP Translator converts the question in a formal request, including the definitions of filters, projections and quantitative measures to be considered in the query. Then, the Query Manager performs the request on the DW to return the OLAP cube with the strategic information to decision makers. The semantic inferences performed in the process can be combined with information from the DW. The Knowledge Base serves as a central element in which the functional modules rely to complete each task. The following section describes the main SBI modules.

## Knowledge Base

The Knowledge Base comprises knowledge resources required in all the steps from the interpretation of decision makers' questions to the queries execution on data sources, as follows:

- Knowledge Base and Inference Rules: Repository formed by the instances of the Domain Ontology, the organization's business rules and instances of the BI Ontology.
- Functions: Consist of functions that must be associated with some specifics words used by the decision maker and with some domain ontology concept. A function assigns one output (e.g. dates, numbers, etc.) to each specific input text. For instance, the words Today, Tomorrow, Yesterday could produce a date as output in order to create an instance of the ontology class called Time.
- Heuristics and Linguistic patterns: It represents regular expressions, lexical and syntax patterns, heuristics designed by a specialist according to the language and the distance between words. These resources must be stored on the Knowledge Base in order to support OLAP Translator identification of measures, projections and filters in the question introduced by the decision maker.

## Linguistic Analyzer

In the first step, the Linguistic Analyzer proceeds with a lexical, syntactic and semantic analysis of the question. The Linguistic Analyzer executes a set of tasks to analyze all textual elements contained in the question in order to classify them and get information needed to interpret the question formulated by the decision maker. As Question Answering systems, this work applies classification tasks and also introduces particular kind of classes to interpret the question and to support OLAP queries on Data Marts. These classes are grouped in six categories as shown in the table below:

Table: Classifications and features of textual terms.

| Classification or feature | Description |
|---|---|
| Stop-word | Words with a high frequency in texts and usually with no relevant content in traditional QA works. In this research, the stop-words are particularly useful in the identification of OLAP constructors, such as measures, projections and filters. |

| | |
|---|---|
| Position or Order | It identifies the position or order of each token in the question. This information is used to recognize the linguistic patterns and heuristics, in which are stored on the Knowledge Base, according to distances between classes of words. |
| Function | When a term is associated with a function defined in the Model and Knowledge Base. |
| Conclusion of inference rule | When the term is contained in a conclusion of inference rules. (E.g. the concept "Alumni" presented in the listing). |
| Entity or Domain concept | It represents a domain ontology concept, such as, a class, a relationship, a property or an instance of a class. |
| Unknown token | Tokens not classified by the Linguistic Analyzer. |

Linguistic Analyzer executes some techniques of natural language processing to classify question terms, namely, POS-Tagging, Lemmatization, Stemming, Named-Entity Recognition, Co-reference and search into dictionaries.

During the classification task, some textual elements can generate ambiguities. That is, Linguistic Analyzer can identify two or more classifications for the same term. Likewise, a term classified as a domain concept may represent a class, a property of class, a relationship or an instance of class as well. These ambiguities are not resolved by Linguistic Analyzer and they are processed and eliminated by the module called Similarity Search Engine afterward.

After of the classification tasks, the question can be reformulated and expanded by the Query Formulator module presented below. The Linguistic Analyzer performs a process with emphasis on each specific term of the question without focusing on the semantic relations among words. The Similarity Search Engine, by verifying the relationship between words and contextual information, can reduce or even eliminate the ambiguities. Therefore, the disambiguation is delayed and performed only once through the Similarity Search Engine. In practice, the Linguistic Analyzer identifies an ambiguity in the question when:

- The textual entity is an instance of two or more classes of the domain ontology.
- The textual entity is a class and is similar to two or more classes of the ontology. This case appears when two or more classes have the same name or synonyms in common and are mentioned in the question.
- The textual entity is a relationship or property and belongs to two or more classes involved in the question. This case is commonly found as the concepts can share the same properties or have equivalent relationships in a given context.
- The textual entity has similarity between classes, instances, properties or relationships of the domain ontology. This occurs when the term has the same textual description of a class, also a property or a class instance.

Once executed the process of linguistic analysis and obtained ratings for all the terms, the question can be reformulated or expanded through the Question Formulation module.

## Question Formulation

Once the lexical-syntactic and semantic classifications are obtained from the elements of the text, the question is reformulated. This process aims to enrich and expand the original question in order to generate all the information necessary to create the OLAP request later. The reformulation process is also a characteristic of Question Answering systems. It comes to finding important facts related to the domain that have been omitted or reported differently by the user and that should be incorporated to complete and formalize the question. This work uses two types of reformulation that can be applied successively. The first strategy is based on the class hierarchy and synonymy relations and the other applies a rule-based inference approach.

The synonyms as well as super classes and subclasses of the entities found in the question are necessary in the question reformulation because there are different ways to express the same request through natural language. Thus, the terminology that was reported in a given question can be exchanged for another that is more adherent or closer to the domain context.

The reformulation by inference rules is applied when the query terms are classified by Linguistic Analyzer as being conclusions of inference rules. At this stage the facts contained in the conclusions or consequents of the rules are used to reformulate the question. That is, the triple of concepts that is in the consequent of a rule is used to replace the term classified as conclusion of the inference rule by Linguistic Analyzer.

From the classification and reformulation tasks made by linguistic analysis and query reformulation respectively, the next step is finding which path or set of relationships between concepts that best fit the question.

## Similarity Search Engine

Based on the question reformulated in the previous step, the Similarity Search Engine performs a search on the model of the domain ontology to discover which path is closer to the context of the question. The textual elements used in the question are confronted with the concepts represented in the domain ontology by Similarity Search Engine in order to check the best path (or the only set of relationships between concepts used in the question) that can resolve the question. Therefore, the concepts of the domain ontology, along with their synonyms and hierarchies are used to evaluate possible alternatives to extract the information required by the decision maker.

The Similarity Search Engine analyses the sequence of concepts or classes (vertices) mentioned in the question and their relationships (edges) in the domain ontology. The Similarity Search Engine chooses the best way to solve the question considering all the terminology given by the decision maker. In this research, as applied by Lopez et al., the best path is characterized as the one that presents the greatest amount of relevant concepts and relationships according to the terms informed in the question.

The Similarity Search Engine may find more than one possible path to tackle the question. Thus, in addition to previously scenarios of ambiguities solved by Linguistic analysis, this module is responsible for resolving ambiguities among candidate paths. Therefore, two types of disambiguation are likely to be made by the Search Engine Similarity: disambiguation of concepts (i.e. considering classes and properties ambiguous) and disambiguation of paths (i.e. considering relationships ambiguous).

Both disambiguation processes may require decision maker intervention to complete. According to the user's choice in this process, the question is refined iteratively until there is no doubt the meaning of the elements mentioned in the question and about which is the best path to solve the information request.

The Similarity Search Engine, as its name indicates, performs searches on the domain ontology, relying on synonyms, class hierarchy, and other types of relationships defined in the ontology. Searches are supported by a textual index in order to speed up the path retrieval. After discovering the best path as well as the concepts related to the terms mentioned in the information request, the final query can be built and processed on the data sources. The work of translating the best path in a request to explore the Data Warehouse is performed by the OLAP translator described in the next section.

## OLAP Translator

The OLAP Translator, based on the path chosen in the last step, identifies the measures, groupings, filters and connections between concepts that may be applied in order to extract the data needed to solve the information request. a translation of the best path found by the search engines to an OLAP request, which will be performed later by DW Query Manager module.

Measures represent numerical measurements (sum, average, minimum, maximum, etc.) on a particular domain concept. Measures classified by the OLAP Translator are associated with facts and attributes of dimensions defined in the dimensional model. The concepts translated as groupings identify the descriptive information used to group or categorize the measures in the queries. These concepts should generally be associated with attributes of the DW dimensions and are the classes' properties.

When the concepts are translated as filters, the values related to these concepts are used as selection criteria in the OLAP request. Usually, the element of the question is translated as a filter when referring to a class instance, or when a value of a property identifier (name, initials, date, etc.) is given. In addition to the measures, grouping and filters, the OLAP translator should also define how should be represented the relationships of these items. Each relationship between the classes denotes joins or connections that must be used between objects of the data sources. All relationships between concepts, including those resulting from the inference rules in the process of reformulation, must be presented on the result produced by the Similarity Search Engine.

In order to make the translation of the path in a query, OLAP translator uses a set of patterns and heuristics based on distance or position between the concepts of the question and stop-words. Although the words classified as stop-words are ignored by most IR systems, they are essential at this stage of translation. Generally, research on QA applies stop-words to classify the type of question and also to identify the syntactic pattern to answer it correctly. In this work, the stop-words also help the discovery of the elements of OLAP query, such as measures, grouping, filters and joins.

All syntactic patterns and heuristics along with a list of stop-words used by OLAP translator must be configured according to the language in the knowledge base. This setting allows regular expressions and criteria based on the position or distance between tokens and stop-words to be used by the OLAP Translator. Thus, there is greater flexibility in the recognition of elements of the query according to the idiomatic patterns or writing mode of decision makers.

To perform the translation and to set standards in the Knowledge Base, this paper adopts three types of stop-words arranged as shown in Table below.

Table: Types of stop-words for OLAP translation.

| Stop-word type | Query element | Description |
|---|---|---|
| Quantification | Measure | Stop-words that deal with numeric values summarization or calculations and data quantification.<br>Expressions such as *how many*, *how much*, and its variants, such as *which and total* are considered. |
| Projection | Grouping | Stop-words used to categorize or group content typically descriptive, without the need to quantify them, such as the dimension attributes. Examples are the stop-words *by, for, as, grouped by, second*, etc., on questions like "how many students by age and by city study in the South?" |
| Selection | Filter | Stop-words used to filter a data set – relational operators such as *above, equal to, greater than, less than*, etc. and even logical (logical operators), such as *AND* and *OR*. Example of question with relational stop-words: "How many specialists *over* 40 years and *below* 50 years have published articles in 2010?" Example of question with logical stop-words: "How many teachers *and* students study Human Physiology *or* Occupational Health?" |

## Applying SBI on Science and Technology Management

Let us discuss an application of the architecture for the Science and Technology management, including the evaluation and analysis of intellectual productions and academic and professional activities of researchers, teachers and students of Federal University of Santa Catarina (UFSC). The sample data used as data source comes from the Lattes Institutional Platform (LIP), from UFSC. Thus, the main concepts and terminology - such as person, degree, educational institution, academic and professional activity, production, among others - are modeled in the domain ontology.

From the domain ontology, a structure similar to a textual index was created so that the best path can be located by Similarity Search Engine. As in IR models, this index forms a matrix with the set of terms and their synonyms extracted from each path of the domain ontology. Figure below illustrates how some of the paths (concepts and relationships of domain ontology) are organized into an IR Boolean model. This type of model is adopted in the construction of the architecture to demonstrate how the paths can be discovered in practice. However, the architecture does not limit the adoption of other forms and structures for organizing and finding paths. Thus, other mechanisms and methods can be used to support the construction of the Knowledge Base module, in order to fulfill the goal of the Similarity Search Engine module.

Due to the presence of synonyms and class hierarchies in the matrix of paths, the process of reformulation based on class hierarchy and synonyms is treated at once by Similarity Search Engine. Thus, the Similarity Search Engine developed also acts as a reformulate, except for cases of reformulation by inference rules.

Based on the matrix created, the question, after passing through the stages of linguistic analysis and reformulation, is used as input vector by Similarity Search Engine to perform a search. Here, all stop-words are ignored and only they are exploited later by OLAP Translator.

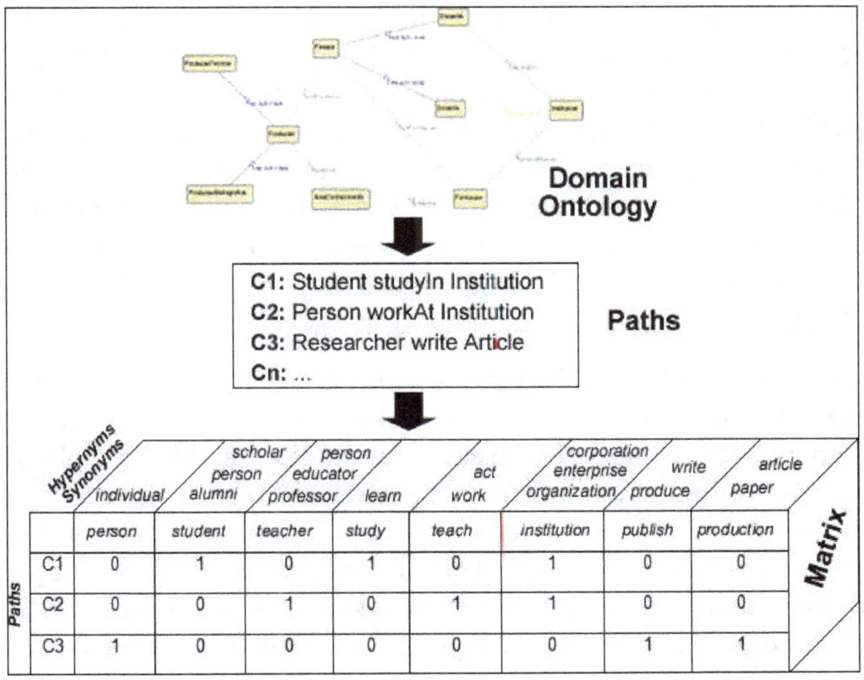


Illustration of the matrix of paths obtained from the domain ontology.

Based on the domain context and in the language used, Knowledge Base should also contain the knowledge of how to identify the elements of OLAP queries, such as measures, groupings, filters and joins. This knowledge is formed by the lexical-syntactical patterns, the relative positions of the query terms and by heuristics based on the types of stop-words previously described in Table above. The representations of these patterns and heuristics are formalized in the Knowledge Base by means of regular expressions that match the positions of recognized entities of the question and the types of stop-words. The patterns and heuristics used by the OLAP Translator module are detailed in Table below according to each element of the associated query (measure, grouping, filter or join).

Table: Patterns and heuristics used to formulate OLAP requests.

| No. | Query element | Description of the pattern or heuristic |
|---|---|---|
| 1 | Measure | All terms classified as classes and class properties positioned immediately to the right of stop-words of quantification, which are followed or not by the tokens AND or OR, are classified as measures. |
| 2 | Grouping | All terms classified as classes and class properties located to the right of stop-words of projection, which are followed or not by the tokens AND or OR, are classified as groupings. |
| 3 | Grouping | The direct classes of terms classified as instances of classes are always used as groupings. |
| 4 | Filter | All terms classified as instances of classes or identified as class property values are used as filters.<br><br>If the term is not to the right of a stop-word of selection, the criterion of equality (=) is used to filter the content; otherwise, the stop-word of selection will be considered. The tokens AND and OR present between the values of properties or instances of classes are used as logical operators of the filter criteria. |
| 5 | Join or relationship | All relationships between the concepts of domain ontology are used as joins or relationships in OLAP request. In own BI Ontology mapping, these relationships must be matched with joints or relationship between the tables and dimensions in the query. |

To clarify how heuristics and patterns are applied, consider the following question: “How many students, by gender and academic training, study at CSE or CFH?” The terms superscript numbers refer to the number of the respective pattern or heuristics. In this example, the term “students” refers to the class “Student” and is classified as a measure because it has proximity to the right of the stop-word How many (by Rule 1). The attribute set in the BI Ontology as a standard measure of the class “Student” should be used to quantify the information in the query. Yet, the two terms “gender” and “academic training”, although with the same numbering (number 2), the first represents a property of the class “Person” and the second represents directly the class “Degree” on the domain ontology.

In this case, the first (the term “gender”) is used directly as a grouping, the second (the term “education”), the default attribute of the class “Education” is defined as a group that should be applied. The terms “CSE” and “CFH”, instances of the class “Instituition” in this example, are used as filters (by rule 4) and also presented in the return of the query (by rule 3). Again, the attributes of the class “Institution” as defined in the BI Ontology should be used as a filter and aggregate by the OLAP translator. As the terms “CSE” and “CFH” are not involved with the stop-words selection, the equality criterion (=) is used in the filter of data comparison in the query. The logical OR is used to build the filter criteria, because the token “or” is informed in the answer between the terms in question. Finally, by applying the pattern number 5 in Table above, the word “study”, which symbolizes a relationship in the domain ontology, is used as a join for the OLAP request. Once this relationship is given in the path returned by the Similarity Search Engines, the OLAP Translator recognizes that the term “study” relate the concepts “Person” and “Institution” in this example.

As the dictionary that helps the terms classification, the stop-words are arranged according to their type in the Knowledge Base. These stop-words are defined according to the previous classification given in Table above. Then the set of stop-words used for the examples of questions in the S&T scenario is shown in Table below.

Table: List of stop-words used according to type.

<table>
<tr><th>Quantification</th><th>Projection</th><th colspan="4">Selection</th></tr>
<tr><td rowspan="6">How many; how much;<br>Amount of; which the amount of;<br>Total of; number of</td><td rowspan="6">By; according to; grouped by; as;</td><td colspan="2">Relational Operator</td><td colspan="2">Logic Operator</td></tr>
<tr><td>Term</td><td>Operator</td><td>Term</td><td>Operator</td></tr>
<tr><td>Above, greater than</td><td>></td><td rowspan="2">and</td><td rowspan="2">AND</td></tr>
<tr><td>Below; less than;</td><td><</td></tr>
<tr><td>From</td><td>≥</td><td rowspan="2">or</td><td rowspan="2">OR</td></tr>
<tr><td>Equal to</td><td>=</td></tr>
</table>

The stop-words applied as filters are related one by one with a specific operator. For example, the stop-word formed by the tokens “Above” is associated to the operator “>” the stop-word “From” and its variants are associated with operator “≥”, and so on. Others stop-words could be added as required and organization´s standard writing. However, this work is limited to the set of stop-words.

The following figure shows a prototype analytical tool to support user’s interaction on top of SBI QA components, where the domain ontology of S&T is illustrated along with the regions of the

input query and display the results. This figure shows an example of a question in the context of S&T with its own answer. The steps to obtain the OLAP cube from this question are detailed below:

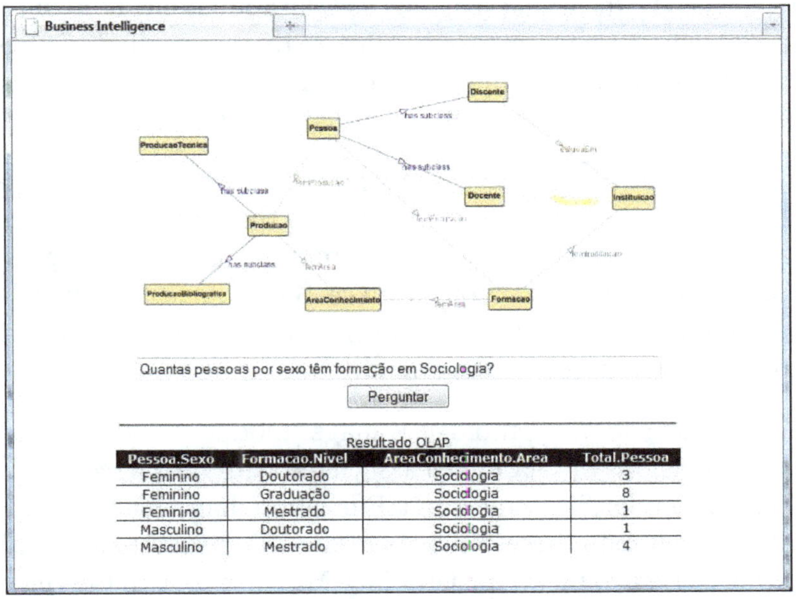


Illustration of a prototype analytical interface.

The question "How many people by gender have education in Sociology?" is a simple example which presents no ambiguities, conclusions of inference rules and no functions. That is, only the class properties, classes and their relationships domain ontology of S&T are involved in the question.

Initially, this question, after being informed at the interface must go through the process of lexical analysis, syntax and semantics of Linguistic Analyzer. By consulting the dictionary and concepts of the S&T domain ontology, the Linguistic Analyzer determines the classification of each term in question, in this case: "How many" (stop-word of quantification); "people" (Person class); "by" (stop-word of projection); "gender" (class property of Person); "have" (token not recognized); "education" (Education class); "in" (token not recognized) and; "Sociology" (instance of Knowledge Area class). The tokens not recognized (on this example, have and in) are not between the dictionary terms and classes of the ontology, so, do not have defined classification.

Before finding the best path based on the domain ontology, the Query Reformulation module in this example replace the instance "Sociology" by respectively class "Knowledge Area". Since the question does not have classified terms as conclusions of rules there is not reformulation based on inference rules. However, for this example reformulation by using synonyms and class hierarchies are performed. This reformulation is performed by Similarity Search Engine that performs also the role of the Query Reformulation module.

The reformulated question that should be used as input to the search for Similarity Search Engine show only the terms: "Person gender have education in Knowledge Area". Note that some terms classified as stop-words were ignored in the input vector for the search. The terms have and in, even not being classified, are used in the search, and special characters are removed.

Only the paths that have the highest number of concepts identified from the input vector are returned by the Similarity Search Engines. So, the best path the S&T domain ontology in this example is (represented in N3): (Person has Education Education) - (Education has Area Knowledge Area). Note that the other paths, such as those formed by only a single vertex (Persona; Education or Knowledge Area) and those formed by the triple; (Person has Education Education) or (Education has Area Knowledge Area) should not return in the search. Thus, in this case a single path is obtained without the need for participation of the decision maker for the disambiguation of entities and paths. Otherwise, the alternatives found are presented to the user that should pick one of the options.

With the best path defined, the set of patterns and heuristics presented in Table is applied by the OLAP translator. Thus, from the classified elements and the types of stop-words, the generated OLAP request has as a measure: the Person class, as grouping: the property gender and the classes Education and Knowledge Area, and as a filter: the term Sociology, instance of the Knowledge Area class. The relationships (has Education and has Area) are also translated in the request as relationships (joins) that connect the concepts of the domain.

Thus, Query Manager works with the Ontology Manager module to assemble and execute the derived query with the dimensions or fact tables associated with the concepts identified in the last step (in this case, Person, gender, has Education, Education, has Area and Knowledge Area). The instances of BI Ontology that map these concepts to the DW structure are retrieved by Ontology Manager. After locating these instances, the Ontology Manager tells to the Query Manager the dimensions, attributes, fact tables and how they are interconnected to create the SQL query.

As seen, the properties of classes are most often associated with the dimension attributes in the BI Ontology. However, only one property (gender property from Person class) were reported and recognized in question. According to the translation from OLAP Translator, a default attribute must be set to measure, group or filter for the class. Thus, when a class has no property explicitly informed the default attribute is set to the BI Ontology to be used in the query.

Thus, considering the configuration of the BI Ontology and the question of this example, the dimension attribute PERSON_SK from DI_PERSON dimension is used as the standard measure and corresponding to the Person class. Since the class Education, which corresponds in BI Ontology to DI_EDUCATION dimension, has as attribute group EDUCATION_LEVEL. Finally, the Knowledge Area class has as group and also filter AREA_NAME attribute from DI_KNOWLEDGE_AREA dimension.

To find out the joins that link the dimensions DI_PERSON, DI_EDUCATION and DI_KNOWLEDGE_AREA in the query, Query Manager Uses the relationships has Education and has Area obtained from the identified path. Also, Query Manager gets the information through the BI Ontology through Ontology Manager to identify the joins between the tables. This information configured in the BI Ontology indicates which attributes of the dimensions is used to describe the join and the type of join (inner join, left join, etc). Finally, the resulting SQL query is performed by Query Manager in order to answers the question.

## Business Intelligence Software

In the current innovative world, the data being produced on a daily basis from numerous sources is massive. Data analytics is not only for large-scale businesses anymore, businesses of all sizes are taking their investigations to the next level. This can involve significant data that can assist business make successful decision.

The best organizations are reaching these new levels by benefiting from rising creative business intelligence (BI) services. Organizations use BI to take this into account and the proper usage of BI can allow them to improve probability and incomes. But the need to overcome the challenges in BI is showing its face.

Business Intelligence (BI) software helps all businesses in measuring and boosting Key Performance Indicators (KPI). BI software extracts, analyzes, creates reports, calculate and display KPI of data. In large organizations, the data created by BI software can be offered to those who are accountable for, or who have conferred interests in return margins such as business investors, business board members, CEOs, executive administrators, marketing managers, operational teams and sales managers.

The main aim of BI software is to cut costs and speed up decision cycle within a business with actionable intelligence. Another use of BI software is to leverage big data and cloud-computing to simplify intricate data analysis and assist companies adopt business intelligence practices across departments. The BI solutions used today are easy to set up, use and incorporate with existing systems. They can be standalone apps or as a part of an enterprise suite like CRM, ERP and ecommerce systems.

## Reasons for using BI Software

- Gain Insight for Growth: Business Intelligence can be optimized for sales opportunities, lead generation, customer segmentation, and market analysis. Merging interactive database and multidimensional data prototypes with cross-departmental and real-time data collaboration, businesses can manipulate massive amounts of data and surface insights in unlimited ways. Businesses can identify growth areas, measure product viability, assess supply and demand and determine their market position among other things. Additionally, data is sourced in real time and analyzed through collaboration, further boosting marketing knowledge.

- Get the Big Picture: Scoreboards and Dashboards are typical features in BI solutions. They offer a clear view of the company's overall performance. Metrics can be modified to line up with the key performance pointers and reports generated in real time. Dashboards can be used to align the health of your business across a threshold range. On the other hand, scorecards are set to deliver regular snapshots of the company's progress against its goals.
- Address Urgent Issues: Problems can be addressed immediately if you have the right information. BI solutions feature impromptu reporting that lets you input data and create insights as fast as possible. More informed actions can be taken before an emergency can further escalate. Through a wizard interface, these solutions allow you to detect and excerpt crucial information off volumes of datasets and produce reports fast.

## Top Business Intelligence Challenges in an Organization

## Ensuring Data Quality

Data Quality and completeness are important success factors for all BI efforts. It is critical for organizations to perform basic auditing to ensure the validity of the data. This is especially vital for data that will be used for measures and indicators. Since data is utilized differently for Business Intelligence than it is in other user cases, auditing often reveals data quality issues that would mostly go undiscovered without these efforts. When an issue is recognized and the root cause determined, the project is launched to close the data quality gap.

## Absence of Execution and Training

Many times, businesses have all-around enunciated necessities, a decent apparatus setup, a sound BI systems, but still require specialized abilities. There is a need to have personnel that is well trained to handle the BI systems but many organizations lack this.

The reason for absence of execution frequently are different and fluctuated, similar to it cures. This requires extra training in data administration applications. Organizations need to focus on understanding their assets, why BI service is required, and the benefits of a BI solution. The most important training that they would require is getting comfortable with the visual interface after picking the right BI stage.

## Unifying BI Across all user Groups

One of the main challenges is having a unified BI tool that includes central governance, security, and management across all users inside or outside your organization. There is not a single BI platform that can offer every capability that users require but an upgraded BI tools, helps businesses to overcome the challenge of reaching out to only a few users.

## Targeting Big Needs with a Centralized Team

Another BI challenge faced by organizations is the lack of a centralized team. The lack of such a team means that the needs are not well looked into and some area are neglected which may lead to the failure of BI.

The work of the centralized team is to drive organizational alignment on the big deals by initiating and managing BI deliverables and working to enable successful integration into the organization's operations. The team will gather requirements for each participating department and develop a prioritized roadmap for implementation.

## Self-service BI

The ability to deliver self-service reporting and analysis across an organization is a big Business Intelligence challenge. One of the biggest problems with traditional BI tools is that they are complicated to use to an extent that only a few key individuals within the company know how to use them. Problems can quickly form around these key individuals which can slow down the entire reporting process.

To address this issue, organizations need to work to deliver full self-service BI data stewards and other end users. This way, users can access data models within the organization data mart and create their own reports. They can also download the data models into their personal sandbox areas after which they can add or remove data, create their own relationships, restructure models, calculated columns, measures and KPIs.

## Extending Value with BI "Soft-serve"

Unlike the self-service BI, soft-serve Bi doesn't allow end users to access and manipulate data from the data warehouse, only reports. But, the soft-serve Bi model has considerable value since an organization can standardize data, indicators, measures, visualizations, and reports while empowering end users to adjust reports as needed to take care of their unique requirements.

## Unlocking Data Buried in Systems

Regardless of whether you have the data already in place and know where to get it does not automatically mean that it is easily accessible. Accessing the information you need, when you need it can be quite a process when the data is buried in complex systems and software. In order to gain any real value from your data, you must transform and manipulate it into the right shape. You can clean up your data using a data warehouse and an effective ETL process and get it into the right shape and apply any business calculations or rules.

## Cost - TCO

Business Intelligence is costly—assets and expenses plans have always been tight especially for small businesses. However, this has changed with the introduction of SSBI stages. The cost of transmitting BI is a worry only among the SMEs. SMEs are weakened by the obstructive costs of obtaining the correct programming.

Currently, a few stages make SSBI open to small businesses without causing anyone to spend a substantial amount of cash. Similarly, constrained assets means looking for qualified professionals. In this case, small businesses should look for BI dealers offering adaptable arrangements with minimal TCO.

## Huge Infrastructure Investment

In the past, expensive BI solutions required huge hardware resources. In addition to increasing the installation price, these data marts and processors also increased the time required for setting up. However, with modern solutions, you can implement BI either with the existing hardware or by running on virtualized infrastructure in the cloud. The fact is that most SSBI channels can ably use the hardware resources of an office computer for all data processes. There is no need to buy a SQL server or an additional hardware to start using BI to empower your decision-making.

## Unstructured Data of BI

Organizations may invest into massive data analysis but can't complete the tasks in time. Business owners are switching to creative BI devices to tackle this BI challenge. This may result in endless hours of cleaning and organizing data first and then using the BI service. This can undoubtedly blend distinctive datasets without the need to rebuild databases or set up a data supply center. A BI service could be loaded with programmed ETL abilities to process datasets that need to be rebuilt. This allows small business to interface all their data sources, see past the numbers and find new connections and identify patterns to eliminate the mystery from crucial business choices.

BI is no longer an indulgence that can be afforded by only big establishments. The need for Business Intelligence driven insights might be more prominent in firms that deal with large amounts of data. Today, even Small and medium sized businesses and entrepreneurs need to make data-driven decisions.

# Financial Intelligence

Finance intelligence is a skill set comprising of the following four competencies; understanding the foundation, understanding the art, understanding the analysis and understanding the big picture. All the four competencies need to be put into practice and implemented for whole hearted success of finance intelligence. Finance is the business language recognized and used across all organizations. It is common denominator on which all the organizations are measured.

Financial intelligence sounds like something that only a few chosen people possess, but actually, it's a little bit in all of us. The difference is that not all of us are aware of it and even those that are might not know how to use it to its full advantage. Some people have it more than others and have a keener insight into how to use their money to generate more money. Experts on the topic will tell you there are no top secrets or quick schemes to get rich. That doesn't mean you have to overwork yourself either. You just need to understand it better and start making changes in how you deal with money.

Chances are you won't find someone successful who is also not aware of financial intelligence. This is regardless of how you want to define success. You might not have a lot of cash on you, but you're happy and happy with what you work and make do with what comes out of it; this can be considered success. By the same token, you can have loads of money, but be spendthrift and waste it on nothing till it runs out, and that could be classified as unsuccessful.

So, let's break it down for you to know exactly what financial intelligence is and why it's so important to have it, and how it can turn your life around.

## What is Financial Intelligence?

The good news is this type of intelligence is a skill to be learned. It's basically about knowing the ins and outs of a financial situation, be it your personal finances, your company's finances or a company you work for. It is basically understanding and gaining knowledge and skills in finance in the business world. It's a relatively new term that has gained increasing popularity to help increase financial results, lessen employee turnovers by including employees in financial decisions within companies.

Actually, many companies offer courses to their employees about it as a leadership skill. Financial understanding has to do with understanding numbers of budgets, payrolls, sheets, profits, interest and more. Because it's a very technical science, we want to show how it can apply to you and why you would need it.

## Increases your Wealth

Is there anyone who doesn't want to increase their wealth? For business minded people, the most important thing to know is your cash flow. Whether you own a business or not, you need to know where your money is going. One of the reasons rich people get rich and richer is because they have their eye on the cash flow and control it all the time. You don't have to own a business to keep track of where your money is going, neither do you have to be making a lot of money to keep watch. Once you know your cash flow, you will spot where the money is going that can be modified, lessened or cut out altogether. This will automatically increase your money.

## How you Relate to Money

You might not believe it, but how you think about money has a lot to do with financial intelligence and how successful you can be. We all know the old adage, 'money is the root of all evil.' Some of us were brought up to believe that, while others were brought up with an 'easy come, easy go' attitude. While still others were brought up to believe you have to work hard for your money and 'money doesn't grow on trees.' Whichever your belief is in, the one thing we should all believe and be convinced of is that money can be controlled.

Successful people control money, not the other way around. They decide where it's going, what it's going into or who it's going to. Your relationship with money needs to be expanded and not limited to what you learned about it when you were young. Formal education doesn't really address the issue of money in this way, and unless you majored in finance, neither does college. So don't take anything you've learned about money at face value.

## What your Knowledge about Money is

There's a difference between your belief about money and what you know about money. Now, for many of us, we only know about the purchasing power of money, and that's where our knowledge ends. To make use of financial intelligence, we need to know more. We need to understand how money works or what are assets are versus our liabilities. Many of us don't know the difference between a credit card and a debit card. A lack of knowledge is what often forces us into making financial mistakes that get us into debt or enter into a poor financial investment, which can also lead us into debt.

There are many tools out there to help us increase our knowledge about finances, and it's just a matter of using them. If you're a bookworm, read more about finances. There are more than plenty of books, articles, and blogs about increasing your financial intelligence. If you're more of an audio/visual learner, watch shows and interviews with experts explaining the nooks and crannies you don't know about. There are even apps that will make your financial learning easier by tracking your spending habits.

## What you do with Money

Raise your hand if you think you make too little. Most of us do think we make too little money and that's why we always find ourselves in financial predicaments. Yet, it's sort of true that no matter how much we make, we never think it's enough. This is because the more you make, the more you begin to spend. Then it becomes a race between what you make and what you spend, and we know that what we spend always gets the better of us and wins. But what are you spending on is that one question you most definitely need to ask yourself.

We've at least heard about a 'rags to riches' story. We've read factual stories about people who made it from nothing to something big. And we've read about the complete opposite of people who blew all their money and wound up as the poor pauper. These stories aren't just for entertainment purposes; they're lessons to learn from. They're meant to show you that success doesn't depend on how much you make or earn, but rather on what you do with those earnings. A simple example of what many financially intelligent people do is save at least 10% of their earnings automatically.

They never see that 10%. They use that percentage for future investment purposes or keep it for long-term gains.

## What's the best Thing to Invest in?

That's a popular question for people. Should you invest in real estate? Stocks? Bonds? These and more can be good investments, but not before you invest in yourself. This is the best investment you can make during any time of your life. When you do that, you're much more likely to achieve the success you want. This is why people take courses in a multitude of subjects, for example. The person who is going to grow your wealth is you, so developing yourself is something worth the time and effort.

When you focus on self-development, you will know what you're good at and what you can be successful in. For many people, self-development changed their entire life and lifestyle. People have left their careers to other types of work or investments and totally succeeded in areas they might have never thought they'd be in. This can happen because the mindset has shifted, making people more enlightened.

## Control what you can

There are lots of things that are not in our hands. It's not in our hands how the stock market is acting. It's not in our hands if real estate goes down or up. Your salary, though it reaches your hands, is not in your hands. With so many things not in our control, it's easy to despair. But you need to focus on what you can control. What you want to invest in is in your control. How you spend your salary is also in your control.

These days, we live in a world of very rapid changes and the future will always be full of uncertainties. But financially intelligent people know that what they do today will affect their tomorrow. Try to tune up your foresight and realize that every financial step you take today will have either a positive or negative impact in the future.

## Hire Financially Intelligent People

Without the intelligence, not only will your money not last, but you won't even be able to make it in the first place. It's easy to believe that you don't have it in you to be financially intelligent. You're not alone in this. Actually, it's part of intelligence to know that you don't know everything. And though most of us have it within us, we still don't know how to utilize that intelligence to make it work for us.

If you really are at a loss, there is no harm in paying someone to help you understand and shed some light on the subject. Yes, you would rather have free advice, but that free advice from someone you know might lead you to pay a heavy price later on if that advice is wrong.

## Short and Long Term Goals

You probably have short term goals you want to reach, we all do. You need to differentiate them from your long term goals as that will keep you focused and balanced. They are both money goals. Yet, we usually get caught up in the short-term and forget about the long-term. For a long time.

It cannot be stated enough that so many people are better at blowing money than doing well with it. And this is because we don't have a plan of action set. You need to protect your future self and wealth and use or invest your money in things that will also serve your long-term goals.

There are insurance blogs available such as this one that will go over the Pros and Cons of Guaranteed Universal Life Insurance. This might be one investment you want to look into to help your long-term goal. At one point, after a lifetime of working, you will want to rest or retire and enjoy your time and live well and make sure everything is being taken care of by professionals in the business of life insurance.

### Mingle More

When you expand your network of people to include people who are financially intelligent, this will help you even more. When people want advice on financial matters, they tend to talk with someone they trust, but might not know much more than you, or even less on money matters. It's a sort of the blind leading the blind scenario which will definitely not help you reach future success. You need people who are in the field, who manage and understand money well. The wider your network becomes, the bigger the edge you'll get by learning new things and picking up good money habits.

### The Blame Game

The last point to mention is our love of playing the blame game. We blame our work, our boss, our family, our circumstances, the weather and our dogs and cats for why our money just seems to disappear. A big part of financial intelligence is to man up and be accountable for our own mistakes with money. We cannot be successful if we don't admit our faults and limitations and do something about them.

## Accounting Intelligence

Accounting Intelligence is a form of Business Intelligence that is used to extract, analyse, interpret, and present actionable insights from ERP Applications viz., SAP FI/CO, JD Edwards, Epicor, CODA, or Oracle E-Business Suite. These Accounting Intelligence Applications focus on 'Deep Learning' and disclose the pertinent information beyond the 'Financial Statements' and also finding out the unstructured documents, identifying trends, patterns, anomalies and relationships.

The 'Seeds of Accounting' were sown in Babylonia and Egypt around 400 B.C. and historical evinces reveal that 'Egyptians' adopted 'Accounting for Gold and Valuables'. The Greece 'Revenue Accounting System' and the Romans 'Memorandum or Daybook and Ledgers' for recording Receipts and Payments on monthly basis were the basis for 'Accounting Transactions'. The Chinese 'Government Accounting' as early as 2000 B.C. was considered the 'Sophisticated Form of Accounting'.

In India, the 'Accounting Practices' were traced in 'Kautilya's Arthashashra' and expounded how accounting records had to be maintained. The Book of Luca Pacioli, 'Summa de Arithmetic, Geometria, Proportion at Proportionality', considered as the First Book on Double Entry System of Book-Keeping containing the knowledge of business and book-keeping. Accounting is an art and science of recording, classifying, and summarizing in a significant manner and in terms of money, transactions and events which are, in part at least, of financial character, and interpreting the results thereof (AICPA).

The evolution of AI has been a rich tale of exploration and also a scintillating experience since its origins in the 1950's and AI in the digi-era emerged as a Plug-and-Play Technology for AI-Powered Organisations. Kensho, the 'World's First Computational Knowledge Engine' for the Financial Industry especially dealing with Stock Markets, automatically analyses 'Portfolio Performance and Predicting Market Volatility'. The UK-Based Arria has developed 'Natural Language Generation (NLG)' that is being emulated by 'Real Intelligence' and incredibly fast, incredibly consistent, available 24/7 and this AI System can react and adjust for changes to an economy. The KPMG in collaboration with McLaren Applied Technologies (MAT) addresses the 'Heart of Financial Statements Risks' since 2015 with utmost 'Quality, Effectiveness, Efficiency and Insight'.

## Accounting Intelligence/Expert Systems (AI/ES)

Accounting is an art and science of recording, classifying, and summarizing in a significant manner and in terms of money, transactions and events which are, in part at least, of financial character, and interpreting the results thereof (AICPA). Accounting Intelligence is Ontology of Artificial Intelligence that will propel innovations in Accounting.

The Robotic Process Automation (RPA) enhanced efficiency at higher levels and reduced audit and contractual processing times. In the process of Accounts Payables, the Payments are matched with 'Purchasing Orders' and the Automated Data Entry and Data Categorization analyses 'Financial Trends' and provides insights where 'Natural Language Processing' interprets 'Contractual Information'. In Health Care, the AIS analyses the accounts, identifies complexities in advance, prescribing analytical insights and discloses accurate and timely information to the stakeholders.

The Accounting Intelligence Expert Systems (AI/ES) are software programs that store knowledge extracted from human experts. The first AI/ES System named 'TAXMAN' was developed by McCarthy in 1977 as a competitive tool in the domains of Financial - Cost - Management Accounting as well as in Auditing, Taxation and Personal Financial Planning (PFP). It assesses the financial, operational and leverage status and also gauges the operational performance. The AI/ES relies on expert emulations, postulations and procedures and formulating algorithms and rules. Some of the prominent AI/ES used by the corporate are: (i) CORPTAX, (ii) CASHVALUE, (iii) FAME, (iv) Auditor and (v) FINEX etc.

The journey of 'Accounting' embarked with 'Reckoning', embracing 'Accounting Intelligence' en route 'Spreadsheet Accounting (MS-Excel and Cloud)'. Accounting Intelligence (AI) is an 'Automated Book-Keeping with Robotic Touch'. The Big Data Analytics and Deep Learning stimulated the AI-3.O and offer Jugaad Solutions and Disruptive Technologies. The RPA (NLP, Machine Vision, Speech Recognition etc.), Cognitive Insights and Cognitive Engagement contributing $15 trillion to the World Economy and amplifying Society (Humans 2.O), Service (Cyborg Concierge) and augmenting Management (C-Suite) (PwC).

The AIS drastically reduces invoice approval time (around 80 per cent), minimizes Accounts Payables Overheads in dollars, boosts every performance metric in terms of speed, efficiency, accuracy and productivity (Infosys AIS Platform - AMD). An Intelligent Accounting System driven by vision and purpose makes data more accessible, actionable and operational. The data-driven analytics provide innovative insights and also attract and retain accounting talent pool.

The Industry -4.O is more disruptive with confluence of technologies such as AI, Block Chain, Robotics, 3-D Imaging, Quantum Computing, Gene Mapping etc. The Agile and Disruptive Technologies have profound influence and impact on primary, secondary and tertiary sectors of the economy. AI is A (Algorithms) To I (Information) and AIS an Ontology of AI. The agility, accuracy and transparency are the dynamics of AIS. Mere 'Humanoids' cannot transcend accounting talents and skills. Be ensure the 'Human in the Loop' (augmenting accounting skills by systems to deliver rich insights), ensue Accounting-as-a-Service (Aaas), infuse Emotional Intelligence and instill Human Touch.

## Agile Business Intelligence

Agile Business Intelligence is defined as the use of agile software development methodology for business intelligence projects to reduce the time-to-value of traditional BI and help in quickly adapting to changing business needs. Executives and business users are able to make good decision with Agile BI. The impact of agile business intelligence depends on close collaboration between IT experts and the firm which results in better communication, setting goals and outcomes that more accurately meet business objectives.

Most agencies store data from both internal and external data sources such as databases, e-mail archives, file systems, spreadsheets, digital images and audio files. Most of the data does not conform to a defined pattern. Conventional Business Intelligence systems use a small portion of the available statistics organized information is used primarily.

The main elements of a traditional BI system are: Extract, transform, and load tools, data analysis and reporting system and the methodologies involved in the inspection of firm's data. Agile BI can disseminate precise data in the desired form and to the targeted audience on time.

Modern software projects are threatened by constant changes in requirements and the business as well as the regulatory environment. Agile development addresses this risk through its adaptive approach. It exhibits high flexible response to change, due to the incremental, its adoption of the iterative approach. The increment is also very short, and the software developers are in constant interaction with the end user.

Any change in requirement is discovered early and the project allowed adapting to these changes quickly. Due to the frequent close interaction with the customer, requirements are directly collected during each increment from the customer as opposed to formal documents that represent them as in other traditional development methods. This eliminates any form of ambiguity in understanding the requirements and ensuring that stakeholders uphold the commitments to the requirements they provide. Agile development best fits software projects which lack structured planning, due to its adaptive planning feature which requires minimal planning activities be conducted formally.

## The Problems with Traditional Waterfall Methods

The waterfall method is a long-established model used in system development life cycle to create a network in concatenation. This model is referred to as waterfall because it develops in a sequential pattern from one phase to another in a downward approach. The model is sub-divided into various episodes, and the accomplishment of one step heralds the beginning of the next stage. Every event has to be accomplished before the next starts, and there is no coinciding of the phases.

This model abstracts the essential software development activities of requirements, analysis, design, coding, testing, and operation sequentially. It was proposed to avoid the risks introduced by the code and fix technique by having the requirements and analysis stages come before the coding stage. This ensures that user requirements are defined in advance, thus, reduces the time and effort wasted on several iterations of code and fix. In the original waterfall model, any error that occurs at any stage passes on into the subsequent steps until it is later discovered in the testing phase.

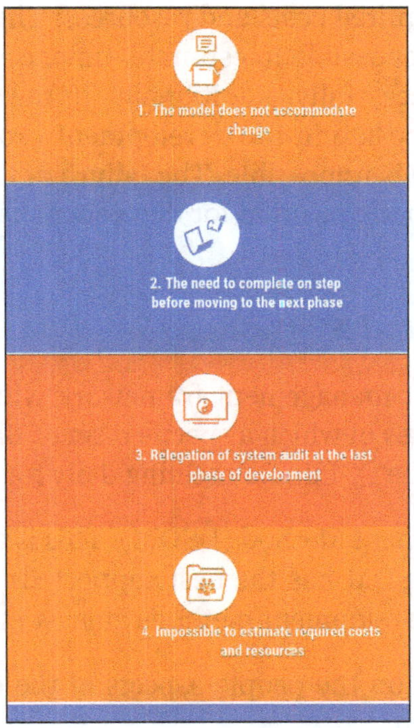


- The model does not accommodate change: The waterfall model is based on constant needs change during the programming phase. The structure of the waterfall model does not accommodate change since it requires that all the conditions are outlined beforehand during the requirements phase to guarantee that no alterations are carried out during the development stage. This belief is idealistic since it impossible for projects to identify requirements beforehand. It is impossible to prevent changes in conditions because continuous requirement change is not a difficulty that needs solving or restricted to the waterfall model. On the contrary, the unstable nature of the software coupled with the restrictive character of the waterfall model makes changes undesirable.
- The need to complete on step before moving to the next phase: Waterfall model requires every step to be completed entirely before moving into subsequent phases. This model fails

to allow overlap between stages. These results in tremendous time, cost, human resources, and other resources, due to the extensive the phases in the waterfall model.

- Team members who are assigned specific roles at the development stages have to spend most of their time waiting for other steps to complete so that they can start doing their work.
- Relegation of system audit at the last phase of development: Lack of quality assurance during the developmental process poses a risk to waterfall methods. The product validation is relegated to a single testing phase that occurs later in the development process.
- The testing phase in the waterfall model is the riskiest phase since it is the last stage where the whole system is subjected to testing. Therefore, all problems, bugs, and risks are detected too late in the development phase and require enormous resources and energy to correct.
- Impossible to estimate required costs and resources: The long stages required in developing this system make it impossible to estimate, time, cost, and other resources necessary to complete each step successfully. Additionally, in the waterfall model, does not have a working product until very late in the development process when the product is almost complete, and any change is impossible. The failure of the product to meet consumer demands presents a problematic position for developers having invested lots of resources in its development.

## Agile BI Project Management Methods

- Scrum: Scrum is a project management framework which focuses on software development in 30-day sprint cycles in which a specified set of Backlog features are delivered. The core practice in scrum is the 15-minute meeting daily for co-ordination and integration.
- Dynamic System Development Method (DSDM): This is an extension of Rapid Application Development practices. DSDM has the best supported training and documentation than any other agile software development methods at least in Europe.
- Crystal Methods: Focuses on the people aspects of the development collaboration, good citizenship and cooperation.
- Feature-Driven Development (FDD): FDD consists of a minimalist, five-step process that focuses on developing an overall "Shape" object model, building a feature list, and then planning-by-feature followed by iterative design-by-feature and build-by-feature steps.
- Lean Development (LD): Lean Development is derived from the principles of Lean production, which extends traditional methodology view that the change as a risk of loss to be controlled with restrictive management practices to a view of change is as producing "opportunities" to be pursued using "risk entrepreneurship".
- Extreme Programming (XP): XP provides a system of dynamic practices, whose integrity as a holistic unit has been proven. XP has clearly garnered the most interest of any of the Agile approaches.

- Adaptive Software Development (ASD): Shows how organizations can respond to the turbulence of the current business climate by harnessing rather than avoiding change.
- Agile Modeling: Agile Data method defines a collection of philosophies and techniques for development of databases using the evolutionary approach.

## Advantages of using Agile Business Intelligence

Agile BI drives its users to self-serve BI. It offers organizations flexibility regarding delivery, user adoption, and ROI.

## Easy to Deliver

The credibility of IT can be damaged by unexpected costs incurred more than budgeted amounts and falling behind schedules which can be costly to a company's revenue earnings. Agile Business Intelligence delivers products within a shorter period with various iterations.

Each iteration consists of independent software which is deployed to production. Agile BI focuses on fractionating projects and is driven by business defined scope and value. Project timelines are tracked in smaller units with clients paying for the amount specified.

## High User Acceptability

In Agile Business Intelligence, IT and business work in collaboration with each other enriching the business need in each iteration. This collaboration enhances user adoption by focusing on the dynamic needs of the non-technical business user, resulting in high end-user engagement and higher user adoption rates.

Unlike traditional approaches which have struggled to place user needs at the core of their processes, Agile Business Intelligence is more concerned with giving users faster and to functionality and more opportunities to provide feedback. Ultimately, user engagement equates to higher user satisfaction and adoption rates.

### High Returns on Investments

Organizations using agile business intelligence achieve an increase in rate-of-return (ROI) due to shorter development cycles. Agile BI minimizes the volume of IT resources and time dedicated to delivering results to clients. Clients and other users achieve satisfaction due to continuous delivery of usable software.

Agile BI contrasts significantly with the traditional waterfall product delivery, where large pieces of functionality are delivered towards the end of the project life-cycle. Throughout the development stages of waterfall method, the project incurs enormous costs with no return on investment.

By delivering working pieces of functionality sooner and more regularly, the users have an opportunity to get a return on their investment sooner. Even if they do not achieve all the functionality, they need upfront; they can put the solution into use and move towards making their lives easier and begin realizing the benefits sooner.

### Low Operational Costs

Due to limited resources and the need for budgets to be aligned with high potential deliverables and outcomes, business leaders turn to agile methods deliver projects within budget and on schedule thus increasing returns on investments. Conventional application development approaches are not suited or business intelligence.

The traditional waterfall methodology encompasses the collection, documentation, and transformation of user requirements into specifications. These specifications used by developers who undertake the design, testing and implementation cycle, while this traditional method works in conventional enterprises, it is not guaranteed to enjoy the same level of success in the majority of business intelligence requirement. In BI, the 'build it, and they will come' mentality is encouraged since consumers are motivated to obtain tangible products and services.

A different approach is therefore required to make BI applications more sensitive to the ever-changing business and legal environment. Agile BI is an essential step towards the goal of designing responsive BI applications.

## Commercial Intelligence

Commercial intelligence or the lack of it can have a major influence on driving behavior in supply markets at all levels. Accurate and appropriate commercial intelligence breeds confidence and conviction of purpose, allowing an organization to approach a supply market and the players within it with confidence and clarity of purpose. Conversely a lack of commercial intelligence manifests itself in uncertainty, trepidation, a mistrust of the market and poor decision making.

Recent events in the subprime mortgage market in the USA have evidenced a lack of commercial intelligence and the impact that this can have. Banks and other financial institutions have lacked the commercial intelligence with regard to who in the market has exposure and at what level to bad debts resulting from the crisis in the subprime market. The resulting uncertainty and lack of confidence has led to extreme caution, putting the brakes on the lending market. Banks are reluctant to lend to other banks because they do not know the financial standing of the other party. Where they are prepared to loan it is at a higher rate of interest than before. What has happened in the USA has had a knock on effect around the world leaving everyone asking the question - who else is involved in the subprime crisis? The problem is no-one really knows. So, credit becomes harder and more expensive to come by for everyone from huge corporations down to the consumer in the high street, panic and uncertainty sets in. In the UK the crisis surrounding Northern Rock with savers queuing in the streets to withdraw their cash leading to the first run on a UK bank since 1866.

Purchasing and supply management professionals use commercial intelligence to inform sourcing decisions, prepare for negotiations, to act as an informed client and to seek out innovation in the market place. However there is often a feast or famine approach. Sometimes key decisions and key supplier relationships are managed with little underpinning by commercial intelligence, at the other extreme the gathering of commercial intelligence can reach a point where it exists for its own purpose with little focus on the activity that it is supposed to be supporting.

It is safe to make the assumption that suppliers are taking advantage of commercial intelligence and therefore it is a key that Procurement uses commercial intelligence effectively to support purchasing strategy and make informed and timely decisions.

Much commercial intelligence is gathered informally by organizations employees. Any employee who visits a trade show, reads a newspaper or talks to friends within an industry is researching commercial intelligence. However many procurement functions are recognizing that a more structured approach to the gathering and application of commercial intelligence is required to realize the potential benefits of commercial intelligence.

Commercial intelligence should not be confused with industrial espionage. Commercial intelligence is derived from the vast source of open source information available and is obtained in an ethical manner, unlike industrial espionage.

## What Commercial Intelligence Could we use?

Commercial intelligence that will support a procurement function will vary from organization to organization. It can include:

- Information on a supplier's financial performance.
- Political developments that impact on a market place.
- Economic indicators.
- New product development.
- Currency market movements and trends.
- Commodity price movements and trends.
- Competitor performance.
- New market entrants.

**Structured approach**

Identify information required

|

Identify sources

|

Manage and deliver

|

Review

### Identifying the Information Required

There is a vast amount of commercial information available today and access to it is made increasingly easier by the World Wide Web. Collecting information can become almost addictive however too much unfocused information will be unwieldy, difficult to apply and lead to "not being able to see the wood for the trees". Just to acquire information and to "leave it on the shelf" is a waste of the time, money and effort taken to collect it. There must be clarity as to why the information is being collected and the benefit that it can bring. Question: can someone use this information to help make better decisions to benefit of the organization?

### Identifying the Ssces

There is a proliferation of sources including newspapers, trade journals, and peers in other organizations, published accounts and organizations who specialize in supplying commercial intelligence. Most sources of news media have huge searchable databases that allow access to reports on companies, supply markets and the organizations and events that influence their behavior. To identify the most appropriate sources it is beneficial to consider: how recent is the information provided; how relevant is the information; how credible is the information and what is the cost of obtaining the information. Organizations can either collect the information or pay for a third party to supply. In practice many organizations will opt for a combination of the two.

## Competitive Intelligence

Competitive Intelligence (CI) is an integral piece of every successful business strategy. It's important for a company to understand where they stand within their market, so they can make Intel-driven decisions. CI avoids operating in a vacuum, instead encouraging decisions designed to place itself as separate from and ahead of the competition.

Competitive Intelligence requires understanding not just the general concepts, but the various nuances and subcategories that fall within. Keep reading to understand the complete picture of what CI entails.

Competitive Intelligence is the process of capturing and analyzing information about your competitors to drive internal strategy changes and tactics. CI is important because, while most companies have a great understanding of what's happening internally, external information is necessary to drive sound strategic decisions.

The key here is making data-based, informed decisions based on the competitive landscape in conjunction with internal factors. CI allows organizations to make more informed business and strategic decisions.

## Competitive Analysis

Competitive analysis is the process of identifying strengths, weaknesses, threats, and opportunities of both your current and potential competitive landscape. You can use your competitive analysis to improve your strategy based on these internal and external factors.

Typically, a competitive analysis is conducted by your product marketing or competitive intelligence teams, and then the findings are shared out to the organization. The insights from the analysis are leveraged by every team to make informed strategy decisions. It's also important to note that this isn't a one-time analysis; you should be conducting a competitive analysis as often as you deem necessary to maintain your competitive edge.

## Competitive Landscape

Your competitive landscape is a breakdown of the companies you compete with. Of course, you have direct competitors, but there are other types of competitors you need to keep an eye on, including your indirect competitors, perceived competitors, and aspirational competitors. You can also dig deeper and analyze your competitive landscape by sales competitiveness, industry focus, company stage, or solution type.

Your competitive landscape encompasses all competitors that might influence your business success. It is important to define not just who these competitors are, but how they present themselves to both each other and potential customers.

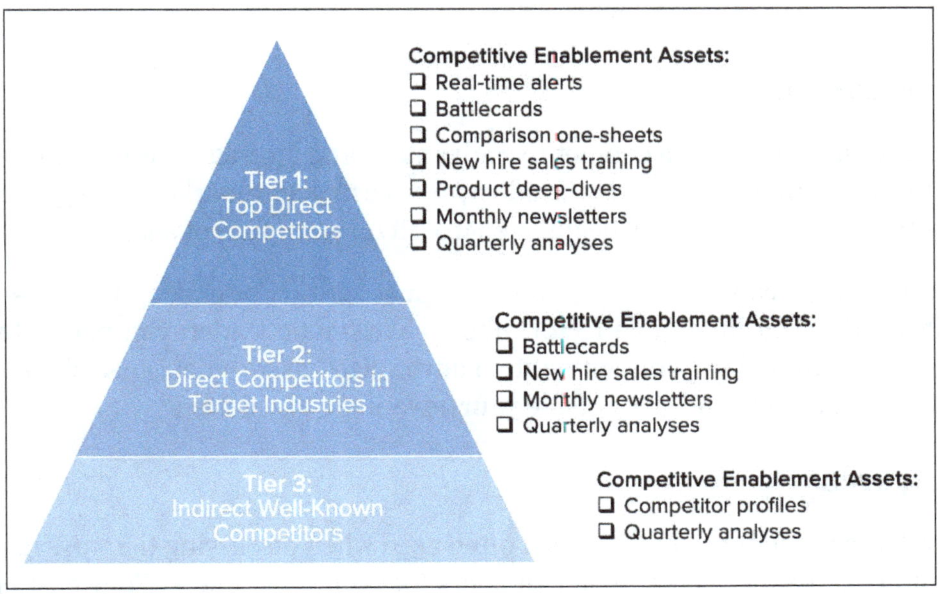

## Competitive Matrix

A competitive matrix is a visualization tool that helps you map out not only your competitors, but how you compare to your market. Competitive matrices can take on a number of forms:

- Feature Comparison Matrices that show each competitor's products and their core benefits and features.
- Quadrants that 'sort' each competitor into one of four sectors based on two tangible metrics, like the ability to execute and completeness of vision. Third-party quadrants such as Gartner, Forrester, or G2 are excellent resources.
- Win/Loss Matrices map out where you struggle as well as where you excel in competitive scenarios.

It's also possible to combine multiple types of competitive matrices for a more in-depth competitive analysis.

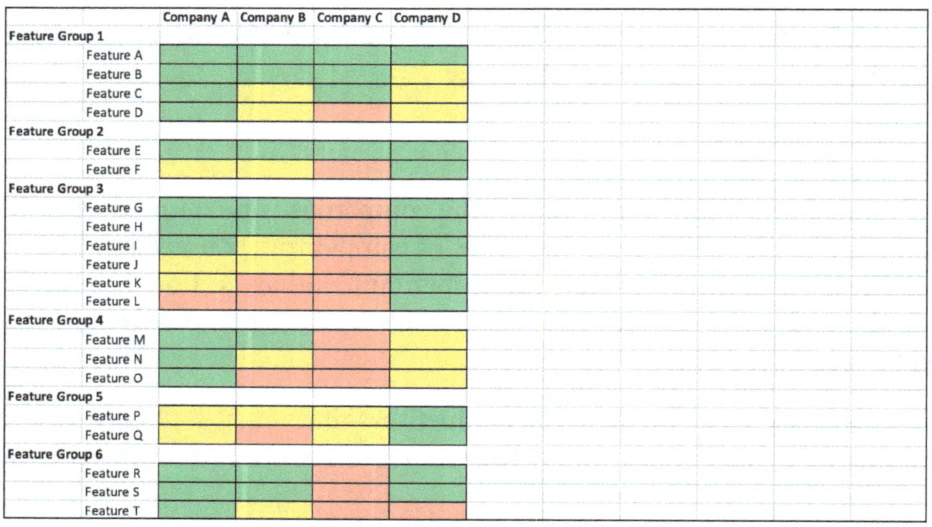


An example of a Feature Comparison Matrix.

## Competitive Advantage

Ultimately, you want to carve out a competitive advantage and leverage it as much as possible. This is the one factor that's unique about your product/service or go-to-market strategy, able to sustain business growth even as competitors begin to encroach on your market share.

A competitive advantage can be anything from a product feature, pricing update, or strategy that's hard to replicate. Even an intangible factor, like a charismatic leader, can play into this factor. However, it's crucial to define your competitive advantage based on an analysis of your market landscape. The more unique and sustainable your advantage, the better.

## Market Research

Market research is a broad term, but it's most often used when discussing the ways to gain insights from the opinions and experiences of stakeholders like your customers. Your customers are the key to taking your go-to-market strategy to the next level. In fact, your customers may even be an excellent addition to your product marketing team.

Good market research is focused on customer needs and preferences. It encourages both qualitative methods, like focus groups and in-depth interviews, and quantitative tools like surveys and polls. Comprehensive efforts should include an evaluation of market needs as well as a deeper dive into top competitors to help you build materials.

## Win/Loss Analysis

One type of market research that deserves particular attention is a Win/Loss analysis. This process takes a closer look at the sales opportunities won and lost by your organization and its competitors during a specific time frame, with the goal of finding the reasons behind those decisions.

Performing a win/loss analysis is complex once you get beyond the basics, but it's far from impossible. The key is visualizing and segmenting your data in various ways, always comparing against your competitors where possible. Focusing on your overall win rate is important, but make sure you're slicing it in additional ways, such as analyzing your overall competitive win rate, and win rate by competitor.

## SWOT Analysis

A SWOT analysis is an evaluation of business strengths, weaknesses, opportunities, and threats. The first two are internal, while the last two take the larger environment into account.

From a competitive standpoint, a SWOT analysis might actually be beneficial to perform for your competitors, as well. Again, the goal here is gaining as much intelligence as possible to 'know your enemy' and make more informed decisions as a result.

INITECH SWOT ANALYSIS

| STRENGTHS | WEAKNESSES |
|---|---|
| • Breadth of Banking Integrations – Their long position as a market leader has allowed them to organically build integrations across a number of banks and their systems.<br>• High Availability – They report to have 99.999% availability which is highly credible for the industry.<br>• Works with Legacy Mainframes – Their on-prem solution work across legacy mainframes. | • Lack of Sophisticated Permissioning– They have a history of giving employees full access to customer systems.<br>• No Threat Detection – They reportedly went months before finding out that a serious breach had occurred.<br>• Understaffed in Support – A series of layoffs has lead to a serious understaffing problem. |
| **OPPORTUNITIES** | **THREATS** |
| • Bank Consolidation – Their existing foothold in smaller credit unions will allow for cross-selling and up-selling as their customers are acquired.<br>• Tightening of Regulations – They have mature procedures in place that reduce the barrier of complying with regulations relative to competitors.<br>• Emerging Markets – They have existing office locations around the world and are uniquely positioned to capitalize on emerging markets. | • Security Focus – Banks are now laser focused on security and their recent breaches have caused them to develop a reputation as an insecure platform.<br>• Migration to Online Banking – Their solution is entirely on-prem, so as Brick and Mortar banking locations continue to decline.<br>• Emergence of New Competitors – New competitors are constantly entering the space. |

## Sales Enablement

Sales enablement is the process of providing your sales teams with the data, tools, and resources they need to sell more effectively. Sales enablement materials can be in the form of collateral, tools (such as battle cards), trainings, or template materials that will prepare your sales team for success.

Sales enablement tools provide your sales team with all of the information they need to execute their sales process, and close more deals. To get there, you have to condense complex information into easily understandable, actionable takeaways.

## Battlecard

One tool that will transform your sales enablement is a competitive battlecard. It is, in essence, that snackable document designed to help your sales personnel better understand the competitive environment and know how to handle competitive sales conversations.

A sales battlecard incorporates information about each competitor's products and services, while also highlighting potential strategies to compete against that company. Done right, they're short, snackable, and actionable, making them an easy reference piece for any member of the sales team.

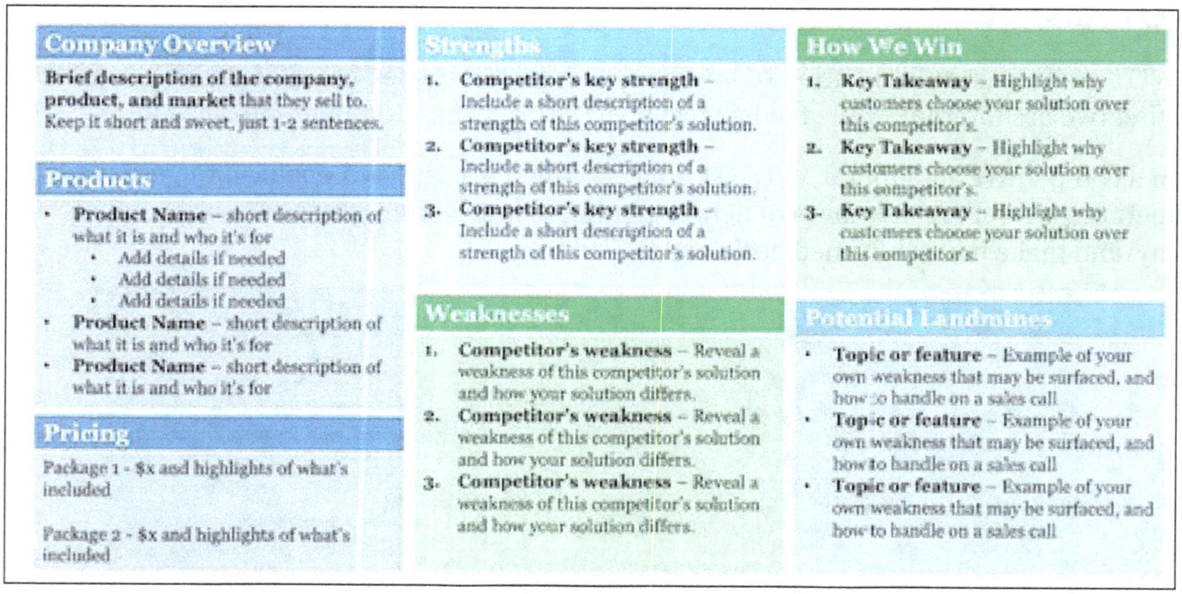


## The Key to a Successful Competitive Intelligence Program

Competitive Intelligence involves a number of individual tactics and processes, all driving towards the same overarching goal. The key is making sure that any complexity gets boiled down to simple, visual, and actionable takeaways.

That's what makes resources like battlecards and competitive matrices such an important piece of the puzzle. The data gathering and analysis is only one piece; if you can turn that piece into a way to help your team on a daily basis, you've achieved a core milestone required for business sustainability and growth.

## Market Intelligence

Market intelligence is defined as the information or data that is derived by an organization from the market it operates in or wants to operate in, to help determine market segmentation, market penetration, market opportunity, and existing market metrics. Market intelligence is a vital aspect to understand the state of the market, as well as helps collect competitor intelligence which in turn aids towards becoming profitable.

For example, A company wants to understand who is the right target audience for a mobile phone they are launching soon. A profile survey can help the company to shortlist its target audience based on the type of mobile device they are launching. For instance, if the colors of the phone are bold and its features are set in a manner to market it as a gaming mobile device, a survey will shortlist participants who prefer gaming, are in a younger age group and people who fall in a specific income range. Such information helps the company to focus its efforts on the right people thus saving costs and efforts.

Market intelligence, however, is not the same as business intelligence. Whilst business intelligence focuses on mostly internal factors such as billing rates, headcount, processes etc., market intelligence gathers data externally providing you a holistic view of the entire market and not just your organization. However, incorporating market intelligence with business intelligence processes will enable a company to have a holistic view of the ongoing corporate performance in specific market conditions.

Market intelligence is closely associated with market research and can be explained in three simple parts as follows:

- Competitor Intelligence: Competitor intelligence can be explained as the collection of data about your competitor using ethical methods such as government databases and public records. For example, Japanese automotive companies were able to capture the US markets and even dominate them using competitor intelligence. Understanding the need for high quality, fuel-efficient cars led them to strategize and penetrate the US market successfully.
- Product Intelligence: Product intelligence is gathering data related to competitor products or similar products in the market. For example, A telecommunications company needs to monitor the prices of competitive mobile phones in the same segment. A price drop in the competitor product can mean the company is introducing a new model in the market. Understanding such information can enable a company to strategically launch their models at the right time and price.
- Market understanding: Market understanding knows the market share of your company, trends in the market, the size of the market and which your target market is. Understanding the demand in the market, and customer wants can help a company tremendously to increase their revenues and market share. For example, A comprehensive market research can give valuable insights to a brand, for instance, the target market is age 20-40, upper-middle-class family and the trend in the market is for Crossfit training to get fit and healthy. A particular gym can use this information and provide services specific to this requirement enabling them to penetrate the market much faster than the usual gyms.

## Market Intelligence: Types and Methodologies with Examples

While market research is a vast topic and can be gathered through various quantitative or qualitative methods, most companies prefer the following basic methodologies to collect market intelligence.

### Data Collection

Some basic data collection methodologies for Market intelligence are as follows:

### Surveys

Survey research involves a set of questions put together in a concise manner to gather data from the target market and analyze the same to create valuable market intelligence. The larger the group of people, the more reliable is the results. There are various methods in which surveys can be conducted depending on what information needs to be collected.

### Online Surveys

These are the best and one of the most economical methods to get data in a swift manner. Such surveys have been associated with unreliable data, but with newer tools coming into the market, this method has become very popular and reliable, to get real-time data fast. Furthermore, the majority of the target audience already prefers online communication; hence online surveys are the best method to gather market intelligence. For example, A mobile company wants to understand the competitor's position in the market to launch its own product in the same segment. A competitor analysis survey can be conducted to understand the competitor's position in the market, their product features, and their market share. Such information will enable the company to decide the right audience, the features, and the correct pricing to capture higher market share.

### In-Person Surveys

These surveys are one to one interviews which can be conducted in high traffic locations such as malls to gather required information. This also allows you to gather customer feedback as you have the advantage of showcasing a product or comparing products and gather valuable information. Such a method has high response rates; however, it is quite expensive as a skilled person is needed at every location with an appropriate device such as a tablet which tends to be costly. For example, A FMCG Company wants to launch a new product in the market for women. In-person surveys can be conducted in malls to understand the trend for particular cosmetic products and preference of its target audience. Accordingly, the product can be modified and launched in the market to have a direct impact on the demand of the audience.

### Telephone Surveys

These surveys are comparatively less expensive as compared to in-person surveys but are costlier than mail surveys. Although, a number of companies use telemarketing and hence the consumer does not respond well due to constant badgering. Therefore, it gets very difficult to convince the consumer to take the survey, thus reducing response rates, as well as the quality of responses. For example, businesses need to understand public opinion about specific products, for instance – laptops. A telephone survey can be conducted with a set of questions that include product features, brand preference, price comfort, and many more, which can help the company to launch the right kind of product in the market.

## Mail Surveys

These are one of the cheapest ways to conduct surveys, especially to a larger audience. Since the advancement in technology, people have stopped reading paper mails nowadays and hence the response rates for such a method are only 3-15%. However, in areas where technology is still inaccessible, such method is still dominant to gather required information from the audience.

- Questionnaires: A questionnaire is a series of questions asked in a printed or online format to conduct research. They can be used for qualitative as well as quantitative research and can be used to gather data from a large set of audience.
- Polls: Polls are somewhat like surveys; however, in such a method there is only one question to answer. Since it takes very less time to answer these, the response rate is extremely high.
- Forms: Forms are a set of questions asked by a researcher to collect very specific information required for the task at hand. Such a method does not include questions that will state opinions or feedbacks from the respondent.
- Focus groups: Focus groups are a set of people selected carefully to represent a target market. Using focus group surveys, a company can evaluate customer demands and opinions or even take feedback from the group. This enables to collect information that can be helpful to a company to penetrate that market or to launch a new product in an existing market. Usually, a moderator is required to ask the question to a set of people where a discussion unveils insights into that topic. However, focus group surveys can now be done online as well thus eliminating the need for a moderator. For example, A focus group is asked about their opinions to understand what would be the most ideal phone for them. A discussion amongst them will give the company information as to what dimension is most preferred in the market and what are the reasons. Reasons such as particular features of the product, screen size, the color of the phone, the speed of the operating system, pricing, etc. can give the company insights in which particular area they need to invest more and accordingly use this intelligence to capture higher market share.
- Personal Interviews: Interviews are generally an expensive affair but provide valuable, reliable information. Such a method is used to understand in-depth about a particular topic or a product. They are unstructured open-ended questionnaires and can last to an hour. However, since they are done on an individual basis, such a method is not preferred to gather market information, as it will not represent the market as a whole. Although, interviews with subject matter experts can give you an understanding of the market trends in a particular industry if you are not well acquainted with such industry information. For example, A company wants to understand what are the current technological trends in the market. An interview with a subject matter expert in technological solutions can give a company

valuable information as to what is trending and what can be expected in the near future. Accordingly, strategic business decisions can be taken to invest in the right direction.

- Observation: Sometimes the data gathered through other types will not give you reliable data or won't give you insights about the customer attitudes or buying behavior. In such a case the observation method provides you with information such as habits of the customer, buying patterns, customer preferences such as quality or price, etc. Understanding this information will enable a company to sell better and make changes in their products according to the demand. For example, Brands have cameras fitted in their stores, which are continuously recording and viewed later to understand the behavior of their consumers. Using this observation, a company can hack into unconscious buying behaviors or attitudes of the target market.
- Field trials: Field trials are like conducting experiments in real time. It involves placing a product in specific stores to understand customer response to the new product. It can be called a pilot run to test the product in the market. For example, A chocolate company wants to test a new product they want to launch. Hence a few select stores are provided with these chocolates to be tested with their target customers. These customers have to represent the target market and hence their feedback will enable the company to understand if the product will work in the market or not.

## Analysis

Information is different from intelligence. Information is not useful until it has some meaning to it. Information is nothing but knowledge about a particular topic or product, while intelligence is about meaningful information which can be used to take action. In order to transform collected data to meaningful intelligence, analysis has to be performed on the collected data. There are various market intelligence software in the market. Such software not only allows you to collect data but also analyze the data using advanced analytical methods. Analyzing the information collected helps you transform it to valuable market intelligence thus enabling a company to understand target market opinions, trends, competition and where improvements or modifications are needed. Advanced analytical techniques such as Conjoint analysis, Maxdiff analysis, Gap analysis, Trend analysis, Text and Sentiment analysis allow a company to understand the market accurately which aid them to make strategic business decisions.

For example, it is important for a company to monitor the market on an ongoing basis. By analyzing and monitoring the trends, measuring customer satisfaction scores and Net promoter scores, a company can stay competitive and manage to increase the market shares, its revenues and also retain its customers. If needed, accordingly decisions can be taken to change or modify the product on the basis of the current trends or the situation.

## Reports and Presentation

Reports and presentation are an important step in using market intelligence. Reports and visual info graphics will enable a company to understand the markets in an easier manner and can answer questions like what do the metrics mean? Wrong interpretation of such data can be hazardous for the company; hence this step plays a vital role in the market intelligence process. The entire market intelligence process has now become much easier using reliable and powerful market intelligence software. Thus using market intelligence effectively can enable a company to penetrate a market successfully and effectively, determine market segmentation, understand the competition and understand the market as a whole.

## Advantages of Market Intelligence

Market intelligence not only helps companies to distinguish their brand from its competitors but also helps in providing valuable information to stay in the game and excel at it. Following are some of the benefits that market intelligence provides:

- Holistic view of the market: Understanding the market completely can lead a company to success in no time. Market intelligence is gathering data in real time from the market and further understanding the customers, trends, behaviors, etc., thus enabling a company to stay competitive and meet market demands.
- Customer retention: No matter how old a customer is to a company, they are always being monitored and attacked by the competition. Understanding when the customer is dissatisfied and the reasons behind it can prevent loss of customers. Market intelligence can help you analyze and give you insights into the areas of improvements that are needed by the customers and thus help you retain them and understand customer lifetime value.
- Improve sales process: Businesses having a variety of products and a large number of customers often face an issue, i.e. which product to target to which groups? Market intelligence helps you to determine market segmentation, thus allowing the company to understand which product will succeed with which group of people.
- Boost process efficiency: Market intelligence helps businesses to boost overall efficiency and productivity by identifying gaps, giving actionable insights to devise crucial strategies and provides an organization with real time data and analytics.
- Gives a competitive advantage: First mover advantage or the launch of a product at the perfect time is a well heard off statement in a lot of business conversation. These are possible only by using market intelligence. Market intelligence helps you keep a watch on the competition, the upcoming trends, and gives a complete picture of the market, which allows a company to penetrate the market or capture the market share by launching a product or a new feature at the right time thus giving them a competitive advantage.

## Importance of Market Intelligence

Market intelligence is vital to the success of any organization, being the foundation on which all marketing is based. Effective use of market intelligence involves the collection of data, analysis and end use of the information. Market intelligence helps you to become customer-centric, understand the market demands and consumer opinions, collect real-time relevant data, boost your upselling opportunities, reduce risks, capture higher market shares and gives you a competitive advantage. These benefits are crucial to the success of any business and hence market intelligence is one of the most crucial elements in executing effective plans for the prosperity of any business.

Following are a few points, to understand why market intelligence is crucial to any business:

- To understand your position in the market: Collecting market intelligence through surveys allows you to understand the market in-depth. It will give you insights into what the competitors are doing, what is the market demand and who will be your target audience and many more. Analyzing this information will enable a company to evaluate its position in the market and make strategies accordingly.
- To evaluate your product: Conducting marketing intelligence surveys will give you actionable insights on the product trends in the market, the demand for specific features and product specification currently in demand. Such information helps you to evaluate your product and make wise business decisions accordingly.
- To know your target audience: Gats based on the competitor's positihering market intelligence will allow a company to understand the needs of the audience and using surveys, businesses can shortlist their target audience for specific products/services.
- To conduct competitor analysis: Market intelligence is a vast field. Conducting surveys to gather intelligence about your competitors is vital in today's business environment. Using such information, businesses can modify their products as per the need, understand competitor's failures or successes, and devise strategies based on the competitor's position.

## Social Intelligence

The old way of gathering social intelligence was very labor intensive. It involved market research from public and proprietary resources, gathering insights from months-long analytics methods, and producing large reports for internal stakeholders (none of which they probably read). Social data was often only visited on a yearly basis because it was that hard to obtain.

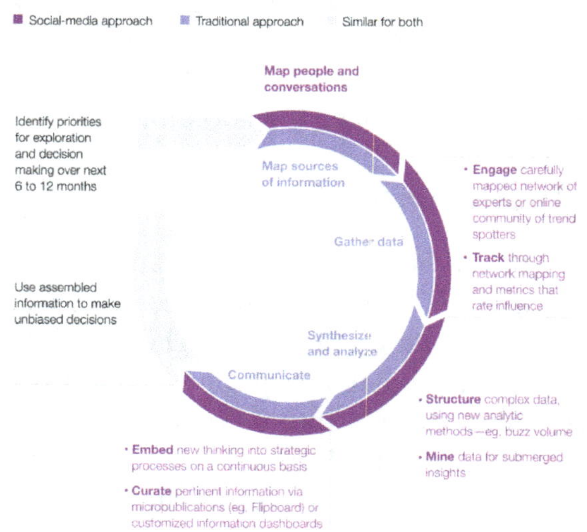


Exhibit 1
Social media is changing the old-school intelligence cycle.

Today, the concept has changed in almost every aspect because the internet produces big social data like never before. Today's social intelligence is more about analyzing conversations and online behavior. This produces a set of data that can lead to greater insight and understanding of business operations. It can make a business the fly on the wall.

Social media has created a new way of mapping information. The old way of collecting data involved information from primary sources like experts, employees, and suppliers. It also looked at secondary sources like articles and market research.

Social intelligence today works on a whole new level. It examines people and their conversations in social spaces. The new "experts" are every single consumer and influencer talking about your brand. That's why there are endless benefits to employing a social intelligence strategy within your business.

## Benefits of Social Intelligence

Although many companies understand the importance of social intelligence and gathering data, they often fail to do anything with it. Perhaps it is because people still don't truly understand the value of social intelligence. It can be applied to many strategies not only in marketing, but in your business as a whole. The following are just a few of the many advantages collecting social data will give you:

### Identifying Micro-trends

Trending is like waves in the ocean. One comes after another and then crashes into oblivion. Micro-trends are like the waves just forming. The ones you can surf the best. Maybe a silly analogy but what it means is that you want to pay attention to the waves that can be surfed. These are the micro-trends that will allow you to get ahead of your competition. The sooner you identify them, the more likely you are to gain market share.

Analyzing social intelligence will help you to identify trends faster. The internet is replete with tools to gather social data in every form, from social monitoring to social surveying; they're at your disposal. Gathering social intelligence will always give you a competitive edge.

### Predictive Analytics

Examining social intelligence allows a company to test various strategies without taking any risk.

For instance, you may have an article you publish that doesn't get a lot of likes. Changing the headline can work wonders. You can even change it a few times and test the social results. Then use that data to curb future decisions.

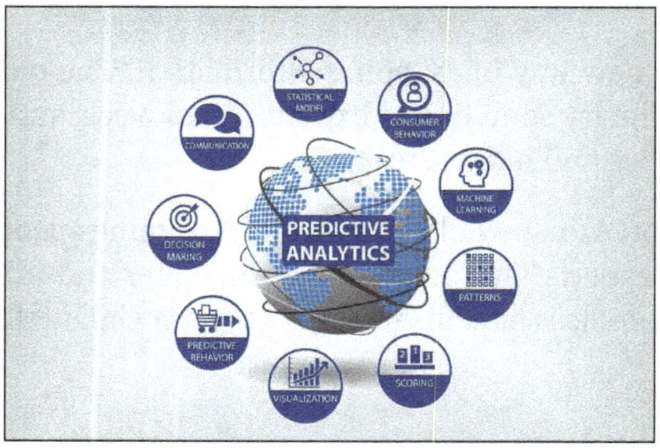


PA Consulting Group is a company that tested their social intelligence to determine the value. They specifically wanted to see if they could predict the future occupancy rate of a hotel using social data. They were able to achieve 98% accuracy just by employing social intelligence. That's predictive analytics at its finest.

## On the Fast Track

A marketing analyst typically spends 80% of their time collecting data, and 20% analyzing. At least they used to. Using social intelligence turns that all around. Analysts have access to a variety of tools that allow them to create dynamic maps to pinpoint expertise within social data. And it doesn't have to be an expert anymore.

General Electric's social campaign is a great example of utilizing social intelligence to gain quick results. In an effort to gather new ideas about what it called a "social airplane," they offered prizes on Virgin Airlines to gather insights. They did this by creating an account and organizing key topics around specific hashtags. The result was more than 90,000 people following and thousands of new ideas within just 2 hours. A traditional campaign like this would have taken weeks.

## Better than Market Research

Social media provides the answers to critical business strategy. This often allows an organization to quickly report progress to board members and stakeholders. It can provide key evidence to back up major business investment. Because of the sophistication and volume of analysis that social intelligence provides, it can never compare to market research which really just equates to studying old numbers.

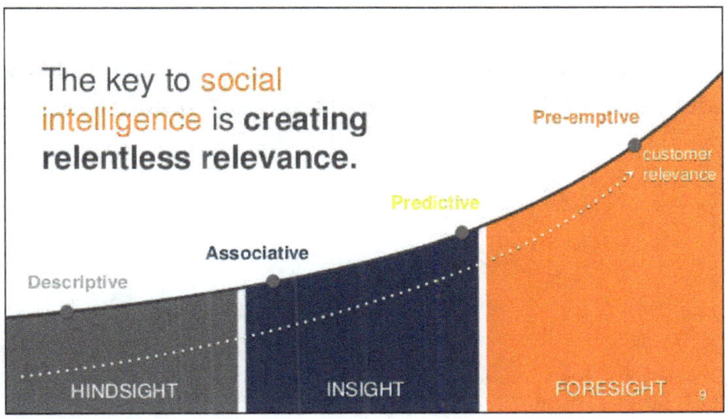


To employ social intelligence that competes with market research, you should understand exactly how it can benefit your company. Social intelligence analysis can give much deeper insight in a variety of ways. It can answer questions like:

- The perception of customer service and how it compares to competition.
- The best ways to reach a certain target market.
- Future product suggestions customers may prefer.
- The key complaints that no one is telling you.
- How your competition is winning and failing.

It's simple. You are using public commentary and behavior to make future decisions. It just happens to be online.

## Competitive Analysis

Social media and the internet allow you a thousand ways to study your competition. It's called "competitive intelligence" and it's right there for the picking. Social intelligence will allow you to not only know what your competitors are planning but have open access to their successes and failures too. This isn't about espionage because the data is public. It's simply about intelligence.

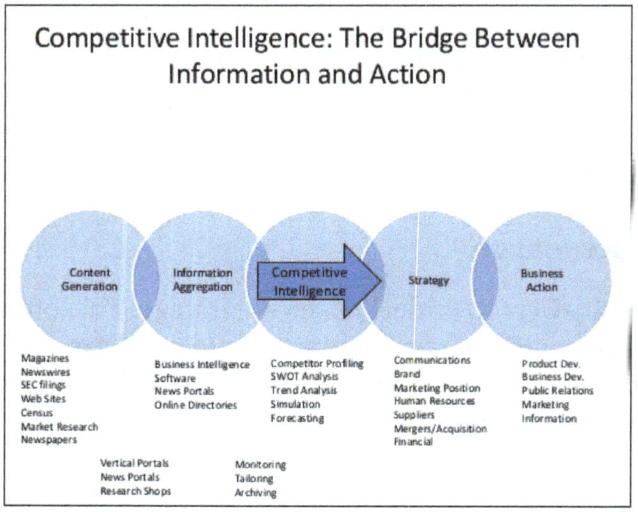


Advanced social intelligence allows a company to study their entire business sector. It permits the opportunity for a broader study that encompasses social data points like:

- Clients,
- Suppliers,
- Employees,
- Stakeholders,
- Competitors,
- Key influencers,
- Potential competitors,
- Potential clients.

These social outcomes can then be used to develop crucial influence tactics. This creates the blueprint for reputation-enhancing signals and content strategy like blogs, press releases, social media posts, etc.

## The Risks of No Social Strategy

Opportunity always brings risk. If you fail to gather the correct social data, at the right time, you may have issues that could affect your bottom line. 78% percent of people say they trust what they read on social media. Even when it's bad. If you don't practice some type of social monitoring that listens to your audience, you may miss a bad comment or review. 72% of people that tweet a complaint to a brand expect a response within an hour.

If you're not looking at social intelligence, how will you answer them so quickly? And it doesn't have to be a live person. Chatbots and automation can address issues on the bottom tier until you have the time. The idea is at least you are responding to consumers and meeting their expectations in a timely manner.

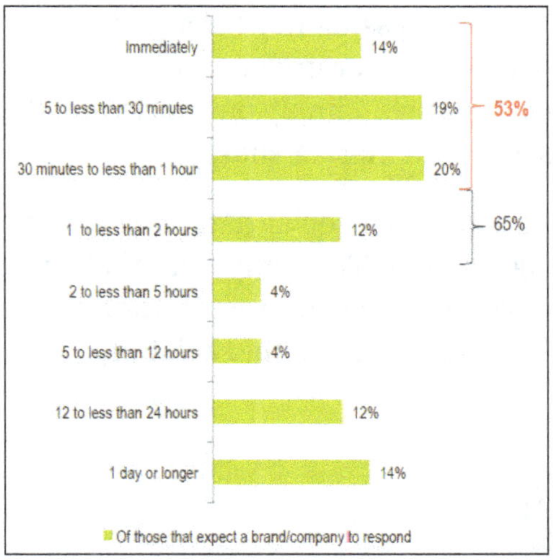


Marketing Land.

Not having a social strategy will also keep you from key insights you can gain from social media. If consumers are talking about a new product they want to see or a better way to offer a service, don't you want to hear that? When you go in the direction of suggestion, it often leads to a higher ROI. It is also powerful data to convince investors on a new project.

## Getting Senior Management Onboard

A popular complaint for marketing analysts is that senior management is not quick to act on information. That may often be due to dated intelligence practices. Reports can be formal processes that are sent through e-mail or newsletters. The information is then dated when it finally gets into the hands of key decision makers.

Social intelligence software changes all of this. It allows organizations to rapidly collect and curate social data that can be sent in real-time to the right people. Decision makers can be dispatched instant market data that allows them to make more informed choices.

One company that has crafted their social intelligence reporting in this manner is Canadian financial cooperative, Desjardins. Using a tool called Flipboard they can deliver social data that is tailored to departmental needs. They do this by allowing key influencers to scan financial services and technology to help them make lightning-fast decisions. Desjardins is essentially curating important social data from the audience itself.

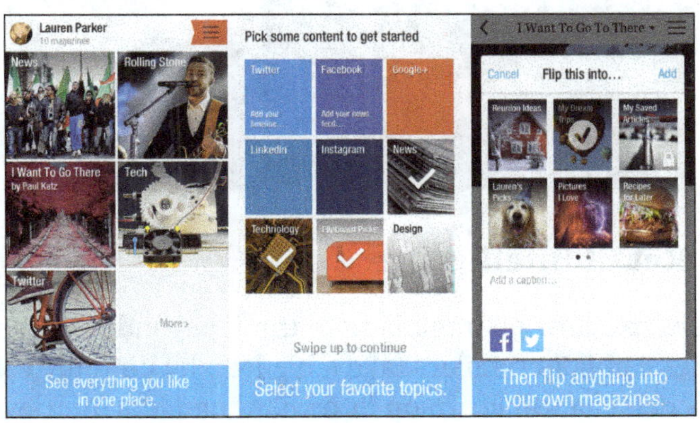

Social intelligence can make your business money because it is the future of marketing. It allows unimaginable opportunities for you to better understand your customers, suppliers, and employees, in a much more defined social context. Simply put, social intelligence is what a company needs to meet competitive challenges and gain market share.

The process requires more than collecting social data. Social conversations need to be had and there must be some aspect of engagement. The companies that succeed build a community around their brand. Social intelligence will immerse an organization with new information, consistently sharpen strategic insights, and strengthen consumer relations.

## Retail Intelligence

Retail intelligence consists of using IT tools to measure consumer behavior within chains or establishments. Retail Intelligence is all set to drive the next wave of disruption in the retail industry by enabling retailers with capabilities to deeply analyze their data, create predictive models and extract incisive insights.

The biggest disruptor in retail is the availability of data. As retail went digital courtesy ecommerce, m-commerce, social commerce, and now connected retail, each customer touchpoint is producing huge amounts of data. The data, if harnessed well, can deliver deep insights into your customer's mind, his motivations, influencers in his purchasing decision, his path to purchase and more. It can also help retailers in building products, processes and providing experiences that delight customers. This provides an exciting opportunity as we look ahead.

The other factor at play now is the mainstreaming of data science technologies like AI, Machine Learning and Computer Vision, etc. Today we see wider adoption of these technologies in business and some fast strides in its innovative applications.

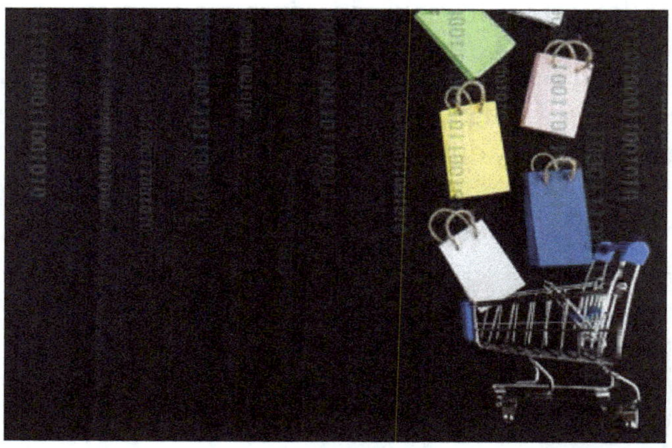

### Retail Analytics to Retail Intelligence

Data Science technologies can now help retailers to think beyond retail analytics to retail intelligence. These technologies can help retailers take a big leap by not only collecting and measuring data but also creating models that can learn on its own. AI and Machine learning can help retailers infer from unstructured data, images, and videos to provide crucial insights and intelligence. It can help them not only understand trends but also predict it with higher accuracy.

### Micro Customer Segmentation

In traditional retail, customer segmentation is done by macro-segmentation. A retailer segments its customers based on age, gender, demography, etc. Retail data intelligence will empower retailers to adopt micro-segmentation by uncovering many layers of customer data to build a 360-degree buyer persona.

### Smart Product Recommendation

Product recommendations will move beyond suggesting items based on purchase history and browsing behavior to context-aware recommendations. Machine Learning driven recommendation engines will self-learn from the data to extract deeper insights into what, why and how of a buyer's needs.

### Real-Time Pricing

Retail intelligence will enable retailers to adopt Predictive pricing wherein pricing will be set at store levels based on the prevailing market conditions. Various internal and external sales drivers like weather, time, demand fluctuations and inventory, etc., can be factored to adjust product prices in real-time.

### Predictive Inventory Management

Data Intelligence will help retailers monitor the stock situation in real-time and predict inventory requirements by analyzing customer behavior, market trends, weather patterns, etc. AI and ML-driven Retail Intelligence offer enormous potential for retailers to build smart, context-aware processes, deliver compelling experiences, drive cost advantages, and empower the workforce. Data has already disrupted the way retailers do business. Data Intelligence will further drive it. Retailers who can optimally leverage their data will get a competitive edge.

## Mobile Business Intelligence

The definition of mobile BI refers to the access and use of information via mobile devices. With the increasing use of mobile devices for business – not only in management positions – mobile BI is able to bring business intelligence and analytics closer to the user when done properly. Whether during a train journey, in the airport departure lounge or during a meeting break, information can be consumed almost anywhere and anytime with mobile BI.

Mobile BI – driven by the success of mobile devices – was considered by many as a big wave in BI and analytics a few years ago. Nowadays, there is a level of disillusion in the market and users attach much less importance to this trend. Survey data from BARC's BI Trend Monitor 2018 shows that market penetration is growing relatively slowly: in 2017, 28 percent of BI users stated that mobile BI is already in use in their company (up from 23 percent in 2016, 21 percent in 2015, 18 percent in 2014, and 16 percent in 2013 and 2012).

## Mobile BI Usage

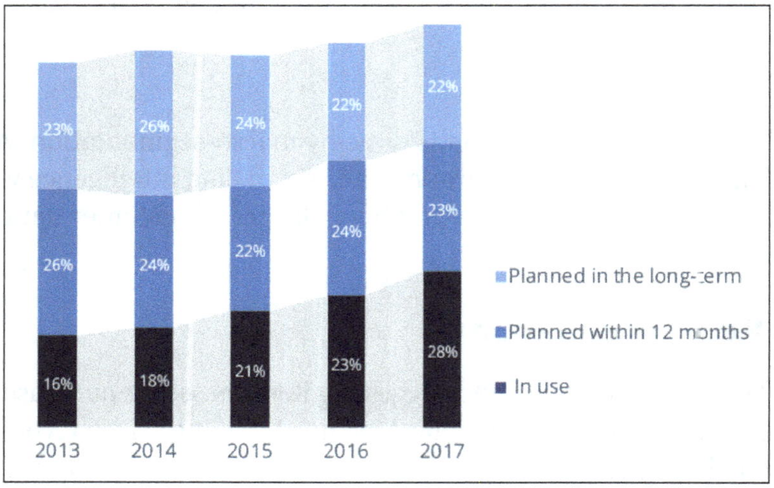


One of the major problems customers face when using mobile devices for information retrieval is the fact that mobile BI is no longer as simple as the pure display of BI content on a mobile device. Moreover, a mobile strategy has to be defined to cope with different suppliers and systems as well as private phones.

Besides attempts to standardize with the same supplier, companies are also concerned that solutions should have robust security features. These points have led many to the conclusion that a proper concept and strategy must be in place before supplying corporate information to mobile devices.

## Benefits of Mobile BI

The first major benefit is the ability for end users to access information in their mobile BI system at any time and from any location. This enables them to get data and analytics in 'real time', which improves their daily operations and means they can react more quickly to a wider range of events. The integration of mobile BI functions into operational business processes increases the penetration of BI within organizations and often brings benefits in the form of additional information.

This speeds up the decision-making process by extending information and reducing the time spent searching for relevant information. With this real-time access to data, operational efficiency is improved and organizational collaboration is enforced. Overall, mobile BI brings about greater availability of information, faster reaction speed and more efficient working, as well as improving internal communication and shortening workflows.

Finally, with the provision of proper mobile applications to all mobile device users, information can be used by people who previously did not use BI systems. This in turn leads to a higher BI penetration rate within companies.

## Mobile BI Technology

A variety of mobile devices can be used to display and actively work with information. Smartphones, tablets and wearable's from brands such as Apple, Samsung, HTC and BlackBerry are the most common today.

A significant difference between these types of device is obviously the size of the screen, which also affects mobile BI. For instance, tablets are comparable to small notebook computers, and are typically not subject to the extreme constraints of the small screen of a mobile phone.

Thus, they offer more space to display content such as dashboards and reports, business data and KPIs compared to the smaller screen of mobile phones. Although BI applications can theoretically run on both tablets and mobile phones, they are not equally well suited to all types of BI. For example, interactive data visualizations require more screen space than displaying KPIs within a table.

There are various ways to implement content on mobile devices. The most common we see in the marketplace are:

- Provision of PDF reports to a mobile device.
- Website (HTML rendering), partly using proprietary technologies (Flash, Silverlight).
- HTML5 site.
- Connection of a native application with HTML5 (hybrid application).
- Native application.

In principle, any BI vendor that can create a PDF or render in HTML (and almost all of them can) can say it supports mobile BI. Most mobile devices include a web browser that can access almost any web page to an acceptable degree of quality. The exception here is when proprietary technologies – which require additional software to display – are used.

BI developers must check how their content renders on a mobile device when creating reports and other visualizations. This means designing their application specifically for mobile use. The main advantage of this is its independence from device types (except when using proprietary technologies), since the content can be consumed on all devices.

Another interesting trend among many software developers is the HTML5 client. BI content is displayed in the browser as previously described, but with several improvements. HTML5 enables Rich Internet Application (RIA) content to be projected across all types of mobile devices without relying on proprietary standards and without having to deal with their disadvantages.

This technology is favored by software manufacturers, and not just because of its browser and operating system capabilities. The end user also benefits by being able to use it without having to install it. Unlike traditional HTML rendering, clients developed in HTML5 also provide some mobile-optimized navigation controls and functions such as zooming, pinching and double-tapping.

In addition, HTML5 can be merged with the features of a native mobile application into a so-called "hybrid" form. This generally refers to a web application that can be downloaded as an app and installed on the device, but at its core includes a web viewer. For this reason, hybrids are often hard to distinguish from native apps. This hybrid category essentially supports more of the native features of the mobile device than a pure HTML5 client, but less than a native application.

The "native" application type is the most expensive way for software manufacturers to support mobile BI because the software has to be tailored to the operating system (OS) of the mobile device.

Native apps are typically downloaded and installed. The advantage of these products lies in their support of device-specific properties, such as the use of cache and navigation controls like "swipe" on the iPhone or iPad. Although the creation of native apps requires effort on the customer and vendor side, they enable interactive and enhanced use of analytics content.

For instance, device functions such as voice recognition can be coupled with the software's natural language generation capabilities to query data ad hoc based on speech. Moreover, app developers are able to use sensors such as GPS to guide a customer to an article which is calculated to be potentially relevant to him. The more operational use and interaction with information that is required, the better the mobile OS support has to be.

In general, the trend in mobile BI apps is veering towards knowledge generation rather than pure content consumption. Analysis and manipulation as well as input options for data are increasingly supported these days. Meanwhile, forecasts based on past data can be statistically calculated and directly reused on mobile devices.

Information should be updated as often as the reader needs it (sometimes even in real time). Especially in operational scenarios, decision-makers often have to react instantly to insights from data or changes in circumstances.

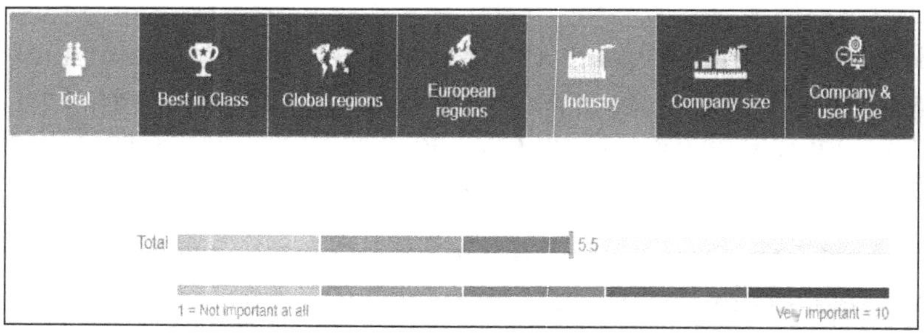


Importance of Mobile BI in 2018 (n=2,637).

Best-in-class companies attach much more importance to mobile BI than other companies. Since 2016 there has been a downturn for nearly all categories, except Best-in-class, Laggards, Eastern Europe, the DACH region and the transport and telecommunications sector.

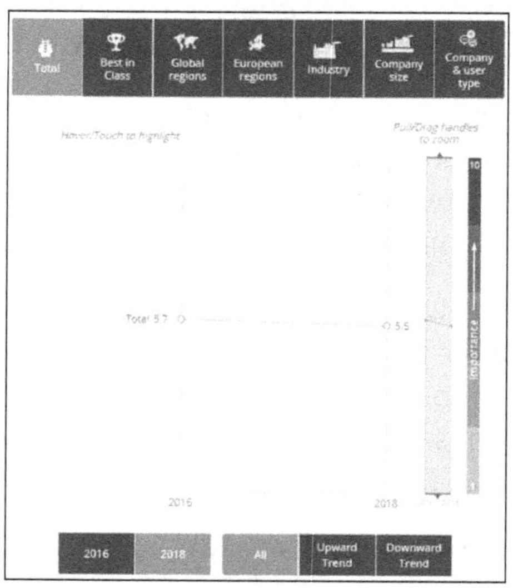


Importance of Mobile BI (Timeline).

## Mobile BI Tools

The requirements and expectations of mobile BI are increasing so the selection of the right product is a key to guaranteeing the maximum return on investment. Since providers are strongly oriented towards the most popular operating systems, they are also aligning their product portfolios for mobile BI.

As well as vendors developing mobile BI solutions for their own BI software, there are more and more companies selling platform-independent systems. Most of them are specialist manufacturers who use the BI systems of popular providers such as IBM, SAP or Microsoft to extract information. Data is then integrated, processed and displayed using their own technologies. This type of mobile software is especially suitable for companies that use multiple BI systems.

## Challenges of Mobile Business Intelligence

Despite all the good things that mobile BI solutions bring, organizations are also exposed to a number of challenges when trying to achieve a successful platform adoption:

- Regardless of the delivery option, customers must consider usability. Displaying familiar content in a mobile browser (even as HTML5) does not necessarily mean that it can be used intuitively. Companies and app developers should take great care in designing the user interface to ensure the app's acceptance, especially in operational scenarios where workers may not be accustomed to using BI.
- When implementing a mobile BI solution, security and privacy may pose problems. Companies have to make sure they implement a strong security configuration in order to protect sensitive business and user data. Furthermore, the mobile strategy should be aligned with existing security procedures.
- Mobile devices can easily be hacked, lost or stolen. Using mobile BI may consequently put sensitive or confidential information at greater risk of being breached.
- Due to the limited screen size of mobile devices, the design of mobile BI applications presents new challenges to developers. Each device and browser works differently.

## Mobile Business Intelligence Software

Mobile Business Intelligence enables to gain business insights through information analysis using applications optimized for mobile devices. The widely used method for accessing BI information is using a GUI of proprietary software or a Web browser on a personal computer to connect to BI applications.

Business Intelligence systems gradually offered alternatives for receiving data, including email and mobile devices. These are through static data push, sata access via a mobile browser, mobile client application and purpose-built Mobile BI apps. In Mobile BI, the users are typically able to navigate dashboard and guided analytics comfortably.

Mobile BI applications can be defined as mobile browser rendered app, customized app, and mobile client app. Mobile Browser Rendered App enables a Web-based, thin client, HTML-only BI applications. Customized App renders reports and dashboards in device-specific format. Mobile Client App provides full interactivity with the BI content viewed on the device.

Mobile Business Intelligence Software extends the traditional business intelligence applications for use on a mobile device. The traditional BI reports are optimized to be viewed easily on a small screen for displaying the key performance indicators and alerts on small screens. Mobile Business Intelligence Software provides real time reporting capabilities on data with analyses, reports and KPIs automatically refreshed in real-time.

Mobile BI presents historical or real time information to its users for analysis on mobile devices such as smartphones and tablets to enable effective decision making and management support. The Mobile BI Software is a tool that is used to connect people and data on the go. It is however, not a replacement for business intelligence.

Whenever it is time to choose a Mobile BI or you want to upgrade to a different version, there are three core competencies which you must bear in mind and they include security; centralization and the architecture involved. The emphasis should never be on the whistles and bells of mobile capability. The security of data is taken seriously because mobile devices expose valuable data to a lot of avoidable risks. If we are to dene Mobile BI Software in the layman's language, it is the software that extends desktop business intelligence (BI) applications in such a way as to be useful on mobile apps.

The traditional BI reports are now optimized in such a way that they can now be viewed on a small screen on mobile devices. There are no unified mobile device standards for the Mobile Business Intelligence for now, this makes effective uniform organization difficult for now. The best of this software will make it easy to integrate BI analytics into the current reporting process in a seamless fashion. It must come with the complements of a web-based front end. They come with a range of filters, slicers, search functions and dropdowns that will permit only valuable data which enables locating needed information easy for the users.

## Mobile Business Intelligence Software Features

The increase in the use of mobile devices across all the divides in the world makes incorporating the Mobile BI Software into the business of today a worthwhile venture. If a business entrepreneur wants to enable easy flow in the chain of business; he will perform better if this software is introduced into the scheme of things.

The data visualization capability is a way of bringing the data to life. It uses charts; gauges; graphs and other visuals to illustrate valuable data in a way that those involved will find easy to understand and digest. This tool will be an asset to business executives who are always on the move because they will be able to access valuable information and carry out due collaborations on the mobile devices while they are on the go.

Everyone among the employees of a business set up that has access to data has the privilege of sharing key information that is up to date even when they are thousands of kilometers away from the office. Every business owner will want his employees to be self-sufficient while handling issues relating to the business; this is what this software will deliver to those who are trained to handle the software. They can operate from anywhere offsite with their internet connections. Such stas will be able to work effectively without looking up to support from the IT department. You are guaranteed topnotch security with this system in place. Your data is secured from the activities of hackers. Every business that wants to make a big difference in today's scheme of things needs this software. It is a profitable tool for business growth.

- Consistent Cross platform experience: Features for consistent user experience across platforms and devices based on the built one and deploy concept.
- Real time capabilities: Real time reporting capabilities.
- User Collaboration Tools: Provides features for user collaboration.
- Mobile apps: Provides mobile apps for ioS, Windows and Android.

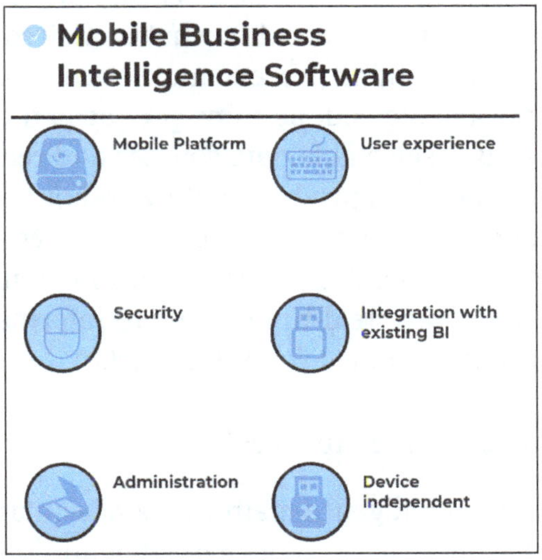


## Real-Time Intelligence

Analyzing data to predict market trends of products and services, and to improve the performance of enterprise business systems, has always been part of running a competitive business. Until recently, these have often been done in the form of monthly and yearly reports by marketing and finance departments. Sometimes market analyses may also be bought from independent research companies. However, this tradition has to start to change. With ever-increasing competition and rapidly changing customer needs and technologies, enterprise decision makers are no longer satisfied with scheduled analytics reports, pre-configured key performance indicators or fixed dashboards. They demand ad hoc queries to be answered quickly, they demand actionable information from analytic applications using real-time business performance data, and they demand these insights be accessible to the right people exactly when and where they need them. Furthermore, since there are too many overlapping data sources with varying qualities, they want more control over the data used for analysis — insights derived from stale, wrongly purposed and poor quality data can do more harm than good.

There are two main reasons that make real-time business intelligence a necessity. Firstly, the conditions and environments in which businesses operate are in a constant state of flux. Sales patterns change from place to place and from time to time. Currency valuations shift and alter profit margins. Suppliers change delivery schedules and their prices. Customers become more educated and therefore more demanding.

Secondly, advances in technology, especially the Internet and modern ICT technologies, make real-time business intelligence seemingly achievable. Indeed, the Internet has revolutionized information sharing. Vast amounts of data are available. Almost all company data sources could be made accessible over an intranet. Nowadays it is very easy to capture all sorts of data and store them cheaply. However, real-time data, analysis and actions still seem a remote reality.

Business intelligence (BI) tries to address these shortfalls by providing software tools that are customized for end business users, and deliver business insights in real time at the point of a decision. However, current BI solutions still fall short of what is desired. They still require specialists to run a statistical analysis, or a data mining process, and set up reports that can then be accessed by business users — they do not enable actions to be propagated back into business processes. BI products also rarely support user selectable data sources and real-time data integration, since almost all current BI products depend on pre-built data warehouses. There are almost no sets of real-time business performance data available because business activity monitoring is still outside the BI domain. Due to these breaks in the BI infrastructure and manual interventions by analysts, end business users do not typically have real-time access to information and cannot change processes in real time based on insights obtained from BI reports.

## What is Real-Time Business Intelligence?

The meaning of real-time business intelligence mainly depends on understanding what 'real-time' means for a business. Not surprisingly there are no agreed definitions here either.

'Real time' can mean:

- The requirement to obtain zero latency within a process.
- That a process has access to information whenever it is required.
- That a process provides information whenever it is required by management.
- The ability to derive key performance measures that relate to the situation at the current point in time and not just too some historic situation.

Based on these descriptions, RTBI provides the same functionality as the traditional business intelligence, but operates on data that is extracted from operational data sources with zero latency, and provides means to propagate actions back into business processes in real-time. Specifically, RTBI could comprise:

- Real-time information delivery,
- Real-time data modelling,
- Real-time data analysis,
- Real-time action based on insights.

## RTBI Vision

The main idea behind our vision of RTBI is the seamless transition from data into information into action. Current BI systems suffer from two bottle-necks in realizing this vision. The transition from data into information is hindered by the shortage of analysts and experts who are required to configure and run analytical software.

The second bottle-neck is the transition from information into action. Today's BI solutions basically do not go beyond generating reports. If the BI software cannot link back into processes automatically and drive process parameters, the transition from information to action can only be manual and can require long periods after which a specific action, i.e. process change, may no longer be appropriate.

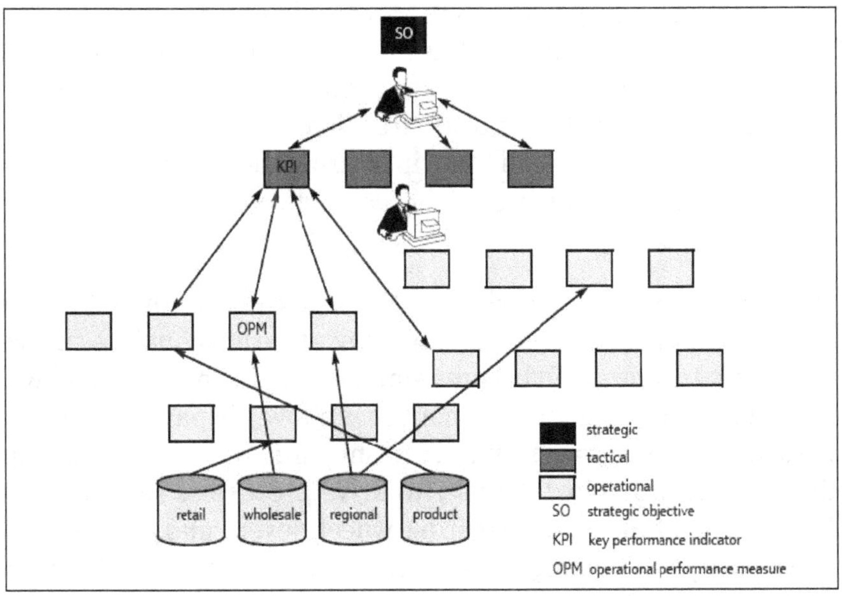


Current business management systems.

Figure above illustrates this situation of current business management systems. The information flow between operational, tactical and strategic layers is broken by manual intervention. RTBI will have a key role in aligning strategic objectives with business operations, and provide cross-organisation alignments to reduce friction between operational units. The challenge is to use intelligent technologies to model the manual intervention present in current systems and automate both the flow of information from operational to tactical to strategic layer, representing data to the information stage of RTBI, and the actions necessary to translate strategic objectives back to operational drivers to effect strategic decisions in real time. Additional challenges exist in areas of on-demand infrastructure configuration, data integration, and unified data models and on demand data warehousing as shown in Figure below:

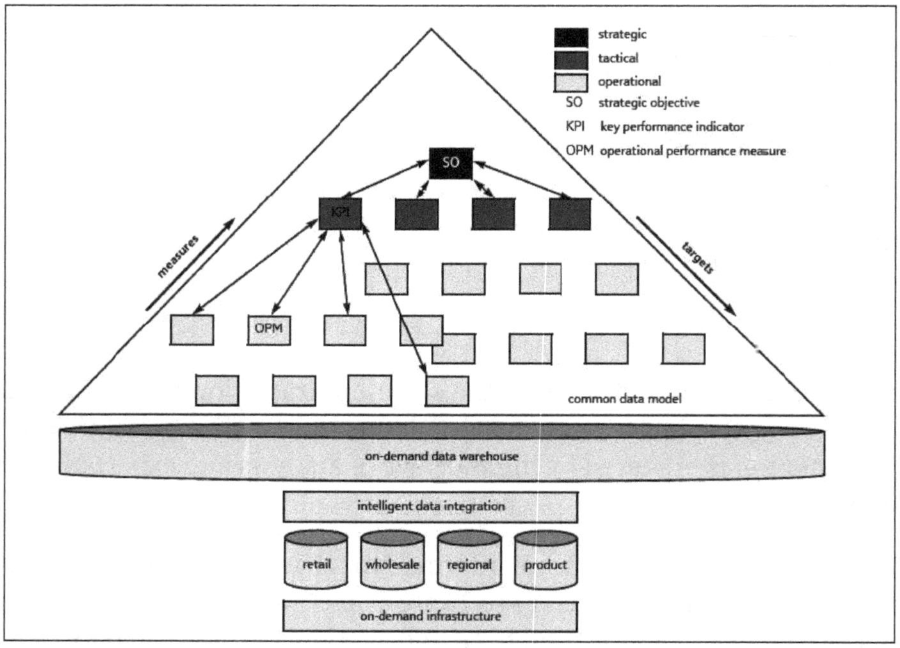


The vision for RTBI.

As an example, consider that a company's new strategic objective is to reduce customer dissatisfaction by 10%. That could, for example, translate into the requirement of handling 20% more calls in a contact centre, which means changing the key performance indicator (KPI) 'number of calls answered per day'. On a process level, that could translate into a mix of operational performance measures such as reducing the average call time, increasing the percentage of callers routed to the correct agent, and increasing the number of active contact centre staff which relates to measures like head count and attendance rate.

Current BI tools are mainly passive and their objective is to cater for the information consumer by providing reports or at most dashboard-like monitoring of various business processes. By moving from BI to RTBI, running a business will become similar to 'flying by wire', and we will see technology similar to that used in IT system management that allows disparate computers and networks to be controlled. Instead of ordinary performance dashboards with drill-down capabilities, we will also see process dashboards that allow the user to drive processes. To expand on the dashboard metaphor, an RTBI system would add a steering wheel, levers and pedals to the control suite, and enable business managers to change parameters of processes in real time. Obviously, RTBI systems need to put intelligent checks in place to prevent harmful changes, similar to the control systems in fighter planes which prevent pilots from killing themselves by turning too quickly. RTBI systems will contain algorithms that can detect unusual or novel patterns, and have the ability to return processes to possibly less efficient but safe conditions.

## Technology Challenges and Gaps

Real-time business intelligence requires many technologies and tools, and needs to interoperate with many enterprise applications and systems. There are many technical challenges to make them work together seamlessly. For the presentation of technology challenges, we have grouped them into three layers. The relationships between them are shown in Figure below:

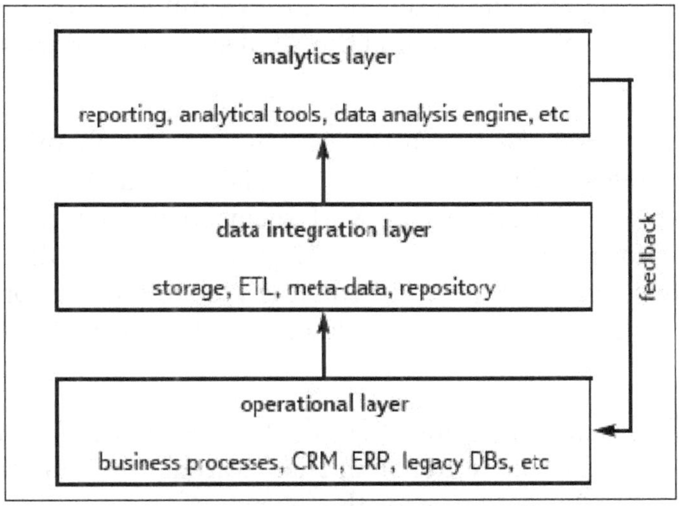


The three layers of the BI stack.

## Analytics Layer

Many BI solutions require expert analysts to drive or configure them. The analyst sits between the BI software that operates on the data and the information that is used by management to make decisions. This 'analyst-in-the-middle' approach prevents RTBI because the analyst represents a time lag that cannot be overcome.

In order to remove the analytical time lag from the process, RTBI software will require a high degree of automation. RTBI software must be able to work based on the specification of the data sources and the requirements of the outcome of an analysis process. The software must be able to select appropriate analysis methods and apply them automatically. The results must then be checked against user requirements. If the requirements are not sufficiently met, the analysis is repeated with different parameters. At the end of the analysis process, the best solution is automatically selected and presented as a high-level report. If the user decides to act on this information, the solution will be wrapped into a software module, for example a decision module that can be immediately deployed into a process, such as the script generation process for a contact centre.

The new role of the analyst will be in the initial setup and configuration of RTBI systems and their constant monitoring and improvement.

## Data Integration Layer

Most enterprises focus on the elements that are visible to the business users — functionality in query/reporting tools and BI applications, training on these tools and applications, and the impact of BI on critical business processes. Far too little time is spent on 'behind the scenes' or 'hidden' aspects of BI — the critical underpinnings that ensure a robust implementation capable of delivering insight in a reliable, scalable and flexible manner. Gartner considers the data integration layer of critical importance when deploying a BI solution.

The data layer needs to provide quality data to the analytics layer, because business intelligence based on poor quality is harmful. However, the data feed to the analytics layer requires data from different operational systems, and very often fused data from these systems. In order for an RTBI solution to succeed, it is paramount either that there is a continuous real time data feed from operational sources into the data warehouse, or that the RTBI system has access to operational sources via an integration layer.

There are many technology challenges such as platform, syntax, semantics and data quality metrics, as well as many products and initiatives. Most available technologies and products are doing well in addressing syntax and platform issues. XML seems to have become a de facto syntax standard. The two main platform technologies are J2EE used by Microsoft's rivals and Microsoft's own.NET. In the area of semantics, the W3C Semantic Web initiative proposes to use ontologies to address data semantic problems. Many vendors are now beginning to add Semantic Web technologies to their products.

The widespread use of BI requires a data layer which allows dynamic plugging in of new data sources, because enterprises cannot afford to build data warehouses for every BI application. Thus the technologies must be developed to provide the following:

- Unified data layer: A common meta-data structure unifies data access by creating a virtual warehouse view of enterprise data so that all users, regardless of their departments or analytical prowess, have access to the same values, field names and sources.
- Streamlined development cycle: This is a step-by-step guide to creating machine process able meta-data repositories and a mapping between meta-data and concept-based data access.
- Automated data mismatch reconciliation: This is a way of combining data while removing any mismatches between the different data sets.

## Operational Layer

For a complete RTBI approach, this layer must provide two functions: business activity monitoring (BAM) and real-time process tuning and change. Some BI vendors have already begun talking about BAM and process refinement based on feedback from operational events, but with limited actual implementation. Current BAM tools provide dashboards and charts that display the process attributes and KPI's, without the ability to make intelligent conclusions about the overall process behaviour. Such high-level conclusions are left to the process manager to discover, usually requiring extensive process knowledge and expertise. Another shortcoming of current BAM provision is in the area of conformance of human actors with the optimum process model. Although some rule-based conformance tools have emerged lately, these are mainly related to regulatory compliance and not with conformance with the optimum execution model.

As far as automated process tuning and re-engineering is concerned, current tools only provide a limited capability that applies in the case of fully automated, service-based processes which do not involve human interaction. An example of this would be selecting the cheapest web service out of the available list. In current practice, real business process change and tuning is carried out through a number of initiatives (e.g. Six Sigma and Total Quality Improvement) that are mainly manual, expensive and time consuming due to the complex subjective nature of process re-design. Furthermore, many of these initiatives fail due to the inability to check whether people are actually conforming to the suggested optimal process.

The challenge for RTBI is to facilitate automated mapping of existing business processes within an organisation, capture the knowledge to automate process tuning, optimisation and re-engineering, and monitor people and systems for process conformance.

## Towards Implementation of RTBI

Let us discuss some example projects and technologies developed as building blocks for the realization of RTBI.

## Advanced Analytics

### Automatic Data Analysis

SPIDA is a platform that uses soft computing methods like fuzzy logic and neuro-fuzzy systems for automating intelligent data analysis. The core of SPIDA is a client/server-based tool-box for data analysis that focuses on modern machine-learning techniques, including data preprocessing and visualisation. SPIDA enables non-experts to run an advanced data analysis without the need to understand, select and configure analysis algorithms. In a simple question/answer dialogue, SPIDA gathers high-level information about the problem to be solved and user preferences regarding the solution and data. It then automatically selects and configures analysis models, preprocesses data, executes analysis processes and displays results.

After an analysis model has been created from data, SPIDA re-evaluates its suitability. If necessary, internal model-learning parameters will be changed by SPIDA to improve the suitability of each model. New instances of each model will be learned from data in an iterative process.

Models that have been created in SPIDA can be wrapped into self-contained software modules. These modules can be integrated into other software applications. This way, SPIDA supports the automatic creation of intelligent data analysis solutions that can be used in daily business operations, either as a standalone tool or integrated into existing tools.

SPIDA can be used as the core analytical engine for future RTBI systems. It provides a high degree of automation which is essential for RTBI. SPIDA's capability to be driven by intuitive high-level targets will enable it to interface to the strategic objectives of the enterprise.

## Decision Optimisation and what-if analysis

RTBI systems must provide facilities for conducting a what-if analysis at any time. If managers decide to change strategic objectives based on the latest analysis results, they must know in advance how these changes will possibly affect the enterprise. By running an RTBI system in simulation mode, a what-if analysis can be run on the most recent data. The effect of proposed changes can be studied and, if approved, the changes can be propagated into the operational layer.

We have implemented a software platform that can be used as a decision optimisation and what-if analysis module in an RTBI system. DecTOP is a decision table evaluation and optimisation tool. It can monitor the performance of a decision model not only on an overall level, but also on the level of individual decisions. DecTOP enables the user to identify individual decisions of poor performance, and to optimise them manually or automatically. The user can study any number of variants of the decision model in parallel and compare their performance. By changing individual decisions, the user can conduct a what-if analysis. The automatic optimisation of the decision model can be based on different measures concurrently, for example, accuracy or cost. Previously, we have applied DecTOP to analyse BT's fault clearing process.

## Changing Processes

Changing live business processes based on BI results is one of the most demanding RTBI challenges because it requires process automation and possibly reengineering of legacy processes. We have recently deployed a platform in the area of mobile workforce management that can optimise certain process parameters based on analysis results.

The intelligent travel time estimation and management system (ITEMS) is a platform for automatically updating parts of the scheduling process for the mobile workforce of an enterprise. Service industries such as telecommunications, gas, water, electricity, etc., have to schedule jobs for large mobile workforces. Successful scheduling requires suitable estimates of inter-job times that are mainly determined by travel time. However, it is not sufficient to simply use routing software, because it cannot estimate the time that is required to find a parking space, to gain access to the site, etc. It is also impossible for technicians to log detailed information about the routes they have taken — they only log their actual travel (inter-job) time. Thus, it is not possible to compare travel data with recommendations from routing software.

Travel times that are estimated from historic travel data are more reliable, because they reflect the actual travel behaviour of the workforce, even if only point-to-point information is available. However, point-to-point information is also the only kind of data a scheduler can suitably process, because it would be intractable for a scheduler to analyse different routes while computing a job schedule. Recorded inter-job times automatically reflect features of the areas between which the journey took place. Areas where it is difficult to find a parking space, for example, will automatically result in higher values for the estimated travel time. Because workforce travel displays distinct local patterns, only a fraction of all possible combinations of areas has to be considered by a model for travel estimation. If for some areas there is no travel data available, default estimates are used. For areas where travel occurs regularly, estimates will improve over time. Improved estimates for travel will improve job scheduling, which will finally result in a reduction of unnecessary travel and can thus create huge savings.

ITEMS has a learning component that constantly builds new models for travel-time prediction. It compares the new model with the performance of the model currently used by the scheduler and updates the scheduler if the new model performs significantly better. ITEMS can operate in real time, if the travel data of the mobile workforce is recorded in real time.

A customised version of ITEMS has been deployed within BT. In addition to process optimisation, ITEMS also provides visualisation and explanation facilities. ITEMS can therefore already be seen as a limited application-focused RTBI system that provides analytical capabilities, reporting, access to operational data and (only automatic) process optimisation.

The intelligent business process management IBPM platform is being developed to support BAM and automated business process change. Information extracted by the data analysis component will be used to achieve the business goals or, in terms of execution, to optimise the KPI's. Any change in the policies in the enterprise will be reflected in the KPI and consequently will be considered by the optimisation system automatically.

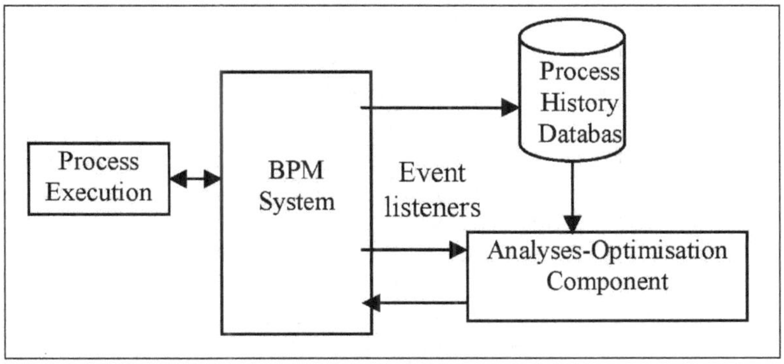


The IBPM platform.

There are three main means to tune a process using IBPM as the base framework:

- Task assignment: The most obvious way to improve the efficiency of a process is to provide a better means to assign resources. Old priority-based scheduling algorithms can be replaced with more intelligent methods.
- Task routing: IBPM processes can define routing nodes where the system can decide which path the instance will take depending on the goals of the systems.
- Process modification: With IBPM the process definition can change at run-time providing great flexibility to the user. Although redesigning the process to improve the performance automatically is theoretically possible, it constitutes a challenge that we are currently far from achieving efficiently.

## Semantics-Based Information Fusion

The DOME project has researched and developed ontology-based techniques to support the building of a real-time data fusion platform. We have developed a methodology, a set of tools and architecture to enable enterprise-wide information management for data reuse. The system retrieves information from multiple data resources, fuses them and resolves mismatches according to the user's queries or application requirements. This section gives a brief overview of the DOME prototype system. Details of DOME can be found in Cui et al.

The DOME prototype consists of a number of key components — an ontology server managing the contents of the entire enterprise data sources, a mapping server which manages the relationships between ontologies and data sources, and a query engine for decomposing queries and fusing sub-query results.

The DOME information model is based on ontology. DOME ontology includes terms used to denote real or abstract entities, and their relationships such as inheritance, formal structures of entities (e.g. attributes), and any constraints. We use the following ontologies to model data sources and applications — a shared ontology, source ontologies and user and application ontologies. The inter-relationships between the various ontologies are shown in Figure below:

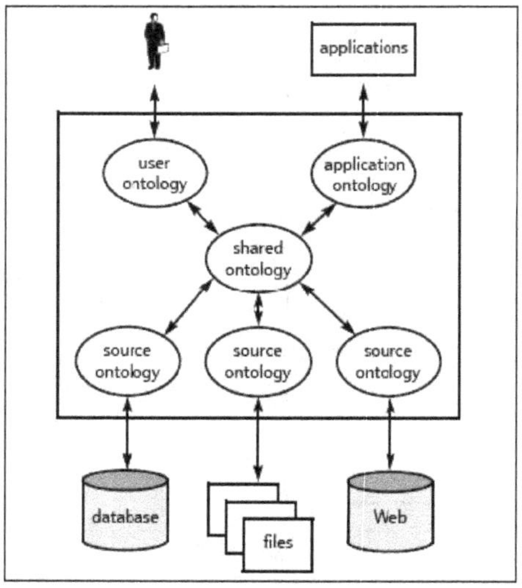


Model of data sources, users and applications, and their relationships.

A shared ontology is a common, agreed vocabulary of both domain users and developers. We treat this ontology as a superset of vocabulary which is rich enough to describe any enterprise data sources. Tools have been developed to update this shared vocabulary.

Source ontologies define the data semantics of their associated data sources. The terms in source ontologies are often taken from a shared ontology, but their definitions could be further constrained. For example, certain attributes may be sub-typed or have fixed values. New terms may be defined, over and above those in the shared ontology.

Shared, source, user and application ontologies are the critical components for DOME to perform context-based mismatch reconciliation at runtime. As an example, products could be priced in different currencies. DOME could automatically convert all product prices into pounds sterling for UK users, and US dollars for US users. Of course, the user could force the system not to resolve any mismatch, if they prefer. We have applied the DOME system to database marketing which uses internal and external data sources, and to e-catalogue management for e-markets to fuse different catalogues.

## Interfaces and Customization

To make RTBI a reality, BI tools need to be in the hands of many more business users of all management levels. This requires simple, intuitive and non-technical interfaces. Current BI tools are either still aimed at the analyst/expert, or have gone down the route of specific applications. In the first case the tools are too complex, and in the second case the tools are too specific, to deliver all the required intelligence.

BI interfaces must therefore be delivered via Webbased interfaces, or plug into standard office tools. Web-based interfaces on a J2EE infrastructure, especially for the enterprise market, seem to be the right way to go because they are very suitable for hosted solutions, and can also easily be administered on the intranet of an enterprise. While these interfaces are also suitable for SMEs that use hosted services, interfaces that plug into office software could provide a competitive advantage for the SME market (compare Microsoft's 'BI for the Masses' programme).

To make BI tools more accessible and useful to business users, automatic adaptive user profiling can help to automatically tailor the software to the user's needs. We should also not forget mobile users. BI can help mobile sales forces or work forces out in the field.

Systems like SPIDA, DecTOP, IBPM and ITEMS are examples of systems that try to make intelligent solutions accessible to non-expert users, each by hiding different aspects of an analytical process and by providing intuitive Web-based interfaces for different types of user.

## Embedded BI

BI will be increasingly embedded in pre-packaged applications and services. Built-in BI capabilities allow monitoring and analysing the performance of an application or service and — even more important —allow changing parameters to fine-tune the performance based on the collected and analysed data.

Figure below illustrates how RTBI should be embedded into a process to use process data and external drivers to analyse and update an internal decision model that drives the process. Based on the complexity of the process, the RTBI module can either run fully automatically or wait for feedback from higher instances that first interpret the generated report before they approve any changes to the process. The report of the RTBI module would also provide alarms and predictions of the future development. Based on business rules, this information can be escalated in real time to the right instances within the enterprise and trigger action immediately.

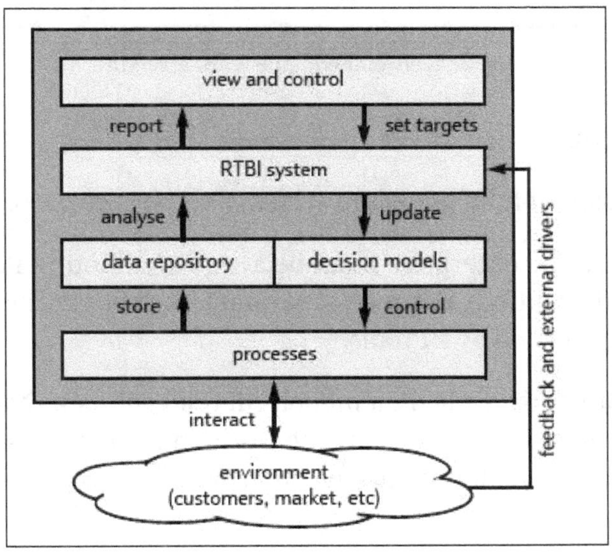


Embedded RTBI.

In Figure below we show how the embedding of RTBI modules can be recursively repeated within an enterprise. RTBI modules within low-level processes directly access process data. They turn this data into information (e.g. measures), and report it upwards to higher ranking or supervisory processes. They can also directly turn information into action by deriving process internal targets and update the process directly. Action in the form of targets is also propagated from higher order processes down the hierarchy. This recursive implementation of RTBI provides the potential for local optimisation as well as global optimisation. Processes on any level have the possibility to tune their performance themselves according to local BI results and prescribed targets. At the same time, the board has access to all key performance measures of the business, can change global targets, analyse the possible impact and cost in what-if scenarios, and finally propagate new targets back into the business, which are then translated into process-specific targets during the propagation down the process hierarchy.

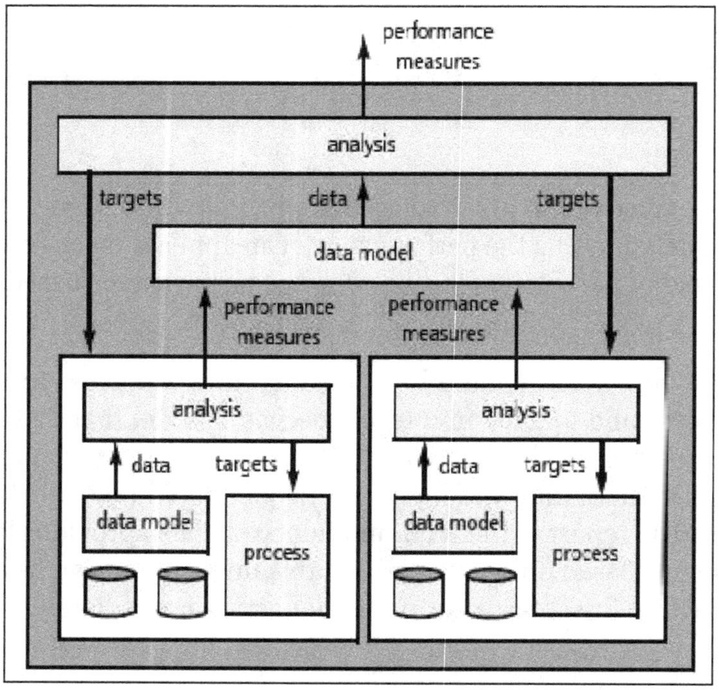


A recursively embeddable RTBI structure.

## BI Tools Development

In order to realise that vision of fully joined up systems, three core prerequisites must be fulfilled:

- Adaptive processes: The enterprise must be aware of all internal processes that are under direct control, and identify the process parameters that can be adapted (bottom layer), based on insights provided by BI tools.
- Infrastructure: Enterprise-wide data model: All relevant data that is generated by internal processes or by interaction with the outside world must be represented and made available for analysis. New data is entered into the enterprise wide repository as soon as it is generated (middle layer).
- Modelling: Flexible automatic analytics: Several layers of BI solutions with increasing degrees of automation are provided to support different analytic scenarios (top layer).

This structure allows data to flow from processes via an enterprise-wide infrastructure to analysis tools that turn data into information and into action by propagating targets back to the process layer. Access to the data model and the analysis tools will be distributed throughout the enterprise.

The top layer of the RTBI model contains BI (modeling and analytics) software that access the middle layer to analyse data and provides new parameters for the bottom layer in order to optimize processes.

Currently we do not see this full picture of turning analysis results into changes of business process. Current BI tools fall into the following categories:

- Report and visualise what has happened: Most of the currently available tools fall into this category.
- Understand why it has happened: Some tools are available at the moment, while more and more tools will become available in the next two to three years.
- Predict what will happen: Although few tools are available today, there are, however, many echniques available for this purpose and more tools will start to appear in the next five years.

In our vision of RTBI, future BI software will encompass all three categories, and on top of that requires different degrees of automation for different user groups and different purposes. Future RTBI will run fully automatic discovery processes that sift through data on a continuous basis in order to find anomalies or interesting patterns. Results are flagged up in automatically generated reports that contain recommendations for changes on a process level.

Currently, BI software is mainly aimed at analysts and provides very little support for managers who have no background in data analysis. While the current generation of BI tools will become more powerful, adding more advanced modelling capabilities on top of visualisation and reporting, the real quantum leap will be represented by automated user-enabling tools.

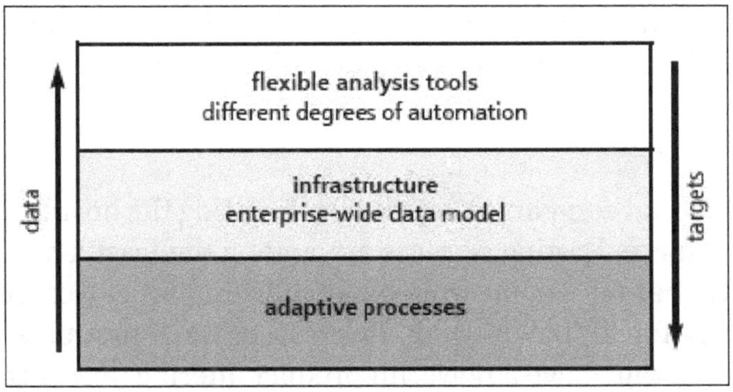


Major building blocks for RTBI.

BI software, that provides this level of automation and user support, can be set up to run in an unsupervised discovery mode as well. This type of software will be able to pick up automatically that there is a significant change in a performance indicator like customer satisfaction, and try to find models that explain this change. Once a model has been found, it can generate the same kind of modifications for the process layer as if it were driven by a high-level user interaction.

As managers become familiar with BI tools and the tools become more and more user friendly, managers will demand access to high-quality data and analysis results. They will want to select data sources and use them according to their requirements. In an analogy to the growth of the Internet and enterprise-wide intranets, we will see an ever-increasing access to BI tools over the next years until they will be available to almost anyone in an enterprise. Finally, everyone could use BI tools to improve their performance.

## Processes and ICT Infrastructure

The ICT (Information and Computing Technologies) infrastructure of the enterprise is a key factor in process performance, and therefore in the overall performance. Businesses try to minimise spend on ICT, and design their infrastructure such that their processes can just operate without problems. However, the question is how ICT infrastructure must change in order to accommodate changes in processes.

When RTBI propagates targets from the strategic level via the tactical level into the operation level, it is eventually the processes that must adapt to achieve new targets. This means that new operational performance indicators are set which result in new KPIs which realise the new strategic objective. For that to work, the dependence of operational performance measures (OPMs) on process parameters must be known. ICT infrastructure can be viewed as contributing parameters to OPMs.

All these measures can have an impact on the ICT infrastructure. Consider the example in Section III. Shortening the call time could mean that the CRM system must provide the customer details faster, i.e. the response time of the data warehouse must shrink. Improving call routing could mean the installation of a new generation of routing software, and increasing the number of staff means buying more terminals and increasing network capacity.

This example illustrates that ICT must become a tuneable parameter of a process, but in an RTBI scenario this must go much further. The level of knowledge, which ICT resources are required to achieve in some OPMs, must be provided and configured. If ICT infrastructure is viewed as a configurable resource, and the dependency between ICT configurations and OPM is known, then a business can automatically and dynamically allocate ICT resources to processes.

## RTBI for ICT

Gartner has found further that companies are underestimating the hosting opportunity. In the BI/DW (data warehousing) space, hosting services are among the least available offerings from CSI companies. End users that are re-engineering or establishing processes (for example, interactive marketing) are candidates for BI/DW hosting. By creating RTBI products on top of hosting solutions, service providers not only have a powerful product offering, but at the same time are in the unique position to be able to fully analyse, understand and control their own ICT products in that space. The same functionality that is offered as an add-on product to the customers can also is used to monitor the performance of the service provider's own business. By using predictive analytics, the service usage can be monitored, and resource can be dynamically allocated. By monitoring development of the utilisation of resources and violations of service level agreements, it would be possible to tailor service level agreements to new products, and adapt them to changing customer needs.

## Data Feed to Analytical Tools

Data warehousing technologies will continue to be the main technologies for feeding data to analytics tools. As more and more data, and new analytical tools, become available, extracting, transforming and loading (ETL) this data to the data warehouse, to be used by analytical tools and reporting tools, will be the bottle-neck to the realisation of RTBI. At the moment, building a data warehouse takes months and even years. Furthermore, data warehouses are often built with a specific purpose in mind. It would be difficult to repurpose these without the loss of information.

To overcome this bottle-neck, real-time ETL will appear that are able to fetch data from operational data sources in real time. These RTETL modules will still be built beforehand using pre-packaged ETL tools available on the market. New vendors might still appear, but existing big vendors will dominate this market.

A significant change in this space will be the development of specific data connectors. At the moment, these connectors are not very flexible, and cannot be used by ordinary business users. Although these connectors will not be exposed to end users, they need to provide end users with declarative descriptions of the data sources to which they are connected, so that users will be able to select data sources based on criteria like quality, context and content.

Meta-data and semantic content repositories will appear. These will provide those capabilities that are similar to 'data shopping malls'. They will contain sets of data arranged by use for each business unit that will allow the business-unit managers to analyse data specific to their area of interest. Data shopping malls will be more accurate, more responsive and less susceptible to the statistical anomalies of large data sets in the data warehouse.

Standards and tools will be available for data source owners to publish their semantic contents. This is in stark contrast to the current ETL and data warehouse practice where data sources have to reconcile their mismatches with the DW schemata. When new data warehouses are built, the whole process repeats again. With the published semantic contents of data sources, tools will become available which will reason over the semantics and contexts, and then ETL data from them will be put into data warehouses. All this will happen in real time as end users choose the data sources to use by their chosen analytical tools.

## Infrastructure Development

The future RTBI infrastructure will include the following elements:

- Static data warehouses and dynamically user configurable data shopping malls where users can select the data sources they require.
- Meta-data information for the whole enterprise.
- Taxonomies and ontologies for describing contents and providing semantic content information.
- Information about the context of data sources.
- Advanced ETL tools for gathering and feeding data to analytical tools — this new generation of ETL tools will be able to extract, transform and load data from unstructured data such as customer feedback, e-mails, reports, etc, in addition to databases.
- Feedback mechanisms to operational systems.

End users will be able to choose data without the need to know the details of the data sources. They will also be able to compose views of information using arbitrary data sources for further analysis. These views will be able to take the end users' context and preferences into consideration.

The infrastructure must be able to change business processes in response to new actions based on business intelligence. This will be realised by controlled feedback mechanisms that allow users to access and modify process parameters in operational systems. Obviously, this feedback mechanism has to be protected by proper checks and bounds.

## Visual Business Intelligence

Visual Intelligence is not exactly a buzzword, but the concept is relatively easy to grasp. Being visually intelligent means being able to process, understand, and express visual information. One's Visual Intelligence is a quotient that can be improved by practice. She often uses art in her training and examples, showing how the effort of examining and expressing visual stimuli can have a positive effect on general communication and understanding. The details are what seem to be her focus; those details that others seem to miss, but can be instrumental in solving the task as hand. She shares real-world examples from her decades of law enforcement and municipal consulting, like crime scenes that were only solved because a detail unnoticed by many; a ceiling fan still turning, or a pair of pants that was mysteriously inside-out.

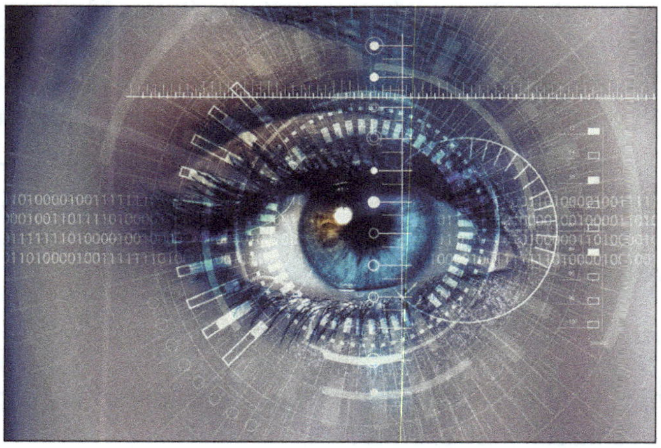

Seeing things clearly, and in a way that others cannot, is valuable in any setting but has particular efficacy in business. Increasing visual acuity, and in turn the communication of the insights gained from visual acuity, can have enormous impact on the success of business initiatives. This is where ideas can generate, where pitfalls can be avoided, and opportunities are uncovered.

### Blending Visual Intelligence and Business Intelligence

Business Intelligence, as a field, tries to make sense of data. Business Intelligence software is one of the main tools in this mission, as it empowers users to blend data from multiple applications and databases, providing a coherent picture of business operations in aggregate. How, though, does that picture come together? How can we assure that the data is being communicated effectively? How do businesses make the connection between "business intelligence" and "visual intelligence"?

Data visualization is an efficient way to process complex information, which is crucial given that the amount of data generated today can feel overwhelming. Visualizing data opens the door to greater comprehension of complicated data points by catering to the fundamentals of visual perception like pre-attentive processing and Gestalt principles. Our brains are uniquely suited to processing visual information quickly and effectively, and well-planned data visualization can communicate more than a table or paragraph ever could.

Dashboards aggregate data from various sources and display that data visually, communicating the message behind the numbers and encouraging viewers to take action on the information at hand. A visual dashboard is synced real time to the data sources the user already relies upon, whether that's Excel spreadsheets, databases, CRMs, online apps like Google Analytics, or a central data repository where multiple sources are blended.

## Data Visualization as Process

One may draw the conclusion that data visualization and data analysis is the same thing, or that data visualization is the resulting product from "successful" data analysis. While it is true that a certain amount of data work is necessary to create a data visualization or dashboard (especially one using several different data sources), that data viz is not the end of the road. In fact, a data visualization can be an effective tool to begin data analysis.

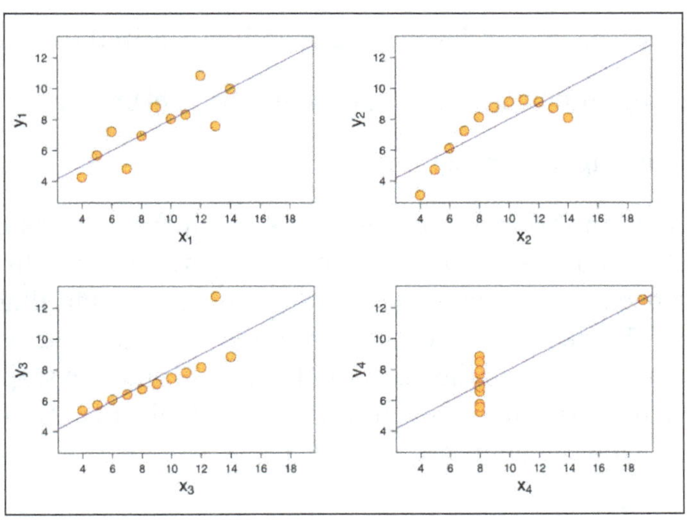

Frank Anscombe, the founding chair of the statistics department at Yale University, illustrated the importance of visualizing data prior to analysis based on research done in the 1970's. Using four similar data sets, Anscombe developed what is commonly known today as "Anscombe's Quartet" which shows the effect of "outliers" within the data set when put in to a graphic representation of that data. All four have many of the same data properties, such as linear regression line and mean values of X and Y, but graph very differently.

Without the ability to use visual intelligence to identify the outliers, the important aspects of the data set might have been missed. A preliminary data visualization can be critical to identifying the real questions one eventually wants to answer, leading to further analysis and potentially further visualizations to communicate the insights uncovered.

If Visual Intelligence is the quotient of one's perceptual acuity, and if indeed practice makes perfect, it would stand to reason that the more data visualizations one makes and analyzes, the more visually intelligent and effective one will be. Data visualization allows us to both exercise our visual intelligence and to benefit from it, uncovering insights and sharing those insights with colleagues and collaborators. The right business intelligence platform will provide the forum for visual intelligence to flourish, leading to greater understanding, communication, and decision-making.

## Organizational Intelligence

Organizational intelligence is a framework for integrating a broad range of business improvement and survival initiatives, combining the latest management thinking with advanced software technologies to produce highly effective organizations. People and technology have complementary forms of intelligence, and in an intelligent organization these abilities are coordinated and mobilized to the best advantage.

Organizational intelligence includes the following abilities:

- Making sense of complex situations and acting effectively.
- Interpreting and acting upon relevant events and signals in the environment.
- Developing, sharing, and using knowledge relevant to its business purpose.
- Reflecting and learning from experience.

These characteristics of organizational intelligence are much the same as the traits we recognize in intelligent individuals — not the narrow form of intelligence as measured by IQ tests but the broad practical intelligence that all people possess to some extent and that some people possess more greatly than others. There is, however, no automatic correlation between the intelligence of an organization and the intelligence of the people in the organization; a stupid organization can be full of brainy people who don't talk to each other, while an intelligent organization can be made up of average people who collaborate effectively.

## Benefits

Intelligence is important for organizations, especially in a complex and dynamic world, because it encapsulates a number of critical and widely acknowledged strategic capabilities, including those relating to knowledge and learning.

This leads to the following two hypotheses: that general improvements in organizational intelligence are desirable and that such improvements are widely possible.

There are three ways in which an organization and its stakeholders can benefit from organizational intelligence:

- The organization is likely to become more successful in the short term and have greater prospects for survival and growth in the longer term.
- Staff morale is likely to improve, and the individual employees will themselves have greater opportunities for personal growth and fulfillment.
- In the broader socioeconomic system, intelligent organizations will create more wealth, not merely economic wealth but in human potential.

Are these benefits available to all organizations or only to those organizations that already possess above average collective intelligence? It may well be true to some extent that intelligence breeds intelligence; in other words, "to those that have, more shall be given." But our working hypothesis is that practically any organization, however dysfunctional stupid on the surface, contains the seeds of intelligence that can be nurtured with sufficient insight and patience.

Organizational intelligence provides a key focus for certain individuals within a large organization. For example:

- The CIO needs to take a strategic view on the use of information within and beyond the boundaries of the organization. Use of simple information within routine business operations is largely taken care of within established application package suites such as SAP and Oracle or homegrown legacy systems. If the CIO is not to be merely a glorified purchasing clerk, acquiring standard commodity software and services from the cloud, he or she needs to rethink and reframe the role of management information within the organization. Organizational intelligence offers a framework for providing a joined-up set of systems, services, and platforms to support intelligent and collaborative business processes across the enterprise and its ecosystem.
- The HR director needs to take a strategic view on the development of creative collaborations and intelligent communities across the workforce and beyond. The deployment of new social tools within the enterprise (such as Enterprise 2.0) represents an opportunity for radical cultural transformation, which calls for sensitive leadership.
- Other key roles may include sales and marketing, product/service, and R&D.
- Meanwhile, the more enlightened software vendors will advise their customers how to align their systems and services with business objectives and organizational culture.

### Detailed Capability Model

Organizational intelligence calls for six connected capabilities as listed below. An informal schematic diagram is shown in Figure below. The six capabilities are:

- Information gathering: How well does the organization collect and process information about itself and its environment?
- Sense making: How well does the organization interpret and understand itself and its environment?
- Decision and policy: How effective are the (collective) processes of thinking, decisions, policy, and action?
- Knowledge and memory: How does the organization retain experience in a useful and accessible form?
- Learning and development: How does the organization develop and improve its knowledge, capabilities, and processes?
- Communication and collaboration: How do people and groups work together? How do they exchange information and knowledge? How do they share ideas and meanings?

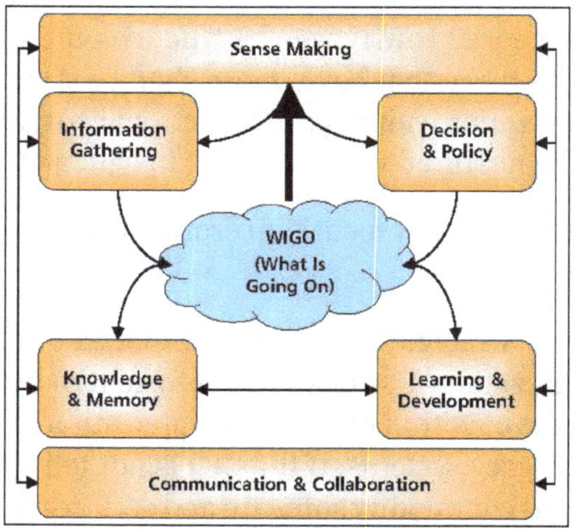


Key capabilities of organizational intelligence.

When an organization lacks intelligence, this may be because one of these six capabilities is weak or marginalized within the organization or because the loops connecting these capabilities aren't working. But when these capabilities are connected and in balance, the organization will make better decisions, respond more promptly and appropriately to key events and trends, and learn efficiently from experience.

## Location Intelligence

Location Intelligence (LI) is the collection and analysis of many sources of geospatial data that are transformed into strategic insights to solve a variety of business challenges. How is it possible?

This technology has the ability to compile and enrich different types of large datasets such as GPS data, transactional data, sociodemographic data, footfall traffic or points of sale data, to be used for deep geospatial analysis. The information is then displayed on a simple and map-centric interface which allows users to visually conceptualise the factors that affect the performance of their businesses in various locations.

In 1854 the first instance of maps being used for geospatial analysis was recorded. John Snow created a map in which he used geolocation to determine the cause of the cholera epidemic troubling London. His map showed the location of a well where local residents who were sick had gone to fetch water and how they were all connected to one single water pump.

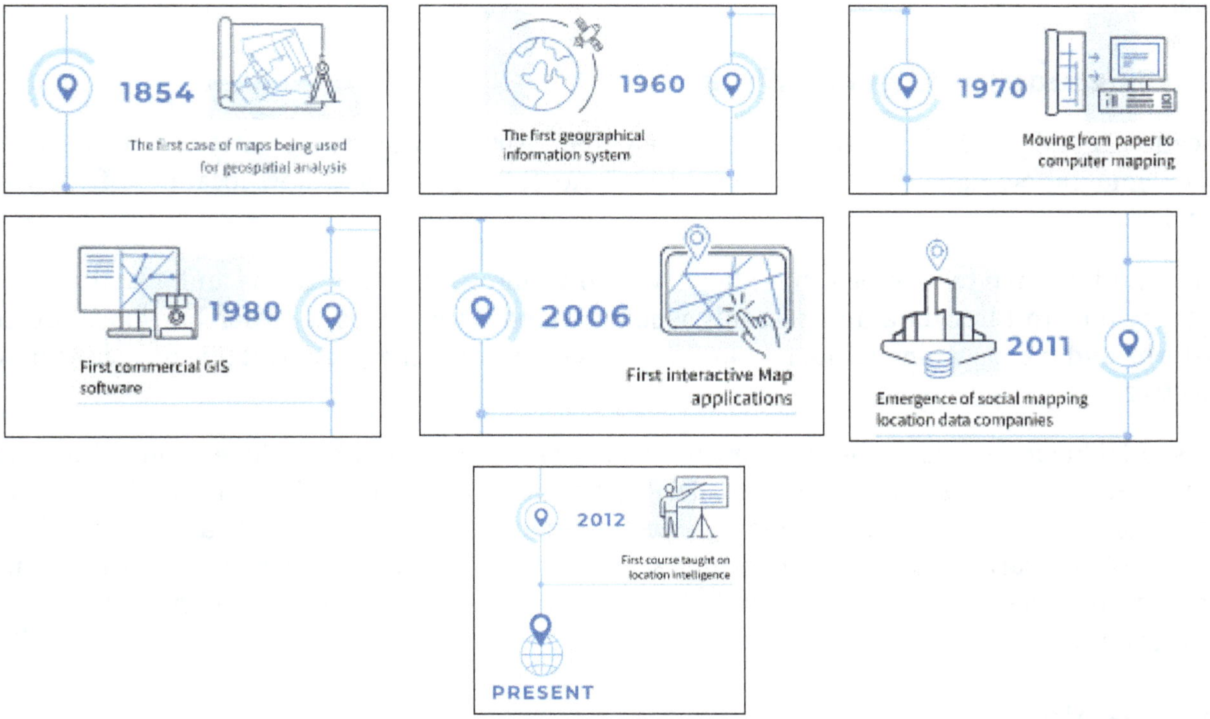


Business Intelligence was first coined in 1865 in a book written by Devens, and how it can be used to analyse data to maintain a competitive advantage. By the late 80s, BI had taken a more commercialised approach, allowing users to become more self-sufficient.

Around the same time, Artificial Intelligence was being discussed at Dartmouth to debate the continuous improvements in technologies capacity to fuel computer research.

The first Geographical Information System (GIS) was created in 1960 by combining geographical data and maps. The benefits of GIS, such as reducing operational costs, led to its progression. In the 1980's the first commercial GIS software was launched. However, this technology has its limits as only select professionals have the know-how to extract the true value of geospatial data. The difficulties GIS applications have faced in regards to ease-of-use and intuitiveness have made its commercialisation challenging—a challenge Location Intelligence technology has overcome with its simple design.

In 2012, the first applied course on Location Intelligence was offered at the University of Texas by Wayne Geary. He defined it as the process of identifying the optimal location that will promote business success and overcome a variety of business challenges.

The evolution of smartphones took location data to a new level. The upsurge of mobile applications which compile massive amounts of location data started to be analysed using Big Data techniques to gain insights on the whereabouts of users. As time progressed, businesses became increasingly more aware of the need to incorporate the insights extracted from location data analysis into their corporate strategies. Only then would they successfully grow their companies and stay relevant in a turbulent corporate environment. The evolution of these disciplines is what has spurred the development of Location Intelligence technology and contributed to its technological makeup.

## How Location Intelligence Works

Location Intelligence is an intuitive technology that gives you access to a variety of data such as sociodemographic data, disposable income and more, to understand how location affects your business.

It is an interactive technology that allows you to generate real-time maps and visualisations, so that you can filter data and see only what matters. This makes it easier for you to detect patterns and trends which relate to your business needs, making your strategic decisions more effective.

Geospatial business intelligence is interdisciplinary and comes from the intersection of three different fields—Business Intelligence, Artificial Intelligence and Geographic Information Systems technology. This convergence has allowed businesses to transform location data into valuable insights, solving various use cases such as maximising store network efficiency, performing sales forecasts and selecting sites with the right location characteristics to support a sustainable expansion strategy.

## Visualisation

Interact proactively with many different sources of data at once and visualise your results at any time. Having information displayed in an easy-to-visualise way means that you can make decisions quickly and easily, without having to cipher through files and lists of information.

## Analytics

Use advanced statistical analysis with big data and machine learning techniques to understand what was previously hidden. This information improves your understanding of the environment and its influencers, so you can make justified business decisions.

## Data

Gain access to multiple sources of data (e.g. demographic, number of competitors, footfall traffic). Geoenrichment is a fundamental factor when developing a business strategy; having the detailed information to target your market is essential to your performance.

# Sales Intelligence

Plenty of sales experts rely on their own knowledge and expertise to drive big numbers. This has however started to change. With data being accessible now more than ever and companies moving to digital sales, the approach is shifting. Companies need to keep growing, and for that reason, being more 'intelligent' about sales approaches are a key to driving up revenue for the years to come. But how easy is it to adopt a smarter, more data-friendly approach?

That, ultimately, is where sales intelligence comes in. In the modern age, clients and customers demand deeper, more personal experiences. People in the modern era do not respond well to assumptions and cajoling. Therefore, more and more businesses and entrepreneurs are seeking to blend their market research and sales channels together.

Sales intelligence revolves around the concept of pooling data about the prospect. Specifically, it is a process which derives data from prospective clients in real-time, and through multiple different channels and platforms. It offers you more than just a quick database of people who you may wish to contact.

Effective, all-encompassing sales intelligence goes deeper than just pulling together contact details. Sales intelligence strategies should work hard to analyze context and behavior, not just face value data. For example, a sales intelligence regime may pool together data that lets you know about a business client's corporate history. Or, it may give you deeper insights into its financial performance. A client's behavior is also a key aspect for determining intent.

Sales intelligence helps to build towards a bigger, clearer picture for all parties in the sales conversation. That not only helps to bridge gaps between sales and marketing but will help to move negotiations with potential clients along with more natural, mutually beneficial milestones. The long and the short answer is, sales intelligence helps us to understand our prospects a little better. That means we can tailor more worthwhile experiences towards their needs.

## Why is Data so Important for Sales Intelligence?

Without data, sales techniques are pointless. It is a blunt statement to make, but data is what helps to propel effective marketing campaigns forward, and it's what also helps us to refine our targets. In the case of sales intelligence, the more data we pool, the better. However, this data needs to be useful – and accurate – which is why it's important to derive information from multiple trusted and worthwhile sources.

Various studies and analyses show that data is crucial in decision-making. With genuinely helpful data, we can understand what our customers and clients are looking for in closer detail. Rather than blanketing them in a stereotype or poorly-researched demographic, sales intelligence can pull together a hyper-contextual data platform, which is neither too broad nor too niche.

What's more, sales intelligence is fantastic at helping to pull together data that is actually relevant. A major downfall of unsuccessful relationship-building lies in focusing on the wrong data, or the incorrect parameters. With a refined sales intelligence program, we can make sure that the data we source is highly relevant. It's worth following up on. The right data can actually help us to understand who our customers are and how we can approach them.

## How can Sales Benefit from Marketing Data?

While it's easy to think that sales and marketing work together hand in hand, this is not always the case. In the modern age, there is more of a push to blend the two departments together. However, marketing tends to be much more hands-off than sales is with the customer approach.

The biggest takeaway from blending marketing data with sales is the fact that it can help both sides of the coin to understand customers better. Marketing tends to be little more behind-scenes than sales after the lead is acquired. Sales, meanwhile, works directly and actively interacts with customers.

Sales can use marketing data to actively establish new scripts and action plans. Rather than muddle through the same tried and tested channels, sales will benefit from marketing data and insights which are thoroughly researched.

That helps to add up to incredible client knowledge. This, of course, is beneficial to all customers. Engagement value increases, as buyers receive tailored campaigns and approaches. That will, eventually, mean that marketing can continue to offer sales well-researched opportunities. Customers receive better experiences and sales – of course – get more sales.

## Defining the Ideal Customer Profile for Qualifying Leads

Before you start qualifying leads, an ideal customer profile needs to be set up. An ideal customer profile (ICP) is a fictional profile of a customer who is a good fit for your business. An ICP is essential to understand defining factors for lead qualification. Now, you probably know your ICP sub-consciously and all you need to do is translate your ICP in terms of these data sets: individual, geographic and firm graphic.

This profile helps you tally your leads with specific characteristics and behavioral patterns that are desirable to you. The derived data can be transferred to sales and it helps them stay updated with relevant information and sales qualify the leads.

## Sales Intelligence Software

Sales intelligence software helps reps to find and understand details about prospects and customers. These tools collect data from all public sources and collate them into easily usable format making it readily available for reps. Reps can slice and dice the data to understand the market, accounts, buyer intent and changes in the organizations without spending too much time on it.

These tools give you information about:

- Firmographics: Firm-level data like revenue, number of employees, growth rate, etc.
- Demographics: People level data like name, age, gender, designation, etc.
- Technographics: Technology level data like technologies the company is using etc.

- Behavioral: User action level data like clicks, views, actions, etc.
- Intent: Buyer intent level data like searches, articles read, etc.

## Who uses Sales Intelligence Software?

- Sales: Sales reps have to maximize time selling and reducing time hunting data and doing research. Intelligence tools can help them do in-depth prospect research, enrich CRM data, avoid junk leads, etc. in less time. They use them to understand the organization charts, key decision-makers, latest projects, and intent signals so that they can pitch at the right time increasing chances of making a sale.
- Marketing: Marketing teams use intelligence tools primarily for data enrichment of their leads and segmentation/targeting helping them improve their conversion rates. For example - Marketers can design smaller forms and with just email have all the other data auto-populated or the can show certain content to a portion of the traffic they want to target by knowing their IP address etc.
- Recruiters: Intelligence tools are mainly designed for salespeople, but they can also be used by recruiters for identifying new employees and filtering them based on criteria they deem fit.

## Benefits of using Sales Intelligence software

- Increased productivity: The biggest advantage of using sales intelligence tools is that they give back time to your sales reps. They cut down time spent on researching and prospecting the potential customer by giving all necessary information in a matter of a few clicks. More time for reps means more selling time, which leads to increased sales.
- Improved customer experience: Today's buyers are very well researched before making a purchase. So the sales rep is also expected to do his homework when engaging a buyer throughout his buying journey especially during the initial stages when the rep is trying to get new leads. Knowing the details such as customer's intent, authority, and designation, existing tech stack, etc. can help the sales rep make a good first impression and personalize every communication. This improves the customer experience, improves the response rates, and shortens the sales cycle and likelihood of conversion.
- Increased (and predictable) Pipeline: Sales intelligence tools help reps generate contact lists of people similar to your existing customers. It helps reps to prioritize the right companies and accounts and give them appropriate time and opportune moment to reach out.
- Better data quality: Intelligence tools can help improve the quality of customer data by enriching it with all the information reps don't have. Just from the email address of the user, you can know his name, designation, company, tech stack, department, etc.

## What Business Problems are Solved by Sales Intelligence Tools?

### Prospecting

Today the sales reps spend a lot of time trying to refine the best customers to go after. Having key insights about the users before the first contact is made is a huge win for the sales rep. Reps can define the parameters such as industry, revenue, technology, etc. and shortlist the companies of interest to them. They can also set up alerts for the changes in these accounts or when anyone in these accounts does a particular action signaling buyer intent. Approaching the potential customers, when the intent and other relevant context is established, improves the chances of conversion much higher.

The above process can also be smoothed out by some of these tools. Reps can enter the list of best current customers and tools can do the heavy lifting to identify the ideal customer profiles, generate the target list of companies and accounts to go after, thus making generating new leads much easier.

Alerts help rep be on top of the changes in terms of technology, org charts, projects, etc. Buying signal alerts helps reps be in front of the buyers at the right time with the right pitch. Reps can create a sense of urgency and right fit by knowing the intent and tech details about the account and that is a huge value adds as it saves a lot of time for both the parties.

Relationships are a key to closing deals and growing accounts. Hence knowing the decision-makers and influencers in the organization, helps sales reps formulate strategies to push new sales.

Reps can get the following type of data from sales intelligence tools:

## Firmographics

- Company performance: Revenue, growth trends,
- Status: Private, VC funded, Public,
- Size: Employee count, sales,
- Industry: Health, consumer,
- Location: US, Europe,
- People: Designation, contact.

## Technographics

- Usage: How much the product is being used within the company?

- Renewal: How many times is the subscription being renewed esp. when not renewed?
- Spend: What expenses are being made on a particular product?
- Adoption: How well a product is being used across the organization?

## Behavioral

- Searches: User searches help reveal intent.
- Articles: Give insights into the type of content being consumed by users.
- Intent: Buying propensity.

## Data Enrichment

Prospects are always on the move from one role to another, from one company to another, from one country to another, etc. It is hard for the individual sales rep to be on top of this. This is where sales intelligence tools come into play and keep track of the changes happening in the B2B universe and updating daily. Data enrichment is another big proposition of intelligence tools. Most of the time sales reps have just the email or contact number of the person. These tools help enrich the information on different dimensions and give a holistic picture to the rep for further action. Beyond enrichment, data cleaning helps reps to get rid of duplicate contacts, cleanse records, ensuring clean information for rep usage.

## Top KPI's for Sales Intelligence Tools

- Increase in response rates,
- New leads generated,
- Improved customer experience.

## How does this Sales Intelligence Software Differentiate them?

- Breadth and Depth of data: This software primarily differentiates them based on the total number of data points they have about the users or accounts or industry. The more data points usually mean wider coverage of accounts, individuals, etc. helping the reps reach out to a larger group.
- Accuracy/Freshness of data: Having incorrect data, having redundant duplicate data, having stale data, etc. are common complaints of users of intelligence software. To solve these issues, some tools even have human teams verifying the data to push the accuracy of the data collected by technology means.
- Other functionalities: Intelligence tools expand their offerings from just being a data provider. Some tools have built-in email outreach capabilities along with the B2B database. Or they have a direct integration with your sales engagement / CRM platform to reach out to these prospects at scale.

## Top Features of Sales Intelligence Tools

- List builder and filters: List builders along with deep filters help you narrow down the targets from a huge list of data to the most relevant ones.
- Lead scoring: Since the tools have detailed information about the clients / prospects, the can easily score the leads based on ICP of rep defined parameters to prioritize the leads which helps reps go after the most important accounts first and maximize the odds of closing.
- Data cleansing: This involves identifying data inaccuracies, correcting them, normalizing data, de-duping it and keeping the data fresh.
- Alerts: Probably one of the most useful features of the intelligence tools. It comes in handy when someone is beginning his buying journey and rep gets an alert so that you catch the user early on. Or if some user stopped using a tool and rep are alerted right then. You can define alerts for any action the buyer takes action, or important events happen or market trends change, etc. so that sales reps are ready to leverage the new change.
- AI: AI is applied by companies very differently. Different tools use AI to answer questions:
    - Will a person be promoted soon?
    - Will the company expand and start a new project?
    - What does the DISC Personality of the users look like?
- AI is also used in identifying ICP based on best customers and automating alerts based on past behavior.

## How to Choose Sales Intelligence Software?

## Who should buy Sales Intelligence Tools?

Sales intelligence tools are mainly used for B2B companies from small ones to enterprise. Some tools do specialize for verticals like Winmo specializes for media and marketing industry so the depth of contact and company data is higher for that vertical. If you need industry-specific data, you should look for a tool that specializes in that vertical. If not you should go after a tool that has more depth and accuracy.

## Coverage and Accuracy of Data

These are the two biggest strengths and challenges for an intelligence tool. What is the breadth and depth of the database and what is the accuracy and freshness of their data? This can single-handedly tilt the buying decision in favor of the vendor. This is a big problem because ~30% of data goes stale every year. Hence the rate at which company updates its data becomes really critical.

Most data is collected by tech scrapping and needs to be human-verified. But humans can verify millions of data points. Hence what % of data is human-verified is a key metric to look at when evaluating these tools.

Account-level relationship structures are extremely critical to decide the GTM for that account. Hence having org charts and key decision-makers and influencers mapped is a huge plus.

### Integrations

Intelligence tools have to integrate with your CRM to update and enrich the lead information. Also, they have to power email engagement campaigns for your prospects. Hence it becomes extremely critical to look for solutions that have good integrations with both CRM and engagement platforms.

If you are a small company, some tools have an engagement module built for your needs, so that you can avoid buying an intelligence and engagement tool separately. Apollo.io, Growbots, Autoklose, etc. work perfectly well for intelligence and engagement needs of small to medium companies.

### How do you want to use AI?

Some companies exclusively focus on using AI to identify growth companies i.e. mining early signals if a company is planning to expand into new businesses or new projects in the near future. Companies such as Gazelle.ai, Cognism do a good job of answering the growth question.

### ROI Concerns

Since users have highlighted ROI concerns with intelligence tools it makes sense for you to do an ROI discussion with vendor before buying an intelligence tool.

## Product Intelligence

Product intelligence is the process of gathering, analyzing, and acting on data related to how customers use your products. It relies on combining product data and operational data to drive product development and improve product experiences. This additional data means your analyses are based on a more complete picture of how customers interact with your product, and you can uncover new insights you would not have surfaced from product user data alone.

One of the challenges of implementing a strong product intelligence strategy is that the data required to derive actionable insights often lives in multiple silos. User behavior data and product metrics, for example, must be combined with customer data from other sources such as CRM systems, marketing tools, and customer experience apps. When all of these data sources are integrated for analysis, the true power of product intelligence can be harnessed.

### What makes a Product Intelligence Platform?

Unlike traditional business intelligence tools, which are typically used to provide a high-level overview of general business metrics and analytics, product intelligence tools home in on product performance and product analytics specifically.

You might think these analyses are only valuable to product managers and product designers, but almost every business department can benefit from having access to product intelligence. Sales can have more effective upsell conversations with power users. Marketing can create more targeted campaigns for new users stuck in the onboarding funnel. And customer success can identify potential at-risk customers when product usage trails off.

Because of its usefulness across the organization, an ideal product intelligence platform provides an easily accessible, collaborative environment in which data can be aggregated and analyzed by multiple teams. And it makes the latest usage data and statistics available in real time, so that decision-makers always have the most up-to-date product information at their fingertips.

## Product Intelligence Tools

Fortunately, there are many analytics solutions that are purpose-built to deliver the insights stakeholders need to make informed decisions. Tools like Pendo, Optimizely, Amplitude, and others excel at aggregating and displaying analytics data in multiple ways to meet the needs of sales, marketing, product, and engineering teams.

However, these tools are only as good as the data they have access to. Your investment in a product intelligence platform will only pay off if it delivers a holistic view of the customer experience both in-product and throughout the rest of the customer lifecycle. If the data needed to obtain these insights is missing or incomplete, the usefulness of your product intelligence initiatives will be diminished, if not eliminated entirely.

## How Data Integration Powers Product Intelligence

Stitch's product intelligence solution supports a range of data sources needed to create product intelligence, including:

- Amplitude,
- FullStory,
- Heap,
- Intercom,
- Marketo,
- Mixpanel,
- Optimizely,
- Pendo,
- Salesforce.

As well as all of the major cloud data warehouse destinations:

- AWS Redshift,
- Google BigQuery,

- Microsoft Azure Synapse Analytics,
- Snowflake.

And you can use any popular analytics tool to create product intelligence reports and dashboards:

- Mode,
- Google Data Studio,
- Looker,
- Microsoft Power BI,
- Tableau.

## References


- Business-intelligence: tableau.com, Retrieved 03, Jan 2020
- Top-challenges-in-business-intelligence: predictiveanalyticstoday.com, Retrieved 11, Jan 2020
- Why-financial-intelligence-is-a-key-to-success: opportunitydesk.org, Retrieved 23, Jan 2020
- The-dawn-of-new-era-in-accounting, accounting-intelligence-336732276: researchgate.net, Retrieved 05, Feb 2020
- The-guide-to-agile-business-intelligence: predictiveanalyticstoday.com, Retrieved 15, Feb 2020
- Commercial-Intelligence: cips.org, Retrieved 20, Feb 2020
- What-is-competitive-intelligence-terms-and-concepts-you-need-to-know: crayon.co, Retrieved 08, March 2020
- Market-intelligence: market-intelligence, Retrieved 19, March 2020
- What-is-social-intelligence-and-how-can-it-make-your-business-money: social.industries, Retrieved 27, March 2020
- How-data-is-disrupting-retail, retail-intelligence: qualetics.com, Retrieved 08, April 2020
- What-is-location-intelligence: geoblink.com, Retrieved 17, April 2020

# 2

# Understanding Business Analytics

Business analytics is the process by which businesses use statistical methods and technologies to analyze past data and predict future states in order to gain new insights and improve strategic decision-making. Business analytics can be sub-divided into prescriptive analytics, predictive analytics, decision analytics, descriptive analytics, pricing analytics, retail analytics, etc. This chapter sheds light on Business Analytics and its related aspects to provide a better understanding of the topic.

Business analytics, a data management solution and business intelligence subset, refers to the use of methodologies such as data mining, predictive analytics, and statistical analysis in order to analyze and transform data into useful information, identify and anticipate trends and outcomes, and ultimately make smarter, data-driven business decisions.

The main components of a typical business analytics dashboard include:

- Data Aggregation: Prior to analysis, data must first be gathered, organized, and filtered, either through volunteered data or transactional records.
- Data Mining: Data mining for business analytics sorts through large datasets using databases, statistics, and machine learning to identify trends and establish relationships.
- Association and Sequence Identification: The identification of predictable actions that are performed in association with other actions or sequentially.
- Text Mining: Explores and organizes large, unstructured text datasets for the purpose of qualitative and quantitative analysis.
- Forecasting: Analyzes historical data from a specific period in order to make informed estimates that are predictive in determining future events or behaviors.
- Predictive Analytics: Predictive business analytics uses a variety of statistical techniques to create predictive models, which extract information from datasets, identify patterns, and provide a predictive score for an array of organizational outcomes.
- Optimization: Once trends have been identified and predictions have been made, businesses can engage simulation techniques to test out best-case scenarios.
- Data Visualization: Provides visual representations such as charts and graphs for easy and quick data analysis.

The essentials of business analytics are typically categorized as either descriptive analytics, which analyzes historical data to determine how a unit may respond to a set of variables; predictive analytics, which looks at historical data to determine the likelihood of particular future outcomes; or prescriptive analytics, the combination of the descriptive analytics process, which provides insight on what happened, and predictive analytics process, which provides insight on what might happen, providing a process by which users can anticipate what will happen, when it will happen, and why it will happen.

Some business analytics examples include the operation and management of clinical information systems in the healthcare industry, the tracking of player spending and development of retention efforts in casinos, and the streamlining of fast food restaurants by monitoring peak customer hours and identifying when certain food items should be prepared based on assembly time.

Modern, high quality business analytics software solutions and platforms are developed to ingest and process the enormous datasets that businesses encounter and can exploit for optimal business operations.

## Business Analytics vs. Data Analytics

Data analytics is a broad umbrella term that refers to the science of analyzing raw data in order to transform that data into useful information from which trends and metrics can be revealed. While both business analytics and data analytics aim to improve operational efficiency, business analytics is specifically oriented to business uses and data analytics has a broader focus -- both business intelligence and reporting and online analytical processing (OLAP) fall under the data analytics umbrella.

Data scientists, data analysts, and data engineers work together in the data analytics process to collect, integrate, and prepare data for the development, testing, and revision of analytical models, ensuring accurate results. Data analytics for business purposes is characterized by its focus on specific, business operations questions.

## Business Analytics vs. Data Science

Data science is a multidisciplinary field that uses scientific systems, methods, and algorithms to study structured and unstructured data in order to determine where information comes from, what it means, and how it can be transformed into a valuable resource in the development of information technology strategies.

Data science combines data analysis, statistics, machine learning, and related methodology in order to manage and understand the data deluge associated with the emergence of information technology. Data scientists are tasked with presenting digital information in a way that depicts its practical value in data-driven decision-making; however, they don't typically endeavor to solve specific questions in the way that business analysts do when seeking out business analytics insights.

## Business Intelligence vs. Business Analytics

While business intelligence and business analytics serve similar purposes, and the terms may be used interchangeably, these practices differ in their fundamental focus. Business intelligence analytics focuses on descriptive analytics, combining data gathering, data storage, and knowledge management with data analysis to evaluate past data and providing new perspectives into currently known information.

Business analytics focuses on prescriptive analytics, using data mining, modeling, and machine learning to determine the likelihood of future outcomes. Essentially, business intelligence answers the questions, "What happened?" and "What needs to change?" and business analytics answers the questions, "Why is this happening?", "What if this trend continues?", "What will happen next?", and "What will happen if we change something?" Business analytics and business intelligence solutions tend to overlap in structure and purpose.

## Benefits of Business Analytics

A business analytics program is essential to the health of a competitive organization. By analyzing key business metrics, the leadership team of the business can make smarter decisions that drive greater value for the business overall. Business analytics can also provide insight to what strategies are working and where to invest in growth. An overview will be provided to describe the specific transactional, informational and strategic benefits offered by a business analytics program.

## Transactional Benefits

Transactional benefits are defined as the tangible direct outcomes of a business analytics system. These benefits include time savings, fewer meetings and reduced headcount. A business analytics program is typically managed via software and online analytical processing systems. By virtue of this type of technology, business metrics can be delivered automatically to end users in a timely fashion. This real-time delivery of data can reduce the need for manual computations and the chance of errors. As a result, the organization can achieve more with fewer meetings, fewer manual processes and in many cases fewer staff, which will dramatically reduce the business cost. As a business is looking to expand into new markets, it will need to continue to manage its agility so that it can scale its business processes to manage new markets. A business analytics program will help the business manage increased workloads while remaining effective in resource allocation.

## Informational Benefits

A business analytics program must be able to turn raw data into usable information; thus, informational benefits of such a program include substantiated facts, the ability to discern business patterns and an increase in transparency throughout the organization. Through the analysis of business metrics, an organization can track customer behaviors and purchasing patterns, improve website design, analyze user-generated content, understand market and competitive intelligence and ultimately begin to forecast the future. Not only will a business analytics solution consolidate all the information about daily operations, but it will also present it to management and business users in an actionable way. Based on a survey of nearly 3000 executives, there is striking correlation between an organization's analytics sophistication and its competitive performance. The biggest obstacle to adopting analytics is the lack of knowhow about using it to improve business performance.

Business analytics help measure how much of a business' Mission Statement will be accomplished; it provides a clearer insight through data visualization; analytics keeps the company up to date; and it offers efficiency. The main benefit a business will realize is an increase in revenue. In some ways this will be immediate and, in other ways, this will take time to occur. This will occur due to a precise understanding of the business and customer needs. "Analytical Insight can maximize loyalty and revenue by extending the right offer at the right time to the right customer, as well as build personal interactions between company and consumer". Ultimately, this will allow Funtastic to focus its efforts on ways to increase the number of sales from its existing customer base, as well as determine new ways to increase with new customers through the trust and loyalty from its existing customers.

## Strategic Benefits

A strong strategy is supported by good business analytics. Business analytics enable organizations to understand business insights, make decisions and resolve key issues that are barriers to success. A business will experience better decision making through the use of analytics. Business analytics is used "to extract information from data to make better decisions and find problems". By extracting this data to make better decisions, organizations are able to focus on what is truly best for the organization, immediately and in the future. This also ties back to an increase in revenue by being very specific with what products and services to offer. After all, "adopting efficient business intelligence and reporting is vital if businesses want to stay competitive and ahead of the game".

The crux of business analytics is the combination of statistical techniques with business savvy. A business analytics program will help an organization understand its business and to deliver good business decisions quickly based on data reflective of the market. A business' strategy should be a reflection of the changing market and business landscape as revealed by its analytics. Business analytics will help a business to stay innovative and ahead of their competition. Most important, the solution is essential to encourage smart decision-making. Decision making is the critical process which makes or breaks a company's goals.

A business analytics program has a number of benefits, ranging from transactional to informational to strategic. When combined, these benefits ultimately provide a competitive advantage to the organization by revealing trends, predicting the future and informing better decisions. A business will benefit from a business analytics program to help it grow over the next few years.

## Successes and Failures of Applying Business Analytics to Strategic Decision Making

The need for continual analysis and innovation to remain competitive through new opportunities is what sets a lot of successful businesses a part from failing ones. The world is constantly changing. Just as new fashion and technology trends change, so does the need for business analytics and statistical analysis within an organization to adapt to an ever-changing landscape. Advances in technology, improvements in efficiencies, and opportunities to save consumers time and money force many companies to explore new ways to improve business practices.

Business Analytics Planning enables an organization to investigate the different types of statistical analysis required to execute a new business strategy and achieve the goals of an organization. The ability of business analytics to be successfully applied to strategic decision making is what enables a supply-chain company to identify ways to get products to consumers faster. It is what allows marketing firms to identify what platforms to use when advertising a product or service within a target demographic. It is what enables retailers to manage inventory more efficiently and understand what goods to stock to fulfill the needs and wants of their consumers.

While the concept of Business Analytics Planning may sound simple, its application is actually very complex. The ability to gain actionable intelligence and apply that into a successful strategic decision-making initiative can be the difference between why some companies become pioneers for new ideas and why some ultimately close their doors for good. The need for the right team with a good blend of industry experience and technical expertise is crucial.

There are successful and failed examples of applying business analytics to strategic decision making in every business section. In this paper, we will examine the examples in two business sectors, retail industry and healthcare organizations because these two business sectors have significant effect on our daily life. The differences in how these organizations utilize their data demonstrates exactly how critical business analytics are to the success of an organization. For the retail industry, we will explore the difference between a highly-profitable retailer: Walmart and a failing competitor within the retail industry: Kmart. For the healthcare organizations, we will examine a successful example: the American Cancer Society and a failed example: the UK National Health Service.

## A Successful Example in Retail Industry: Walmart

With more than 245 million customers visiting almost 11,000 stores and 10 active global websites, Walmart generates roughly $36 million dollars in sales every day. Walmart relies on big data analytics to leverage its ability to manage supply chains and keep inventory levels optimal, perform research on constantly changing customer trends and demographics, and market across a multitude of social media outlets. Business analysts track data consisting of what customers are buying online, outcomes of local sporting events, what is trending on Twitter, and even how local weather deviations impact buying patterns. Walmart collects 2.5 petabytes of unstructured data from over 1 million customers every hour.

Walmart has been able to take such a significant amount of unstructured data and turn it into actionable intelligence by migrating from an experiential 10 node Hadoop cluster, to a 250 node Hadoop cluster allowing data from 10 global websites to be consolidated into one massive data ecosystem. This data is then analyzed to cover millions of products with 100s of millions of customers across several different sources. Data is then analyzed into 100s of millions of keywords to optimize the bidding of each keyword on a daily basis. It is with this actionable intelligence that Walmart strives to reach its primary objectives of optimizing the shopping experience for each of its customers (both online and in-store). The outcome of Walmart's ability to successfully apply business analytics to strategic decision making has resulted in 10-15% increases in online sales in incremental year-over-year revenue.

The quality of Walmart's business analytics plan is excellent as it combines an extremely large volume of data with the speed to analyze it quickly. Walmart's ability to not only obtain this much data, but also store and organize it allows the company to edge its competitors and drive its organization. The three most prevalent characteristics of Walmart's business analytics strategy that has led to its success over the years include its ability to accumulate analytics. Walmart's use of best statistical practice and its capability of collecting and storing data through a complex network of data management systems. This requires strong leadership throughout the organization with a clear vision to truly understand their customer's wants and needs.

Walmart makes data-driven strategic decisions based primarily on four functions: In the box behaviors (understanding what customers are buying), out of the box behaviors (understanding customer behaviors outside of Walmart at other retailers), stated behavior and attitudes (research of online and offline data of what is on customer's minds), and actual cross-channel purchase behaviors (understanding how online behavior influences in-store behaviors and vice versa). By analyzing data multiple ways, Walmart is able to understand and gain multiple perspectives on how customer behaviors impact sales.

## A Failed Example in Retail Industry: Kmart

In contrast to the success Walmart has achieved with effective business analytics, the consequences of ignoring your data or analyzing it inefficiently could have serious repercussions on the overall success of your company. Kmart is a great example of when business analytics fail to be successfully applied to strategic decision making. Once, one of the largest retailers in the United States, Kmart has been on a consistent decline since the 1980s as it struggles to compete with big box retailers like Target and Walmart. Despite efforts to restructure debt, remodel stores, acquire new business partners, and even implement a new Business Intelligence Platform Kmart has failed to adapt to changes in the marketplace and align business analytics with strategic goals.

Kmart is a great example of why simply implementing a new business intelligence system alone is not enough to succeed in business analytics. The importance of performing statistical analysis on your data to truly understand how your customers are being treated and how efficiently you are able to give them what they want is critical in the retail industry. Kmart's inability to analyze data and understand product trends and manage inventory levels would eventually result in a poor customer experiences as customers continuously complain that they are not able to find what they are looking for inside Kmart stores. This is largely attributed by Kmart's failure to adapt to a more modernized "just-in-time" inventory management system (like Walmart implemented), which would have allowed the retailer to restock shelves more quickly and efficiently.

In addition, Kmart failed to differentiate itself from Walmart (low cost retailer) and Target (more focused on value-based products for younger, image-conscious demographic) by offering several low budget designer goods (Jaclyn Smith designer apparel) paired with more high end appliances (IE: Kenmore appliances) with no clear concept on how to cater to a specific target market. Not only does this show Kmart's inability to capture market trends through business analytics and research, but this also shows a clear lack of leadership and organization throughout the company. Without the leadership needed to make data-driven strategic decisions, Kmart lacked the decision-making capabilities, technical practice, and use of best statistical practice to be an effective retailer.

As a result, Kmart's stock price fell 63% between 1998 and 2000 which ultimately would lead the company to bankruptcy in 2002. Despite several efforts to obtain new management and business partners, Kmart has continued to see declines in sales year after year. From $37 billion in sales in its 2000 fiscal year, to $12.1 billion in 2015, Kmart has closed hundreds of stores across the U.S. Kmart once had 2,165 stores to 979 in 2015. Kmart is a prime example of the consequences of poor management and an inability to leverage data to make strategic business decisions and adapt to a constantly changing market.

## A Successful Example in Healthcare Organizations: The American Cancer Society

For over 100 years, the American Cancer Society (ACS) has been leading the fight against cancer illnesses. Some of their biggest assets are their websites and mobile applications that allow users to learn about screening, detection and treatment, as well as volunteer opportunities and accepting donations. The latter being extremely important as the ACS is a non-profit organization. In 2012, senior members at ACS determined they needed a better understanding of their users and a better approach to marketing. They enlisted the help of Google Analytics and marketing company Search Discovery to help them evaluate their current marketing strategy and develop a plan for emerging markets. The goal of the project was to use analytics to understand how current users interacted with the ACS websites and mobile applications, monitor user behavior over time and subsequently remarket to new segments more effectively.

To better understand their users, Google Analytics was employed and the results were evaluated. It was determined that there were three main segments: information seekers, donors, and event participants. The next step was to determine the conversion rate for each of those segments. The conversion rate is where a user visits a website and completes an action. For instance, if a user visited the ACS website to view event details, and then completed a sign-up for that event, that would be a successful conversion. A customer scoring system was developed by Search Discovery that showed when each user was successful or unsuccessful at meeting a goal. The scoring system was used by the ACS marketing team to determine the health of each of their websites and to follow users' trends over time. The biggest gain, however, was that the ACS could use the information provided by the segments and scores to remarket to users by sharing fundraising ideas, or registering for local events among others.

The end result was that within two years, the ACS was able to successfully evaluate user patterns and subsequently develop marketing strategies to specific user segments. In one particular case, the team noticed an uptick in queries on their main site for breast cancer donors, however, they were expecting those donors to instead visit the site directly related to breast cancer. In answer to that data, they created a new promotion on their main site driving those specific donors to the breast cancer website. The result was an increase of 5.4% in revenue year over year. ACS is now using the scoring metrics to measure the performance of other website changes and redesign projects to help in their efforts to increase their reach to a new generation of support, patients and donors in the fight against cancer.

## A Failed Example in Healthcare Organizations: The UK National Health Service

Several years ago, the UK National Health Service undertook a project to integrate all patient medical records into a central healthcare database. The analytics this project predicted from this project would have been significant and valuable to the National Health Service. Information regarding illness, treatments and costs could have been tracked allowing the system to manage its resources more effectively. Illness and health trends among the population could have informed health care providers how to counsel patients and predict illness based on risk factors. The system would have also provided oversight to ensure standard treatment protocols for various procedures, offering better patient outcomes. This effort was originally estimated to take ten years and cost €6.4bn. By 2011, the program was shut down after spending more than €10bn.

The failure of the NHS National IT program is directly related to several challenges. First, the effort to build this analytical platform began with a lack of clear business objectives. Each health care provider within the system had different requirements yet they needed each of their systems to work together. Because the leadership team did not clearly understand, define or communicate the benefit of this effort to those affected, health care providers continued to work within their respective silos and did not find common ground upon which to build such a platform. The program was also challenged by technical difficulties stemming from a lack of expertise within the analytics team. Pointed to relevant technical experience as a critical component of a successful analytics project; NHS did not have this experience and therefore had issues in understanding the complexity of the system it needed to build. This resulted in vendor disputes and overall lack of progress. Finally, the project defined the customer as the NHS itself. While the NHS would clearly benefit from this analytics initiative, the real customers were the patients and the providers. Had the project understood its customers and their journeys from the start, this effort may have been better supported and more reflective of the business model.

## Implementing a Successful Business Analytics Program

Business analytics programs stress the utilization of quantitative analyses, predictive models and statistical tools to help organizational leadership gain a different view of their data, derive maximum value from its interpretation, and utilize the results to improve decision making and problem solving. However, as we can see from the previous section, the implementation of a business analytics program is no small feat. The implementation of this program will require a reorganization of the company, the recruitment of new professionals, and a revamping of organization of company strategies and culture. To reap the decision-making benefits of an analytics program, a business must work diligently to ensure the program is properly implemented. This implementation will include the development of an analytics team and leadership, the integration of analytics into the organizational culture through stakeholder involvement, the utilization of business intelligence systems, and the assessment of business needs and capabilities, and the application of statistical resources.

## Identify Business Needs

In order to properly and successfully implement a business analytics system, a business needs to document its business needs and requirements that it wants a system to be capable of producing. This will help identify the types of analytics systems and processes that it needs to develop or bring in, as well as the staff it will need to hire in order to meet the needs. The immediate business need for a business analytics system is to enable analytics-based decisions that will allow the business to increase its fleet with revenue growth. Furthermore, the business needs a business analytics system that can leverage data to inform their decision on their strategic plan.

## Build Business Analytics Team

The right business analytics team can turn massive amounts of data into insightful business knowledge that can be used to make timely business decisions. A strong business analytics team requires a unique set of skills and qualifications and piecing together these individuals can be difficult. The number one quality that most experts look for when building the team is intellectual curiosity. This quality is difficult to find because it cannot be taught or bought, but is highly desirable because technical skills alone are not enough. Organizations should seek candidates that demonstrate an involvement in a wide variety of projects and are constantly seeking to gain new knowledge. Analysts with these traits are more likely to dig deep into the data and are more effective at asking questions when performing their analysis. Companies should not be afraid to hire individuals that possess this trait but have technical skills that are lacking because skills such as math and science can be taught.

Organizations should be careful to not only focus on candidates that have strong skills in programming languages. The ability to script the various programming languages is vital to data analysis; however, management should also look for candidates that have the ability to communicate data through visualization. The ability to express the data visually can provide greater insights than other presentation methods. Being able to express ideas about how a business can best use the output of a data analysis is vital to the success of the analytics program. The analytics team should also seek out a leader that is the best storyteller when it comes to the data. The ability to tell the story through data is very difficult and should be done by individuals with a strong mind for business. Data can be difficult to understand in its raw format and therefore it needs a human touch added to it so that it can be understood by individuals in other areas of the business.

Another aspect to consider when assembling an analytics team is the use of domain experts. These experts possess the versatile skill of being able to translate the data from specific areas of the company into actionable intelligence. These individuals are necessary to make sure that the insights acquired from analytics will actually make a difference when they are applied to the operations of the business. Experts believe that the required amount of experience can vary from as little as six months in some cases to as much as ten years in industries that are highly specialized. The time required to develop these professionals is worth the investment for organizations because they add a perspective of reality that cannot be obtained from simple data analysis. It is recommended that these domain experts are rotated between the analytics team and the line of business so that they can continue to build their understanding of the day to day operations of the line of business.

## Identify Talent

When selecting among candidates, the organization should select candidates that have strong programming skills because the best data scientists must be able to manipulate the data in addition to just viewing and analyzing it. There is a big difference between a statistician that reviews and interprets the data set and the data scientist that can change the code that collects the data. Organizations should also look for candidates that have excellent communication skills. As mentioned before, these analysts need to tell the story of the data and provide visual representations whenever possible. These candidates should be able to provide real-world examples of how they were able to use their work to improve a business process. Some analysts will provide data that will result in algorithms where a computer makes the end decisions versus others that will result in a decision made by a human. In the case of a human decision maker, the value of good communications increases greatly.

The best candidates will also need to be great innovators. Recruiters will need to see that these analysts can think outside the box and create something new as the business changes. Candidates that have implemented the same processes in multiple companies may not possess the innovation skills that are needed. Finally, good candidates should have a strong understanding of the business to complement their math and analysis skills.

## Identify Skills and Certifications Needed

There are a wide variety of skill and certifications that a member of the data analytics team can possess. The candidates that fill these positions often have different skills and backgrounds, but there are some basic skills that are needed. A data analyst should have a strong understanding of Microsoft Excel so that the data is structured properly. Excel provides a suite of functionality to make data management convenient and hassle free. The data will be useless to the analytics process if it is not properly structured. A career as a data analyst can overlap with a career in higher mathematics and statistics at one end of the spectrum or can merge with a career in programming and software development. All candidates should possess some basic skills in SQL language and have some basic knowledge of web development.

R and Python are two of the most popular programming languages that are learned by data analysts. R is very useful when supporting statistical computing and graphics while Python is very easy to use and is good to use on large projects. There are also many certifications that are offered directly from companies such as IBM and Oracle. These certifications can help analysts differentiate themselves from the field by showing that they have extensive knowledge of these systems.

## Involve Stakeholders

The development of a qualified analytics team is far from sufficient in ensuring the success of an organization's business analytics program. The success or failure of an analytical endeavor can be due to the level of stakeholder support and involvement it receives. A list of business stakeholders can be found in Table below. To achieve analytics incorporation, organization stakeholders must be involved in analytics processes. The analytics team leader must possess the communication skills necessary to advocate the program throughout the organization. The first step in advocating must be a conversation with organization executives. The analytics leader must convey the benefits of analytics to garner trust and the resources necessary for performance. At the same time, this conversation must identify the goals and needs of the executives. By identifying the needs of the executives, the analytics leaders can ensure an alignment of strategies, further increasing executive's trust in the system, and the use of its results in decision making. While the executives are a linchpin in creating trickle down success for program integration, the program's success will also depend on the involvement of other stakeholders throughout the organization. Leadership and business quants must meet with not only executives, but divisional leaders and all potential users of the analytic results. The analytics team must conduct interviews with these data consumers to identify their needs and build analytical processes to meet them.

After implementation, the analytics team must meet with these data consumers on a frequent basis to evaluate the success of the program in meeting their needs, or identify areas of weaknesses that must be adjusted to meet their business process needs. Additionally, frequent conversations should be had with data consumers to check if their support level of analytics has changed. Through the inclusion of data consumers throughout the organization in the development of analytics, the analytics team will foster relationships that will ensure stakeholder involvement.

Stakeholder involvement will foster buy-in from the data consumers, as well as on-going communication that will help promote new uses of analyses, and increased prevalence of analytics-based business decisions.

## Create Business Analytics Culture

To truly succeed in implementation, business analytics must become an accepted component of the organization's culture. Many studies on business analytics programs have found that companies who fail to integrate analytics into the organizational culture ultimately fail to deliver on program expectations. In order to ensure that the stakeholders of the organization are involved, it is important that a strong analytics-driven culture is developed. Organizations that adopt an analytics culture can create economic advantages over competitors by quickly gaining insight from data and translating it into impactful business decisions. Companies across all industries are aggressively entering into analytics by making large investments in new technologies. Companies must be sure to create an analytics driven culture because large investments in technology are not enough to be successful on their own.

Companies that have created strong business analytics programs have found the proper mix of investment in technology and analytical cultures. There are five recommended steps that organizations follow in order to successfully create an analytics driven culture. A strong analytics culture must be installed using a top-down approach much like any successful business program. The senior management must not only accept the culture of analytics for it to be successful, they must champion it. Users of the business analytics system must be sure that the corporate leaders are fully committed to analytics-based decision making. Leaders that show they are fully committed will make others follow suit by setting a strong example.

An analytics driven culture can ensure that all employees are on the same page about the specific business objective that the analytics system is attempting to solve. Employees must be aware of both the importance of the analytics and the objectives in order to create a successful analytics culture. One of the most common causes of failures for analytics initiatives is a lack of clearly defined business goals. The best companies use analytics to solve very specific business questions. General business goals such as increasing revenue are not enough and do not generate as much success as the more specific goals.

Companies must openly share information and data to develop an analytics-driven culture. Information must be broken down into information silos in order to eliminate multiple versions of the truth. This can only happen when stakeholders throughout the organization openly share data and information and gaps between IT and the lines of business must be bridged. IT teams must ensure that the lines of business have access to the information they need. The lines of business must ensure that they collaborate with IT and amongst themselves to ensure data security and governance. All departments must adopt a shared data approach to make unbiased decisions for the best of the company.

Companies that involve more employees in the analytics process are usually more successful. It is critical that they cultivate and empower citizen data scientists which are non-IT users that can be embedded in the lines of business. The users will ultimately be responsible for driving innovation through analytics. Companies must invest in analytics technology that does not require advanced degrees to operate. The best systems allow data scientists to build analytics models and workflows using reusable templates that can later be used by non-IT users. Companies can also share analytics models outside of the organization through the use of online market places. This is an excellent way to empower the citizen data scientists and help foster an analytics-driven culture. Companies that have implemented a strong analytics-driven culture must be sure to make decisions based on what the data tells them. The previous steps will be useless if companies continue to make decisions using gut feelings or past experience.

## Prescriptive Analytics

Prescriptive analytics is a process that analyzes data and provides instant recommendations on how to optimize business practices to suit multiple predicted outcomes. In essence, prescriptive analytics takes the "what we know" (data), comprehensively understands that data to predict what could happen, and suggests the best steps forward based on informed simulations.

Prescriptive analytics is the third and final tier in modern, computerized data processing. These three tiers include:

- Descriptive analytics: Descriptive analytics acts as an initial catalyst to clear and concise data analysis. It is the "what we know" (current user data, real-time data, previous engagement data, and big data).
- Predictive analytics: Predictive analytics applies mathematical models to the current data to inform (predict) future behavior. It is the "what could happen."
- Prescriptive analytics: Prescriptive analytics utilizes similar modeling structures to predict outcomes and then utilizes a combination of machine learning, business rules, artificial intelligence, and algorithms to simulate various approaches to these numerous outcomes. It then suggests the best possible actions to optimize business practices. It is the "what should happen."

Prescriptive analytics is the natural progression from descriptive and predictive analytics procedures. It goes a step further to remove the guesswork out of data analytics. It also saves data scientists and marketer's time in trying to understand what their data means and what dots can be connected to deliver a highly personalized and propitious user experience to their audiences.

### Benefits of Prescriptive Analytics

If you're a senior executive, looking to further optimize the efficiency and success of your organization's operations is always top of mind. Prescriptive analytics is the smartest and most efficient tool available to scaffold any organization's business intelligence. Prescriptive analytics affords organizations the ability to:

- Effortlessly map the path to success: Prescriptive analytic models are designed to pull together data and operations to produce the roadmap that tells you what to do and how to do it right the first time. Artificial intelligence takes the reins of business intelligence to apply simulated actions to a scenario to produce the steps necessary to avoid failure or achieve success.

- Inform real-time and long-term business operations: Decision makers can view both real-time and forecasted data simultaneously to make decisions that support sustained growth and success. This streamlines decision making by offering specific recommendations.
- Spend less time thinking and more time doing: The instant turnaround of data analysis and outcome prediction lets your team spend less time finding problems and more time designing the perfect solutions. Artificial intelligence can curate and process data better than your team of data engineers and in a fraction of the time.
- Reduce human error or bias: Through more advanced algorithms and machine learning processes, predictive analytics provides an even more comprehensive and accurate form of data aggregation and analysis than descriptive analytics, predictive analytics, or even individuals.

### The Cloud and the Future of Prescriptive Analytics

In order to analyze data comprehensively, you need a robust and versatile location for data storage. Enter the cloud data warehouse. Cloud data warehouses make massive undertakings like understanding prescriptive analytics not only possible, but user-friendly. With its ability to house information while also supporting an endless selection of external tools and proprietary integrations, cloud data warehouses gives users an all-in-one solution to data analytics.

Imagine if businesses currently using on-premises system data as the basis for their predictive and prescriptive analytics could harness the power of the cloud? Not only would they gain more data, they would gain more accurate, secure, and real-time data. For example, a manufacturing company could draw on more than company data. It could leverage both historical and customer industry trends and predictions, and general economic predictive analytics. The power of the cloud is pushing prescriptive analytics into new, exciting possibilities every day.

## Predictive Analytics

Predictive analytics is the branch of the advanced analytics which is used to make predictions about unknown future events. Predictive analytics uses many techniques from data mining, statistics, modeling, machine learning, and artificial intelligence to analyze current data to make predictions about future.

It uses a number of data mining, predictive modeling and analytical techniques to bring together the management, information technology, and modeling business process to make predictions about future. The patterns found in historical and transactional data can be used to identify risks and opportunities for future.

Predictive analytics models capture relationships among many factors to assess risk with a particular set of conditions to assign a score, or weightage. By successfully applying predictive analytics the businesses can effectively interpret big data for their benefit.

The data mining and text analytics along with statistics, allows the business users to create predictive intelligence by uncovering patterns and relationships in both the structured and unstructured data. The data which can be used readily for analysis are structured data, examples like age, gender, marital status, and income, sales. Unstructured data are textual data in call center notes, social media content, or other type of open text which need to be extracted from the text, along with the sentiment, and then used in the model building process.

Predictive analytics allows organizations to become proactive, forward looking, anticipating outcomes and behaviors based upon the data and not on a hunch or assumptions. Prescriptive analytics, goes further and suggest actions to benefit from the prediction and also provide decision options to benefit from the predictions and its implications.

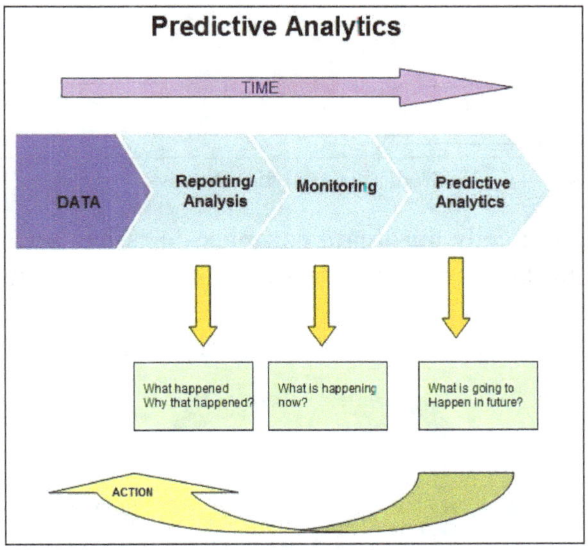


Predictive analytics value chain.

## Predictive Analytics Process

- Define Project: Define the project outcomes, deliverables, scoping of the effort, business objectives, identify the data sets which are going to be used.
- Data Collection: Data mining for predictive analytics prepares data from multiple sources for analysis. This provides a complete view of the customer interactions.
- Data Analysis: Data Analysis is the process of inspecting, cleaning, transforming, and modeling data with the objective of discovering useful information, arriving at conclusions.
- Statistics: Statistical Analysis enables to validate the assumptions, hypotheses and test them with using standard statistical models.
- Modeling: Predictive Modeling provides the ability to automatically create accurate predictive models about future. There are also options to choose the best solution with multi model evaluation.

- Deployment: Predictive Model Deployment provides the option to deploy the analytical results in to the everyday decision making process to get results, reports and output by automating the decisions based on the modeling.
- Model Monitoring: Models are managed and monitored to review the model performance to ensure that it is providing the results expected.

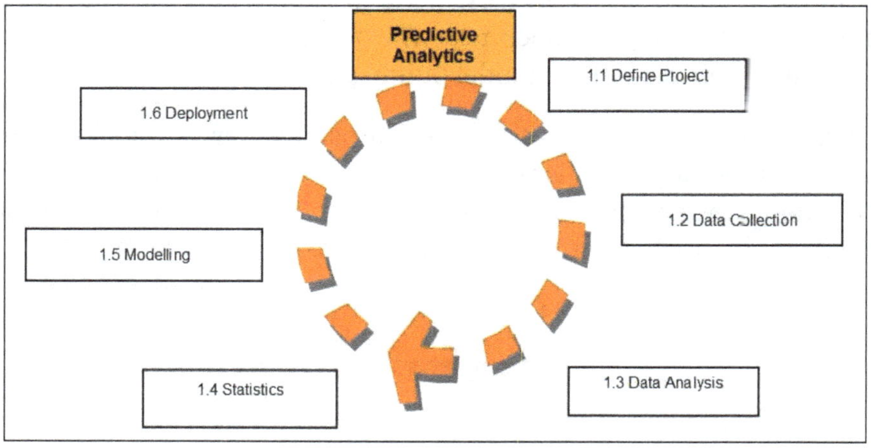


Predictive Analytics Process.

Prescriptive Analytics automatically automate complex decisions and tradeoffs to make predictions and then proactively update recommendations based on changing events to take advantage of the prediction.

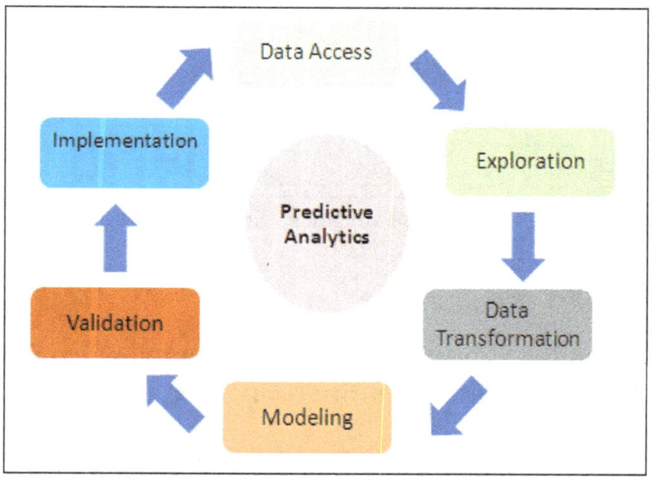


## Applications of Predictive Analytics

- Customer relationship management (CRM): Predictive analysis applications are used to achieve CRM objectives such as marketing campaigns, sales, and customer services. Analytical customer relationship management can be applied throughout the customer's life cycle, right from acquisition, relationship growth, retention, and win back.
- Health Care: Predictive analysis applications in health care can determine the patients who are at the risk of developing certain conditions such as diabetes, asthma and other lifetime

illnesses. The clinical decision support systems incorporate predictive analytics to support medical decision making at the point of care.

- Collection Analytics: Predictive analytics applications optimize the allocation of collection resources by identifying the effective collection agencies, contact strategies, legal actions to increase the recovery and also reducing the collection costs.
- Cross Sell: Predictive analytics applications analyze customers spending, usage and other behavior, leading to efficient cross sales, or selling additional products to current customers for an organization that offers multiple products.
- Fraud detection: Predictive analytics applications can find inaccurate credit applications, fraudulent transactions both done offline and online, identity theft and false insurance claims.
- Risk management: Predictive analytics applications predict the best portfolio to maximize return in capital asset pricing model and probabilistic risk assessment to yield accurate forecasts.
- Direct Marketing: Predictive analytics can also help to identify the most effective combination of product versions, marketing material, communication channels and timing that should be used to target a given consumer.
- Underwriting: Predictive analytics can help underwrite the quantities by predicting the chances of illness, default, bankruptcy. Predictive analytics can streamline the process of customer acquisition by predicting the future risk behavior of a customer using application level data.

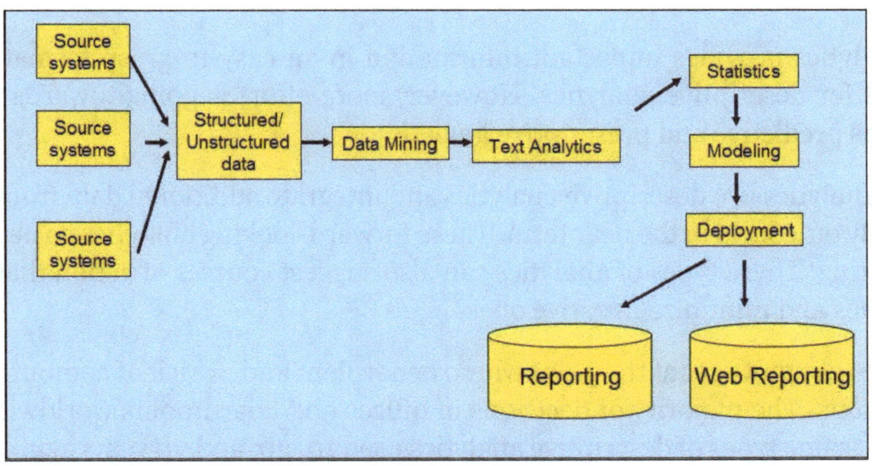


Predictive analytics.

## Descriptive Analytics

Descriptive analytics is the interpretation of historical data to better understand changes that have occurred in a business. Descriptive analytics describes the use of a range of historic data to draw comparisons. Most commonly reported financial metrics are a product of descriptive analytics—for example, year-over-year pricing changes, month-over-month sales growth, the number of users, or the total revenue per subscriber. These measures all describe what has occurred in a business during a set period.

Descriptive analytics takes raw data and parses that data to draw conclusions that are useful and understandable by managers, investors, and other stakeholders. A report showing sales of $1 million may sound impressive, but it lacks context. If that figure represents a 20% month-over-month decline, it is a concern. If it is a 40% year-over-year increase, then it suggests something is going right with the sales strategy. However, the larger context including targeted growth is required to obtain an informed view of the company's sales performance.

Descriptive analytics uses a full range of data to give an accurate picture of what has happened in a business and how that differs from other comparable periods. These performance metrics can be used to flag areas of strength and weakness to inform management strategies.

Descriptive analytics is an important component of performance analysis so that managers can make informed strategic business decisions based on historical data. Descriptive analytics is one of the most basic pieces of business intelligence a company will use. Although descriptive analytics can be industry specific—such as the seasonal variation in shipment completion times—analytics use broadly accepted measures common throughout the finance industry.

Return on invested capital (ROIC) is a descriptive analytic created by taking three data points—net income, dividends, and total capital—and turning those data points into an easy-to-understand percentage that can be used to compare one company's performance to others. Generally speaking, the larger and more complex a company is, the more descriptive analytics it will use to measure its performance.

Descriptive analytics provides important information in an easy-to-grasp format. There will always be a need for descriptive analytics. However, more effort is going towards newer fields of analytics such as predictive and prescriptive analytics.

These types of analytics use descriptive analytics and integrate additional data from diverse sources to model likely outcomes in the near term. These forward-looking analytics go beyond informing to decision-making. These types of analytics can also suggest courses of action that can maximize positive outcomes and minimize negative ones.

That said, we are not quite yet at the point where benevolent and prescient computers will helm all major corporations. The majority of decisions in offices and boardrooms worldwide are made by people using the same types of descriptive analytics used 10, 20, and 30 years ago, such as whether sales were up or down compared to last month, is the product getting to market on time, and does the company have sufficient supply based on last month's numbers.

## Marketing Analytics

Marketing analytics is the study of data garnered through marketing campaigns in order to discern patterns between such things as how a campaign contributed to conversions, consumer behavior, regional preferences, creative preferences and much more. The goal of marketing analytics as a practice is to use these patterns and findings to optimize future campaigns based on what was successful.

Marketing analytics benefits both marketers and consumers. This analysis allows marketers to achieve higher ROI on marketing investments by understanding what is successful in driving conversions, brand awareness, or both. Analytics also ensures that consumers see a greater number of targeted, personalized ads that speak to their specific needs and interests, rather than mass communications that tend to annoy.

Marketing data can be analyzed using a variety of methods and models depending on the KPIs being measured. For example, analysis of brand awareness relies upon different data and models than analysis of conversions. Some popular analytics models and methods include:

- Media Mix Models (MMM): Attribution models that look at aggregate data over a long period of time.
- Multi-Touch Attribution (MTA): Attribution models that provide person-level data from across the buyer's journey.
- Unified Marketing Measurement (UMM): A form of measurement that integrates various attribution models including MMM and MTA into comprehensive engagement metrics.

## Importance of Marketing Analytics

In the modern marketing landscape, accurate analytics is more important than ever. Consumers have become highly selective in choosing the branded media they engage with and the media they ignore. If brands want to catch the ideal buyer's attention, they must rely on analytics to create targeted personal ads based on individual interests, rather than broader demographic associations. This will allow marketing teams to serve the right ad, at the right time, on the right channel to move consumers down the sales funnel.

## How Organizations use Marketing Analytics

Marketing analytics data can help your business make decisions on matters including product updates, branding and more. It's important to take data from multiple sources (online and offline) to prevent a fragmented view. Using this data, your team can gain insights into the following:

- Product Intelligence: Product intelligence involves taking a deep dive into the brand's products as well as how those products stack up within the market. Typically done by speaking to consumers, polling target audiences or engaging them with surveys, organizations can better understand the differentiators and competitive advantages of their products. From there, teams can better align products to the unique consumer interests and problems that help drive conversions.
- Customer Trends and Preferences: Analytics can tell a lot about your consumers. What messaging/creative resonates with them? Which products are they buying and which have they researched in the past? Which ads are leading to conversions and which are ignored?

- Product Development Trends: Analytics can also offer insight into the types of product features consumers want. Marketing teams can pass this information on to product development for future iterations.
- Customer Support: Analytics also helps uncover areas of the buyer's journey that could be simplified or improved. Where are your clients struggling? Are there ways you can simplify your product or make the check-out process easier?
- Customer Support: Analytics also helps uncover areas of the buyer's journey that could be simplified or improved. Where are your clients struggling? Are there ways you can simplify your product or make the check-out process easier?
- Messaging and Media: Data analysis can determine where marketers choose to display messages for particular consumers. This has become especially important because of the sheer number of channels. In addition to traditional marketing channels such as print, television and broadcast, marketers must also know which digital channels and social media networks consumers prefer. Analytics answers these key questions: What media should you is buying? Which are driving the most sales? What message is resonating with your audience?
- Competition: How does your marketing efforts compare with your competition? How can you close that gap if there is one? Are there opportunities your competitors are capitalizing on that you may have missed?
- Predict Future Results: If you have a thorough understanding of why a campaign worked, you'll be able to apply that knowledge to future campaigns for increased ROI.

## The Challenges of Analyzing Data

While marketing analytics are critical to successful campaigns, the analysis process poses key challenges because of the immense quantity of data marketers are now able to attain. This means that marketers must determine how to best organize the data into a digestible format to derive actionable insights.

Some of the biggest marketing analytics challenges faced today are:

- Data Quantity: Big data emerged during the digital age, enabling marketing teams to record every consumer click, impression and view. However this quantity of data is irrelevant if it cannot be structured and analyzed for insights that allow for in-campaign optimizations. This has left marketers grappling with how to best organize data to evaluate its meaning. In fact, research shows that experienced data scientists spend the majority of their time wrangling and formatting data, rather than analyzing it.
- Data Quality: Not only is there a problem in terms of the vast information organizations must sift through, but this data is often viewed as unreliable. 21 percent of respondents' media budgets were wasted due to poor data quality. This means one dollar out of every 5 dollars was not being utilized effectively. Over the course of a year, these dollars can add up, resulting in \$1.2 million dollars and \$16.5 million dollars of

wasted budget for mid-size and enterprise level firms. Organizations need a process to maintain data quality, so that employees can leverage accurate information to make the right decisions.

- Lack of Data Scientists: Even if companies have access to the right data, many don't have access to the right people. In fact, according to a survey by The CMO, only 1.9% of companies believe they have the right people to fully leverage marketing analytics.
- Selecting Attribution Models: Determining the model that provides the right insights can be tricky. For example, media mix modeling and multi-touch attribution offer entirely different insights – aggregate campaign-focused data and person-level consumer data respectively. The models that marketers choose will dictate the types of insights they receive. Engagement analysis across so many channels can create confusion when it's time to choose the right model.
- Correlating Data: In this same vein, because marketers are collecting data from so many different sources, they must find a way to normalize it to make it comparable. It's especially challenging comparing online and offline engagements, as they are typically measured by different attribution models. This is where unified marketing measurement and marketing analytics platforms demonstrate true value, organizing data from disparate sources.

### Uses of Marketing Analytics Software

Marketing analytics software combats these challenges by collecting, organizing and correlating valuable data quickly, allowing marketers to make real-time campaign optimizations. Modern marketing platforms are valuable for the speed at which they can store and process massive amounts of data. One of the major drawbacks of having access to so much data is that marketers cannot possibly parse through it all in time to make real-time optimizations. That's where the processing power of advanced analytics platforms comes into play, enabling marketers to adjust creative or ad placement as needed before the campaign ends, enhancing potential ROI. Additionally, many platforms now leverage unified marketing measurement, to normalize and aggregate marketing data from across various channels and campaigns, simplifying analysis.

Finally, advanced analytics platforms go beyond measuring consumer engagements to offer insights into brand equity and how certain audience segments react to creative elements. This helps marketers better determine brand-building ROI, as well as how to further personalize branded experiences.

## Marketing Analytics Software - Features and Capabilities

When implementing a marketing measurement solution, consider these key features and capabilities of marketing analytics software:

- Real-Time Analytics and Insights.
- Brand Measurement Capabilities.
- Granular, Person-Level Data.

- The Ability to Correlate Online and Offline Attribution Metrics.
- Contextualized Customer and Market Insights.
- Annual Media Plan Recommendations.

## Skills that Marketing Analytics Managers Need

As marketing teams seek to conduct quality analysis that lead to more engaging, profitable campaigns, they must focus on employing analytics managers who can:

- Conduct Quality Analyses: First and most obvious, an analytics manager must have experience evaluating large data sets to discern insights including buying patterns and engagement trends within the target audience.
- Make Optimization Recommendations: Once data insights are gained, the ability to come up with recommendations to improve underperforming campaigns based on trends is crucial. For example, data may show that one consumer engaged with branded content only in the evening, informing a strategy shift to serve the ad on the consumer's commute home, rather than the morning commute.
- Understand Consumer and MarTech Trends: Analytics managers should also stay abreast of consumer and MarTech trends. Understanding consumer demands for a seamless omnichannel experience and how buyers are engaging with augmented and virtual reality will certainly play a role in determining next steps for optimization opportunities.
- Work with Analytics Tools: Next, analytics managers must be on-boarded and comfortable with various automation tools and analytics platforms, because of the vital role these tools play in reducing the time from consumer engagement to consumer insight.
- Collaborate with Stakeholders: Finally, members of the analytics team must be able to use the data they work with to tell a compelling story to stakeholders, and demonstrate the ways other departments, such as sales or product development, can use these findings to drive engagement and conversions.

## How to Start the Marketing Analytics Process

If you're looking to enhance analytics capabilities, here are four steps to take at the outset of your program:

- Understand What You Want to Measure: There are many aspects to a marketing campaign you can measure: conversion rates, leads captured and brand recognition, to name a few. Understand the problem you are trying to solve or insight you are trying to glean when beginning to analyze your data.
- Establish a Benchmark: What does a successful campaign look like? This will determine the types of data and metrics marketers collect. For example, if the goal is to increase brand awareness – the success benchmark might be an increased percentage of brand loyalty demonstrated in a customer panel, rather than an online click or impression.

- Assess Your Current Capabilities: What is your company doing today? What are your weak spots? Whether assessing offline campaign results or identifying media most likely to convert, understanding these weak points can help you strengthen your program.
- Deploy a Marketing Analytics Tool: Marketing analytics tools will increase in importance as consumers become more selective and datasets grow. An advanced platform, such as our Marketing Measurement and Optimization Platform uses unified marketing measurement to help marketers identify the messages that resonate and the types of media that converts. This provides a holistic view of which campaigns are successful and which are underperforming in real time.

## Pricing Analytics

Pricing analytics are the metrics and associated tools used to understand how pricing activities affect the overall business, analyze the profitability of specific price points, and optimize a business's pricing strategy for maximum revenue.

### Why Pricing Analytics are so Important for SaaS Companies

Companies across just about every business sector and industry vertical—from manufacturing and distribution to retail and ecommerce—can benefit from pricing analytics. One general rule of thumb, though, is that pricing tends to become a bigger challenge as companies grow. Companies with lots of products sold at different price points, different customer tiers, or complex product bundles tend to see the greatest benefits from analysis.

Subscription billing in particular makes SaaS businesses the perfect candidates for pricing analytics tools like ProfitWell. Revenue in a SaaS company is built one subscription at a time and paid in small increments; therefore, success in SaaS means understanding the factors that drive subscription and churn rates more than just knowing which factors drive one-time sales. Pricing analytics solutions give you the data to make better pricing decisions, so you can stop guessing and start growing.

### How Pricing Analytics Improve Profitability

Big data alone won't solve your pricing problems. Having a strong handle on the reasons behind past performance—in other words, basing your decisions on pricing analytics instead of guessing—can go a long way towards improving your future performance.

- Acquire more insights on customers: Going after the wrong customer segment can mean significant lost revenue. For companies dipping their toes into improving their pricing for the first time, even simple tools like customer segmentation can be a huge improvement.
- Pricing analytics show which customer segments are the most (and least) profitable and which respond best to specific pricing strategies. Aligning your pricing with those customer segments increases both revenue and profit, keeping customers happy and helping reduce churn.

- Optimize your pricing for value: Many businesses rely on the "sounds about right" pricing method. But basing your decision-making on hard data gets you much closer to value-based pricing. Data lets you quickly learn which customers are most likely to buy and exactly how much they value your solution to their problems. The insights from your pricing analytics drive more effective (and profitable) business and pricing decisions for you, and a fair price for customers that matches the value you provide. Everybody wins.
- Identify quick pricing wins: Nearly every company has holes in their pricing strategy just waiting to be patched—pricing leaks, underpriced or overpriced product tiers, or missed upsell opportunities. Pricing analytics tools comb through the data, finding the low-hanging fruit that can be fixed quickly and creating extra revenue in just a few short months.
- Discover which channels are most profitable: Pricing analytics can also show, for example, that posting videos on YouTube might bring in fewer qualified leads than written content, but that video helps those leads trust you more, meaning customers who are more willing to pay a premium for your product. Based on that discovery, you might choose to pursue video more aggressively, even though your customer acquisition costs might end up higher.
- Recognize which pricing tiers work the best: Tiered pricing models are incredibly common in subscription businesses—most SaaS companies offer some form of pricing tiers to meet the needs of different customer segments. Pricing analytics tools really start to shine when breaking down what those tiers should look like. Having insight into how many tiers you should have, the optimal price for each tier, and who uses which tiers can unlock new levels of profitability for your SaaS product without needing to add new products or features.
- Plan promotions: Pricing promotions need to be carefully planned for the most optimal time to acquire the most number of paying customers. Predictive analytics let you keep a close eye on the market, waiting for the perfect time to pounce with your promotional campaign. Most pricing tools will also calculate price elasticity in real time and predict revenue at different price points, making it a piece of cake to set your prices and discount levels for maximum demand.

## Four Important Pricing Metrics you Need to be Tracking

Here we will explore some details on how you can get started tracking your pricing analytics. It's worth noting that while some of these metrics are relevant to all business models, a few are specific to SaaS and other subscription businesses.

## Willingness to Pay (WTP)

Willingness to pay (WTP), sometimes called price sensitivity is the maximum amount a customer is prepared to pay for your product or service. WTP is easily the most important component of your pricing strategy. Without an understanding of the price sensitivity of your product, you have no way of knowing whether or not your product development efforts are yielding an augmented product value (i.e., if customers are really interested in the features you're creating). In fact, a study at Harvard Business School revealed that a 1% improvement in pricing can improve your revenue by 11%.

The chart shows the monthly willingness to pay of over 6,000 current, former, and prospective

YouTube Premium customers based on age group. Two things quickly become clear: 1) Older audiences are less likely to pay for YouTube, and 2) YouTube Premium's current pricing of $11.99 per month is exactly what their target demographic—millennials—is willing to pay.

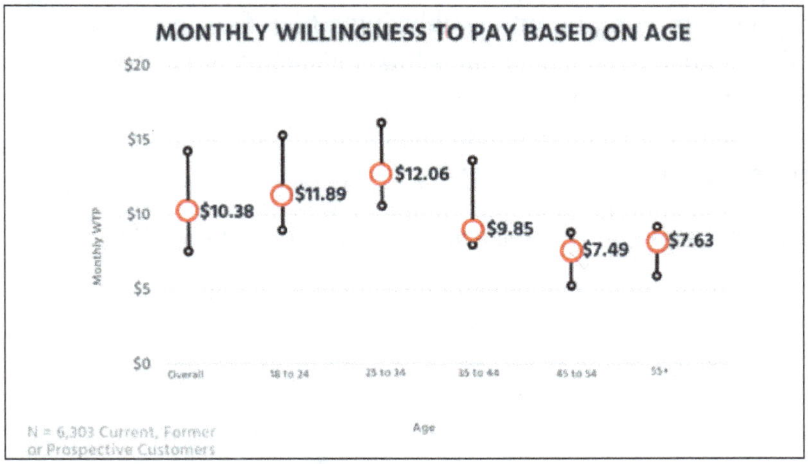


This chart shows the monthly WTP of 6303 current, former, and prospective YouTube Premium customers based on age group.

Tracking willingness to pay—especially when you segment customers by age group, as with YouTube above, or other factors like product features or job title—can ensure your products are priced competitively for maximum profit and that your prices stay in line with current market conditions.

## Feature Value

Feature value analysis, also called relative preference analysis, measures which features are more or less important to customers relative to other features. The same idea also applies to value propositions (high-level benefits that prompt purchasing decisions).

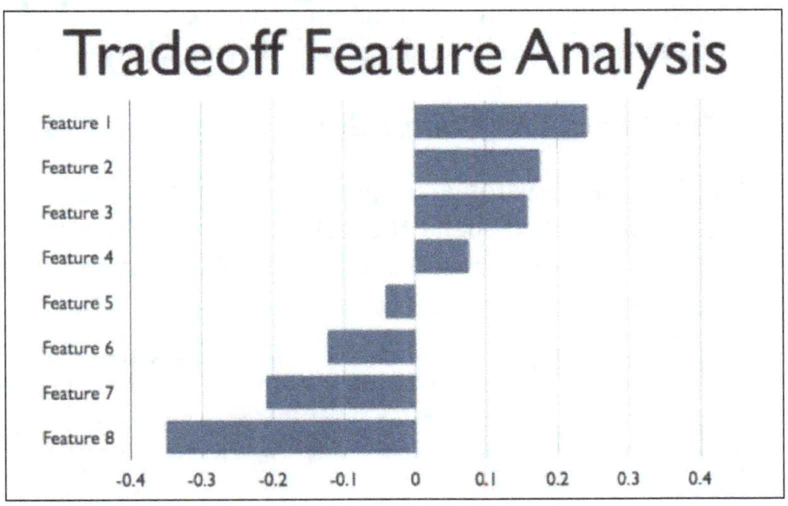


Asking customers to choose their favorite and least favorite features can quickly show which features customers care about.

You can't just guess which features customer's value— you have to ask them directly. Here at ProfitWell, we like to take the simple approach of asking customers to choose their favorite and least favorite features. This eliminates the "more is better" mindset that makes most customers check more boxes and masks which features are truly valuable.

If you're a SaaS company, your pricing page is likely tiered based on a sliding scale running from basic attributes to premium components. Analyzing which features motivate your customers to buy helps you establish how you package and bundle each pricing tier accordingly, helping you capture the most value for that section of the market.

## Average Revenue Per User (ARPU)

Average revenue per user (ARPU) is a measure of the revenue generated each month from each user.

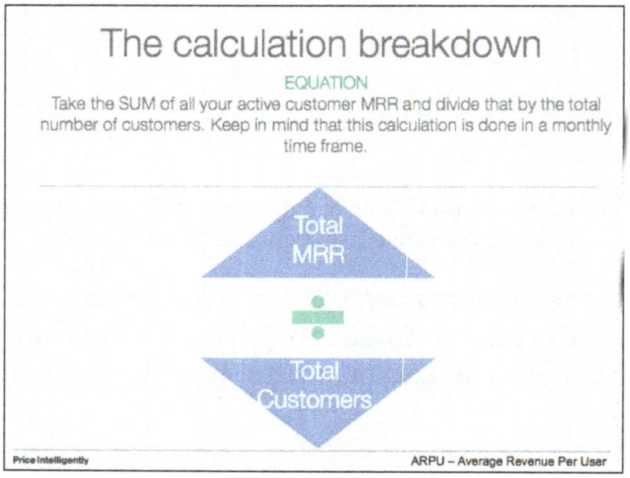


Average revenue per user (ARPU) is calculated by dividing the total MRR by the total number of customers.

ARPU gives you a bird's-eye view into how well your SaaS Company is actually doing. The higher your ARPU, the better the chance that the company is able to extract more cash in the future. ARPU also reveals the relative value of your product—if you have a high ARPU relative to the revenue of the company, you know you have a product that's driving a better value ratio.

## Customer Acquisition Cost (CAC) and Lifetime Value (LTV)

Customer lifetime value (LTV) and customer acquisition costs (CAC) go hand-in-hand when it comes to pricing analytics. You want to spend the right amount to drive new customers to your service without jeopardizing the revenue from that customer. This is known as the LTV/CAC ratio, and it's the "god metric" of many successful SaaS companies.

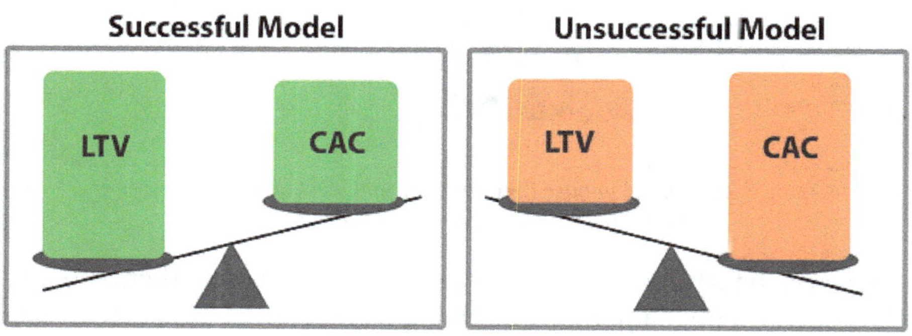


Lifetime value needs to remain higher than acquisition costs for a SaaS company to be sustainable.

Calculating CAC and LTV for each customer persona will help you understand your buyers even more, letting you make more informed decisions about your pricing strategy.

### Get to Know your Pricing

Collecting and analyzing data on your product's pricing does take work, but its necessary labor if you hope to craft an effective pricing strategy for your business. You can use your pricing analytics to find and fix the holes in your pricing strategy, driving revenue higher and reducing churn. The key is to start tracking your pricing analytics today. You can collect all the data in the world, but it only becomes valuable once you start using it to drive meaningful pricing decisions.

## Retail Analytics

Retail analytics is the study of consumer data as it relates to the retail industry. Retail analytics helps merchants to respond appropriately to the needs and wants of their target markets. Before the advent of the Internet and advanced technology, retailers relied on broad market information published by marketing research firms, or more specific—yet still general—data gleaned by their own marketing teams.

In essence, retail analytics is all about understanding the customer:

- It is focused on the future: Proper analysis will yield crucial data that allow retailers to make an informed decision about which products to make and sell to which customer segment. The past, or sales history, can only tell you which products moved fastest, and not much else.
- It gives retailers a clearer picture of their customers: Retail analytics can provide you with a more specific profile of your target market—their lifestyle, spending habits, eating habits, and other things. It's no longer just "people in their 30s and 40s who are working with families." It's "Sarah, a 34-year-old married mom with two kids who loves to go hiking with her family and needs water-resistant bags to hold her kids' snacks."
- It allows retailers to check if their products still match their target market: You started with dresses aimed at the young female professional and marketed them accordingly. But then a deeper analysis showed that it's the older female professionals who are buying those dresses. All right then, you say, time to switch marketing gears and cater to the market actually buying our goods, instead of wasting dollars enticing a customer segment that is largely ignoring you.

### Retail Analytics for Online Shopping

With the rise of online shopping, it's actually much easier now for retailers to get a glimpse of who their customers are. Have you ever bought something online—or even just browsed online without purchasing anything—then find that the next time you log on to that website, it shows you similar products?

Technology has allowed retailers online to probe further into the habits and movements of their customers. What products were the most viewed? From what part of the country or world did the most sales come from? Which items were viewed a lot but were not purchased? What did the customers end up purchasing? The answers to these questions help retailers make better decisions about their strategies, making advertising and marketing campaigns more cost-effective.

### Retail Analytics for Brick-and-Mortar Stores

What about the stores that only operates with physical branches, or gets most of their revenue from brick-and-mortar stores? The good news is that technology has also opened up new ways to analyze customer data for these types of retail stores:

- Time data capture: How long do people typically spend at the store?
- Traffic flow: What is the foot traffic like inside the store? Outside the store? Do more people linger around specific product racks?
- Movement vector: What kinds of movements do certain groups of people make in and around the store? What do they do?

There are companies that offer to track these metrics for retailers, using GPS from users' smartphones. It is important to note, however, that this is still a tricky line because of data privacy laws. Still, these kinds of information would be very valuable to a retailer. Some data will even include competitor analysis if the information shows where a potential customer ended up buying what they needed.

### Impact of Retail Analytics

In the end, it's not only sales and marketing that will benefit from a good retail analytics system. Inventory will also benefit from it, as it will allow merchants to manage inventory more efficiently according to forecasted sales from an analysis. The technology we have today also means increased automation, leading to more insights for better planning.

Retail analytics is a worthwhile and practical tool for retailers to understand their customers better and give them what they want. The retail industry is highly dependent on the behavior of their markets, and so to understand them will likely lead to improved performance, if not outright success.

## Behavioral Analytics

Behavioral data is data generated by, or in response to, a customer's engagement with a business. This can include things like page views, email sign-ups, or other important user actions. Common sources of behavioral data include websites, mobile apps, CRM systems, marketing automation systems, call centers, help desks, and billing systems.

Customers can either be consumers, businesses, or individuals within a business, but behavioral data can always be tied back to a single end-user. It's important to note that this user can be a known individual (logged-in) or anonymous (not logged in).

This type of data is typically created and stored in the form of an "event," meaning an action that was taken, with "properties," meaning metadata used to describe the event. For example, an event could be "site visit" and a property for that event could be "device type." It may help to think of events as the "what" and the properties as the "who, when, and where."

Behavioral analytics examines the "what's" and "how's" of customer behavioral data to inform the "why's" of customer behavior. This can include tracking page views, email sign-ups, or other important actions like registration. These critical day to day insights allow us to further optimize for conversion, engagement, and retention.

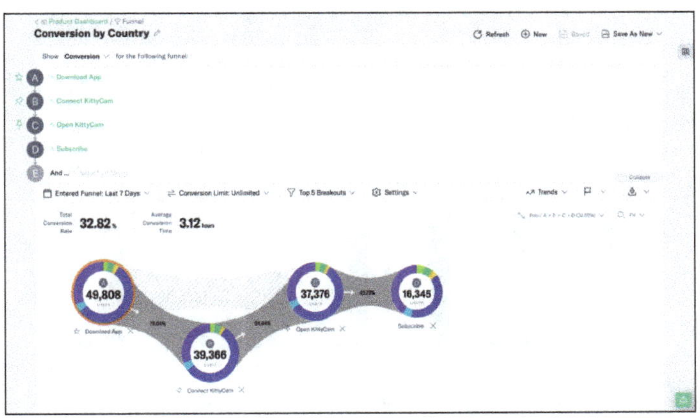

For example, if a business is looking for insight into why users bounce before subscribing, they can build out an analysis that aims to isolate points of friction within a specific conversion funnel. The example Funnel above compares user flows of those who open an email and begin their journey to creating an account.

With Indicative marketing, product, and data teams can gain deep behavioral insights that they need to understand their customers and grow their business.

## How can you Benefit from Behavioral Analytics?

Behavioral analytics is crucial in optimizing your company's conversion, engagement, and retention. With the right behavioral analytics tool, every member of your team should be able to gain the actionable insights they need to answer their own questions and leverage data in ways that didn't seem possible before.

## What are Behavioral Analysis Tools?

There are three main behavioral analysis tools involved in building a complete picture of your customer journey: segmentation analysis, funnel analysis, and cohort analysis. Each of these tools serves its own importance when examining users conversion, engagement and retention.

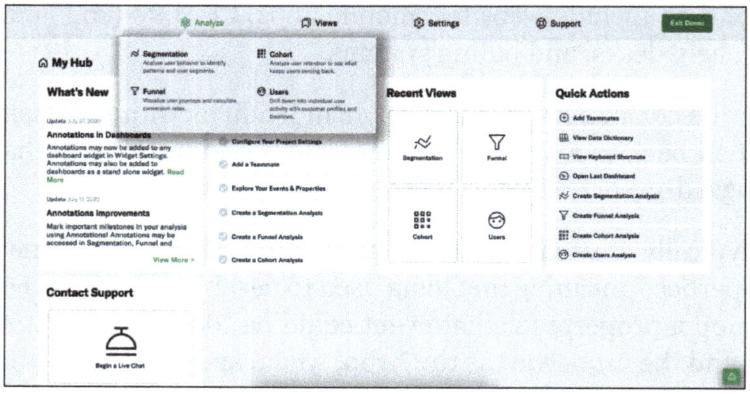


## Segmentation Tool

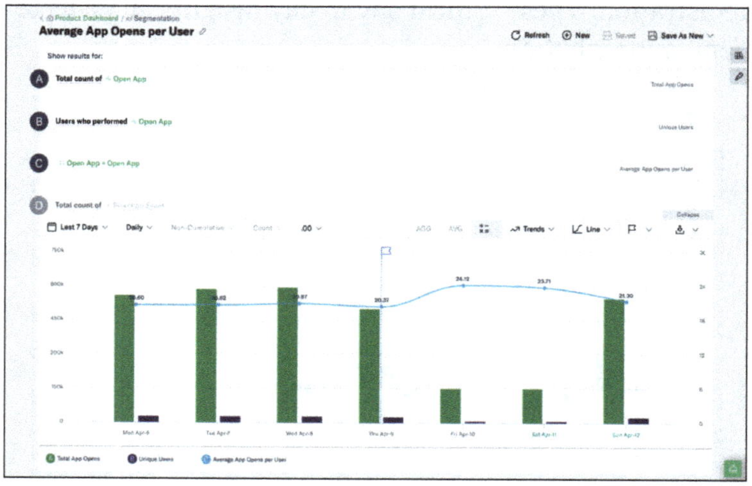

The segmentation tool helps you build out key KPIs and metrics, create custom calculations, and identify behavioral trends. For example, if you're interested in tracking your site subscriptions, you can monitor each marketing source to track the number of subscriptions they bring in over time. This allows you to optimize your marketing channels by enhancing the ones that work and improving or removing ones that are less effective.

## Funnel Tool

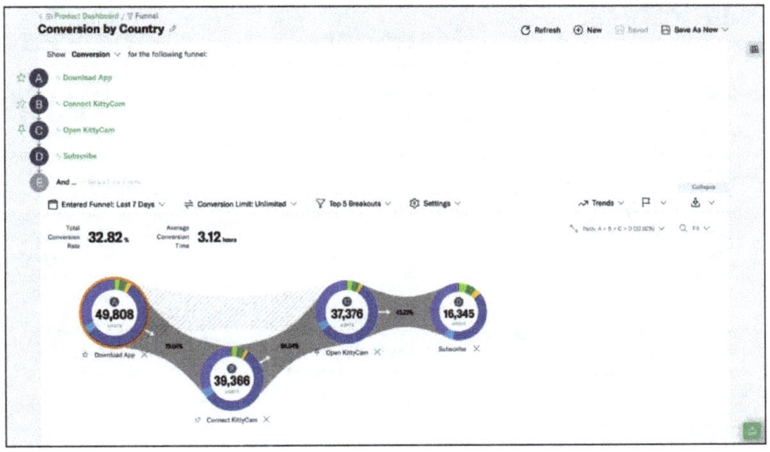


The Funnel tool is used to analyze conversion funnels, visualize multidimensional user journeys, and see what's working and what's not. Funnel analysis is a great way to examine user drop-off. For example, you could explore users who create an account, but then never go one to visit your blog page. This could help you optimize your site so that users are more clearly directed to your blog page.

## Cohort Tool

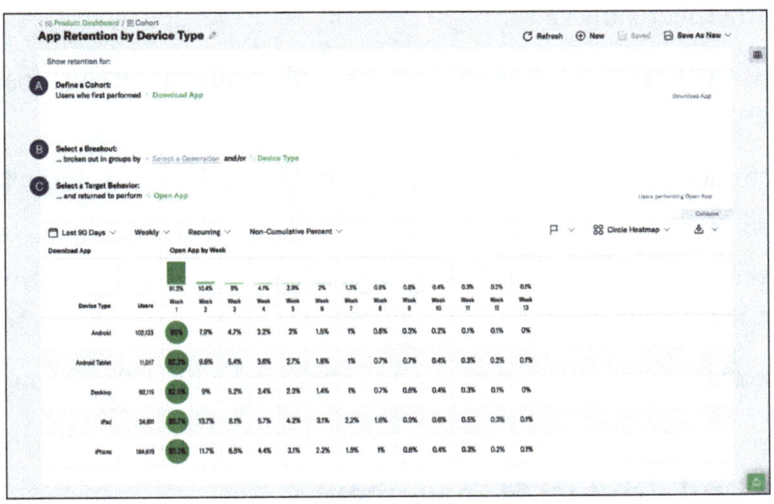


Cohort analysis is used to analyze user retention over time to see what keeps users coming back. For example, you could analyze and group users who purchased items from one category and then came back to purchase a product from a different category. This allows you to build more accurate profiles of your users and their interests and needs.

## Who should use Behavioral Analytics?

Data is the new currency of modern business. Everyone, in any industry, should be able to use behavioral analytics to drive their business. Marketers, product managers, and data analysts can begin to see their customers as people, not just data points when they begin to use behavioral analysis tools.

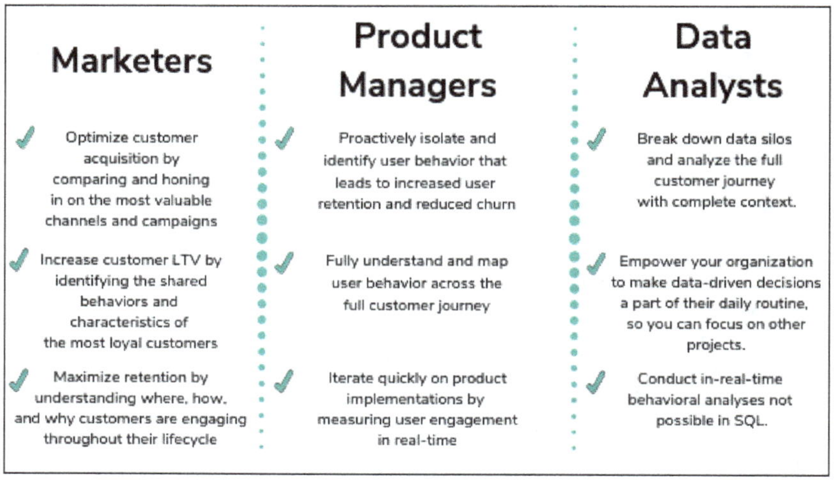


## Behavioral Data and Marketing

Marketers can use behavioral data and analytics to get the most out of campaigns, optimize customer acquisition, and grow customer Lifetime Value (LTV). As a marketing team, it's important to know which campaigns are successfully increasing engagement and revenue. For example, a marketing team that sends out an email campaign with the intent to increase blog traffic can track the success of the email, visitors to the blog, and which blogs are gaining the most views.

With Indicative, marketing teams can:

- Optimize customer acquisition by comparing and honing in on the most valuable channels and campaigns.
- Increase customer LTV by identifying the shared behaviors and characteristics of the most loyal customers.
- Maximize retention by understanding where, how, and why customers are engaging throughout their lifecycle.
- Build dashboards on the fly to monitor and share valuable KPIs throughout the customer journey.

## Behavioral Data and Product Management

Product managers can use behavioral data and analytics to build out a product roadmap, optimize user engagement, and reduce churn. For example, if you're a product manager of an app developer looking to monitor the success of a new feature on an app, behavioral analytics can help you track and isolate users who use the new feature and the process that led them to use the new feature. If the new feature is unsuccessful, the product team may be able to identify points of friction that are causing problems with new feature engagement.

With Indicative, product teams can:

- Fully understand and map user behavior across the full customer journey.
- Iterate quickly on product implementations by measuring user engagement in real-time.
- Proactively isolate and identify user behavior that leads to increased user retention and reduced churn.
- Build dashboards on the fly to monitor and share valuable KPIs throughout the customer journey.

## Behavioral Data and Data Analysis Teams

Data analysts can use behavioral data to gain complex analytics without having to build complex SQL queries and analysis capabilities that are not available using SQL. This allows business users to devote more time to other projects and streamline their workflows. For example, if you're looking to build a report on conversion time vs. new features, you can use create a conversion over time funnel and flag the dates when new features were rolled out.

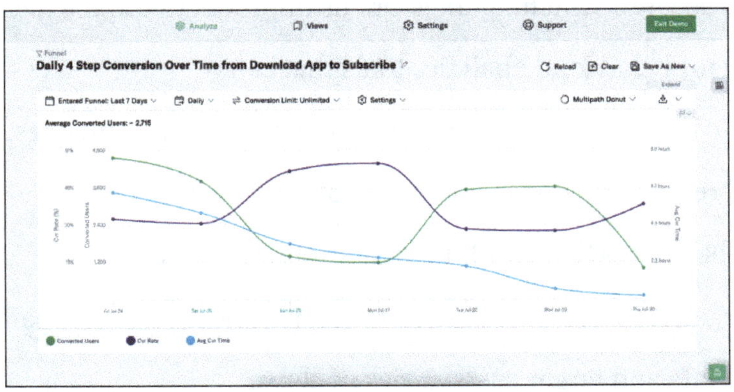


With Indicative, data teams can:

- Conduct in-real-time behavioral analyses not possible in SQL.
- Break down data silos and analyze the full customer journey with complete context.
- Empower your organization to make data-driven decisions a part of their daily routine, allowing you to focus on other projects.
- Build dashboards on the fly to monitor and share valuable KPIs throughout the customer journey.

## Which Behavioral Analytics Product Should you Choose?

As the data and analytics market continues to expand, the number of behavioral tools to choose from can be hard to select from. Providers like Amplitude, Indicative, and Mixpanel are all popular choices in the behavioral analytics space, and each one has its respective differences.

| | indicative | Amplitude | mixpanel |
|---|---|---|---|
| Data Limit | 50 Million Events | 10 Million Events | 5 Million Events |
| Data Retention | 6 Months | Unlimited | 90 Days |
| Multipath Funnels | ✓ | ✗ | ✗ |
| Segmentation Analysis | ✓ | ✓ | ✗ |
| Cohort Analysis | ✓ | ✓ | ✗ |
| Calculator | ✓ | ✓ | ✗ |
| Email Support | ✓ | ✗ | ✗ |
| Customizable Data Dictionary | ✓ | ✗ | ✓ |

If your company is searching for the right behavioral analytics provider, it's important to take your time and do research on each product that you are considering. Some products offer a free plan which can help you gain a better idea of how the tools work and if the product makes the most sense for your business and analysis goals. Trialing several products can be the most time and cost-effective process because switching tools can be unproductive and expensive.

It's important to look for behavioral analytics tools that can:

- Optimize behavior among different paths and isolate successful ones.
- Diagnose and remove friction-heavy steps for customers.
- Focus on key behaviors that result in higher total customer value.
- Use highly targeted customer segments to inform and launch campaigns.
- Proactively isolate and target users at risk of churn.
- Build at-a-glance dashboards to share with teams and executives.

## Risk Analytics

Risk analytics helps take the guesswork out of managing risk-related issues by using a range of techniques and technologies to extrapolate insights, calculate likely scenarios, and predict future events.

The rise of big data, computing power, and advanced analytics enables companies to gain valuable insights from data. Artificial intelligence, machine learning, the Internet of Things, and drones are just a few innovative tools now available to help companies gain a more complete view of their businesses and make better decisions. For risk managers, using big data and risk analytics provides an unprecedented ability to identify, measure, and mitigate risk.

## Effective Risk Analytics Requires a lot of Data

To get an accurate picture of risk, your risk analytics solution must aggregate and analyze both internal and external data. Relying on internal information alone ignores all of the factors that impact a business beyond its four walls. Take, for example, farming. The value of a crop is determined by internal factors – seeds, water, fertilizers, pesticides, transportation costs, etc.; however, external factors are also important – weather, competitive pricing, geopolitics, market shifts. Farmers need to analyze all this data to completely understand the risks associated with their crops.

## Machine Learning is Essential

Machine learning algorithms are the only way to gain any actionable insight from the massive amount of data generated each day. The volume, velocity, and variety of data produced each day is beyond the capacity of manual analyses, spreadsheets, and programmed algorithms. Machine learning algorithms generate reports in seconds, enabling risk management teams to evaluate risk in real time and avoid costly delays.

## Benefits from Risk Analytics

Tracking and analyzing risk factors in real time provides huge benefits because you know immediately when anomalies occur and can quickly react to make changes to alleviate risk.

Using advanced analytics, you can:

- Create alerts to monitor for anomalies and outliers in real time and know instantly when problems arise. The faster you know where problems are, the sooner you can fix them.
- Utilize real-time portfolio monitoring and evaluate performance across key parameters. Analyzing performance in real time enables you to quickly adjust the portfolio to improve performance when necessary.
- Use machine learning algorithms to identify high risk customers and reduce charge-off losses by screening for risky deals.
- Simulate portfolios and evaluate the potential impacts of possible trades, disruptions, and events and create the portfolio that meets goals for profits and risk.

- Track credit breaches in near real time and analyze risk limit breaches by trader, profit center, and trading desk level.

Big data is changing the way businesses are run, enabling businesses to analyze massive amounts of information about operations in near real time. Risk analytics enables you to take that data to understand and reduce risk.

## Supply Chain Analytics

Supply Chain is a tricky business. One missing entity or a lack of synchronization can break the entire chain and mean millions in losses for a company. However, the use of analytics in this domain is resolving several pain points in supply chain management at the strategic, operational, and tactical levels. "Supply Chain Analytics brings data-driven intelligence to your business, reducing the overall cost to serve and improving service levels." For supply chain professionals, it can only mean one thing – to up skill to be able to use advanced analytics to improve operational efficiency and make data-driven decisions.

Analytics uses data to make predictions to help businesses take advantage of the widely available data in the supply chain industry. Data Visualization techniques ranging from charts, graphs and more help decision making, by uncovering patterns and generating insights.

The different types of data analytics are:

- Predictive analytics: While predictive analytics doesn't actually tell you what will happen in the future, it gets pretty close to that. This process unveils all the patterns and motifs from existing data to present a set of trends that are likely to occur in the future.
- Descriptive Analytics: Descriptive analytics breaks down the insights gathered from any data sets to help businesses understand them better. In a way it summarizes all the information gathered.
- Prescriptive Analytics: Prescriptive analytics helps businesses take decisions based on analytical findings. Since it is based on data it is scalable and can provide businesses with direction.
- Cognitive Analytics: Cognitive analytics tries to mimic the human brain by studying data and understanding patterns and interpreting them to draw conclusions. This knowledge thus gained is further used for future reference.

With modern businesses becoming increasingly global, the demand for an efficient supply chain logistics which can perform at scale is on the rise. Operations and logistics teams have become more complex, and issues pertaining to inconsistent suppliers, delayed shipment and more need a robust solution.

### Challenges of Supply Chain Industry

- Managing Demand Volatility.

- Supply chain and logistics process transparency.
- Tackling cost fluctuations in Supply Chain.

Business analytics and intelligence have improved significantly in the last decade, resulting in a dependable system that can help solve the issues of this domain with meaningful insights, analysis and predictions.

## How Big Data is Transforming Supply Chain Management

Use predictive modelling to control critical process parameters – A Fortune 100 fertiliser manufacturing company produces fertilisers that must meet quality criteria for key natural elements like potassium, nitrogen, and phosphorus to be within a defined range of specification. The results of thorough data understanding and brainstorming determined that for water soluble fertilisers, in 98.4% of instances the prediction accuracy was greater than 95%. For other nutrient products, in 99.9% of instances, the prediction accuracy was greater than 95%. The client saw multi-million-dollar savings through these tools in fine-tuning the manufacturing process.

## Advanced Analytics in Supply Chain

Data is crucial for managing all kinds of supply and storage systems. Predictive analysis, in particular, has emerged as a successful way of ensuring an effective management of supply chain units. Predictive analysis uses copious amounts of data to gain insights on any kind of future scenarios to avert plausible disruptions and prepare for the inconvenience.

Predictive analysis can be used for demand forecasting to understand consumer behavior and anticipate product and consumer demand. Historical data can be used to perform time series analysis and come up with insights that can predict seasonal fluctuations, consumer trends, and weather-date purchase correlations. It is a proven method of predicting and managing supply chain logistics.

Data-powered decisions can help supply chain businesses set the standard for operational success. Fast digitization and ready availability of data has paved the way for big data analytics in the supply chain industry. The use of big data analytics has immense potential to curtail costs, manage demand volatility, and make the process more visible for stakeholders.

## References


- What-is-prescriptive-analytics: talend.com, Retrieved 26, April 2020
- What-is-predictive-analytics: predictiveanalyticstoday.com, Retrieved 07, May 2020
- Descriptive-analytics: investopedia.com, Retrieved 16, May 2020
- Marketing-analytics, marketing-essentials: marketingevolution.com, Retrieved 25, May 2020
- Pricing-analytics: profitwell.com, Retrieved 05, June 2020
- What-is-behavioral-data-and-behavioral-analytics: indicative.com, Retrieved 23, June 2020
- Why-is-risk-analytics-important-14421: finextra.com, Retrieved 02, July 2020
- Supply-chain-analytics: mygreatlearning.com, Retrieved 10, July 2020

3

# Data for Business Intelligence and Analytics

Business intelligence and analytics cannot work without data and it comes in all sorts of shapes and sizes. Data and its related topics like big data, data mining, data warehouse, data presentation architecture, data sampling, data preparation, data visualization, data profiling, data filtering, data clearing, etc. are examined extensively in this chapter for the reader's benefit.

## Data

The modern business marketplace is a data-driven environment. The role of data is to empower business leaders to make decisions based on facts, trends and statistical numbers. But with so much information out there, business leaders must be able to sift through the noise, and get the right information, so that they can make the best decisions about strategy and growth.

### Importance of Data

Data is at the core of nearly every business decision made. Human resources directors are gathering data from online resources to determine the best people to recruit and confirm details about them. Marketing departments are lasering in on market segmentation data to find consumers who are ready to buy, speeding up the sale-closing process whenever possible. Business executives must examine bigger trends in the market, such as changes in pricing of resources, shipping or manufacturing.

By using data effectively, a company is able to streamline the process of getting a product made and putting it in the hands of the customer. The costs savings from not doing shotgun advertising or paying too much for resources can have significantly affect a company's bottom line profits. Looking at the data and incorporating it into the business strategy, is the role of the manager.

### Analytics Strategy

A company needs to develop strategies for marketing, sales, human resources and operations. Getting the right information means knowing what information is important to the company's decision-making process. The strategy starts with basic demographic data; then, it considers pricing based on the education and income of buyers, and how that group speaks. Education and income are important, because the more educated and the higher the income a target group has, the more likely it is that the business can logically sell a higher-end product to the group who can understand, appreciate and afford the product.

For example, a company wants to market a new skin care line to women. There are several key factors the company must know to effectively design and execute a marketing strategy. Although the product might work for all women, will it be branded more for the younger teen crowd? Or, will it be branded for the aging woman who's trying to hold on to her youthful skin? The label design might be different for each group. A higher price point might not be affordable to a younger crowd, but research backing the claims might be required to sell a product with a higher price point to educated, professional older women.

In a scenario like this, the company needs data on the cost of goods sold, with the ultimate product pricing and who is most likely to buy it. It will design the entire packaging around its biggest segment, even though others may buy it. The analytics took not only numbers and group sizes, but what a specific demographic respond to visually. Packaging for a young Millennial group is much different than it would be for a Baby Boomer demographic.

### Effective Data Use

It isn't enough to have the data. Great business leaders use data effectively to make decisions. Assume that a cell phone manufacturer uses components made in China. If tariffs are put on that line of components, the costs of that phone costs will rise. Understanding the effects of that data and what it does to the business owner's profit margin is imperative in developing a strategy that keeps the company profitable. The business leader might seek to find a new resource for components, which are less likely affected by tariffs or international political situations. The business leader might decide to raise the cost of its final product, effectively passing on the new cost to the consumer.

Initially, the company could also decide to do nothing and absorb the higher costs, because it has enough of a profit margin to still be successful, while many of its competitors will need to raise prices. This strategy is one that could reduce the profits-per-sale, but it might increase the demand for products, because it is more competitively priced for consumers; thus, the demand increases.

## Big Data

Every business organization, small or big, needs valuable data and insights. When it comes to understanding your target audience and customer's preferences, big data plays a very important role. It even helps you anticipate their needs. The right data needs to be effectively presented and properly analyzed. It can help a business organization achieve various goals.

In simple terms, Big Data is a combination of all the processes and tools related to utilizing and managing large data sets. The Big Data concept was born out of the need to understand trends, preferences, and patterns in the huge database generated when people interact with different systems and each other. With Big Data, business organizations can use analytics, and figure out the most valuable customers. It can also help businesses create new experiences, services, and products.

## Big Data - A New Competitive Advantage

Using Big Data has been crucial for many leading companies to outperform the competition. In many industries, new entrants and established competitors use data-driven strategies to compete, capture and innovate. In fact, you can find examples of Big Data usage in almost every sector, from IT to healthcare.

When it comes to healthcare, data pioneers have been analyzing the outcomes of pharmaceuticals. Companies have focused on discovering the risks and benefits that were not clear during initial clinical trials. Big Data can lead to a better analysis of the trials, and help predict outcomes. Some other early adopters of the concept have been using data from the sensors embedded in various products, ranging from industrial goods to children's toys. This helps companies determine how products are used in the real world. With such knowledge, it becomes easier to create new services and design future products.

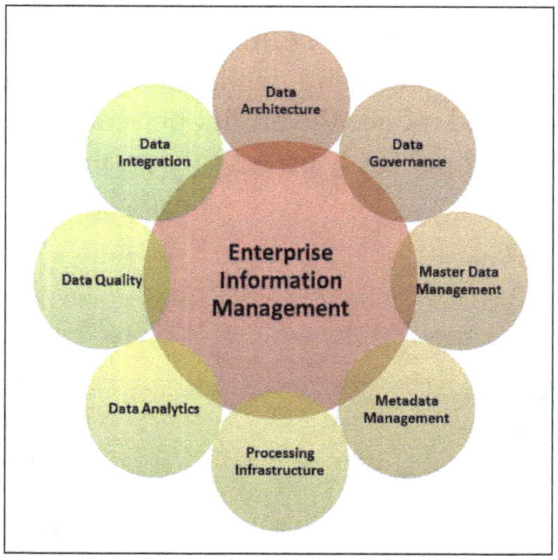


Big Data can create a lot of new growth opportunities. It can even give rise to a new category of businesses, such as the ones that analyze and aggregate industry data. Most of these companies will be sitting in the middle of large information flows about services and products, suppliers and buyers, consumer intent and preferences, and more. Companies across industries should start building their Big Data capabilities aggressively.

In addition to the broad scale of big data, the high frequency and real-time nature of data are crucial. For instance, the ability to estimate metrics, including consumer loyalty, was previously handled retrospectively. With Big Data, such practices are being used more extensively. This adds a lot to the power of prediction. Similarly, high frequency allows businesses to test theories in real-time. Besides these general benefits, Big Data helps a business organization in many different ways. Currently, Big Data is used in both the public and private sectors.

## Dialogue with Consumers

These days, consumers are smart and understand their priorities. Before making a purchase, consumers look around and compare different options. They even talk to businesses through social media channels and demand special treatment. In fact, most customers want to be thanked for buying products from a company.

Big Data allows a business organization to profile such customers in a far-reaching manner. This allows a business to engage in a real-time, one-on-one conversation with consumers. In tough competitive times, this isn't a luxury. You need to treat customers how they want.

A good example is about a customer entering a bank. When a customer enters the establishment, the clerk can use Big Data to check his or her profile in real-time. The clerk can learn about the customer's preferences and desires. This allows him to advise relevant products and services to the customer.

Big Data also plays an important role in integrating physical and digital shopping spheres. An online retailer can easily suggest an offer on the mobile carrier. This can be done on the basis of a consumer inclined toward increased social media usage.

## Re-Develop Products

Big Data is one of the best ways to collect and use feedback. It helps you understand how customers perceive your services and products. Thus, you're able to make the necessary changes and re-develop your products. When you analyze unstructured social media text, it allows you to uncover general feedback from your customers. You can even disintegrate the feedback in various geographical locations and demographic groups.

In addition to this, Big Data allows you to test numerous variations of high-end computer-aided designs within seconds. For instance, you can gather information about lead times, material affect costs, performance and more. It allows you to raise the productivity and efficiency of various production processes.

## Perform Risk Analysis

Success depends on a lot of different factors. It's not just about how you run the company. Economic and social factors play an important role to determine your accomplishments. Since Big Data leads to predictive analytics, it allows you to analyze and scan social media feeds and newspaper reports. Thus, you can permanently keep up with speed on the latest trends and developments in the industry.

## Data Safety

Big Data tools allow you to map the entire data landscape across the company. This allows you to analyze all kinds of internal threats. With this information, you can keep sensitive information safe. It's protected in an appropriate manner and stored according to regulatory requirements.

Due to this, most industries have been focusing on Big Data to ensure data safety and protection. It's even more important in organizations that deal with financial information, credit and debit card information, and other such practices.

### Create New Revenue Streams

Big data provides you with insights from analyzing the market and consumers. However, this data is not only valuable to you but also for other parties. You can sell the non-personalized trend data to large industries operating in the same sector.

There's no doubt that Big Data will continue to play an important role in many different industries around the world. It can definitely do wonders for a business organization. In order to reap more benefits, it's important to train your employees about Big Data management. With proper management of Big Data, your business will be more productive and efficient.

Big data has big applications in the business world. It is no longer surprising that there is a need for people to take a data science course to fully understand the impact of big data on the business environment and how to create real value through analytics.

### Implement Risk Management

Every business needs to have a strategic approach to risk management. While many things can help make this possible, big data is one of the most important. It will also allow companies to quantify and model risks that can confront their operations. With the use of big data, companies can rely on predictive analytics to have an intelligent risk foresight. With this knowledge, it will be easier to implement risk mitigation strategies.

### Understand Customers Better

Businesses must understand their customers, and big data will make this possible. From website visits to social media interactions, big data will reveal a lot about your customers. It will also allow the business to create customer profiles and buyer personas. When you understand them better, you can improve your products and services. It allows you to deliver the highest level of satisfaction. This can also help in building customer loyalty.

### Know your Competition

Big data also provides the opportunity to get to know your competitors. For instance, it can provide information about their pricing models and how it is perceived by the customers. You will also learn about the customers' perceptions of your competitors. Plus, it will help you determine how they are performing online, such as their social media engagement.

### Personalize your Marketing

Marketing can make or break your business. For its success, one of the most important is personalization. This is another area where you can use big data. Because it lets you understand your customers, you can create marketing campaigns that will target a specific niche or segment. It can offer insights that will allow marketers to create high-converting materials.

### Identify Trends

Through big data, it is also possible for businesses to identify trends, which can be useful in product research and development. From customer behaviors to buying patterns, big data will provide the management with the information it needs to analyze how trends will change over time, and in turn, will give the business the time to prepare for these changes.

### Manage Human Resources

Utilizing big data will help you develop a robust approach to human resource management. From hiring decisions to training and development, big data will help have the best people. From staff satisfaction to productivity data, you can have access to the information that you need for understanding and improving your workforce.

Big data has endless applications in businesses. Businesses need to uncover the hidden patterns, correlations, and get insights from unstructured big data to make proper business decisions. From risk management to human resource management, you can use big data in many ways to improve business operations. So, make sure to have the right infrastructure in place for managing big data.

## Data Mining

Data mining is the process that companies use to turn raw data into useful information. They utilize software to look for patterns in large batches of data so they can learn more about customers. It pulls out information from data sets and compares it to help the business make decisions. This eventually helps them to develop strategies, increase sales, market effectively, and more. Data mining sometimes gets confused with machine learning and data analysis, but these terms are all very different and unique.

While both data mining and machine learning use patterns and analytics, data mining looks for patterns that already exist in data, while machine learning goes beyond to predict future outcomes based on the data. In data mining, the "rules" or patterns aren't known from the start. In many cases of machine learning, the machine is given a rule or variable to understand the data. Additionally data mining relies on human intervention and decisions, but machine learning is meant to be started by a human and then learn on its own. There is quite a bit of overlap between data mining and machine learning, machine learning processes are often utilized in data mining in order to automate those processes.

Similarly data analysis and data mining aren't interchangeable terms. Data mining is used in data analytics, but they aren't the same. Data mining is the process of getting the information from large data sets, and data analytics is when companies take this information and dive into it to learn more. Data analysis involves inspecting, cleaning, transforming, and modeling data. The ultimate goal of analysis is discovering useful information, informing conclusions, and making decisions.

Data mining, data analysis, artificial intelligence, machine learning, and many other terms are all combined in business intelligence processes that help a company or organization make decisions and learn more about their customers and potential outcomes.

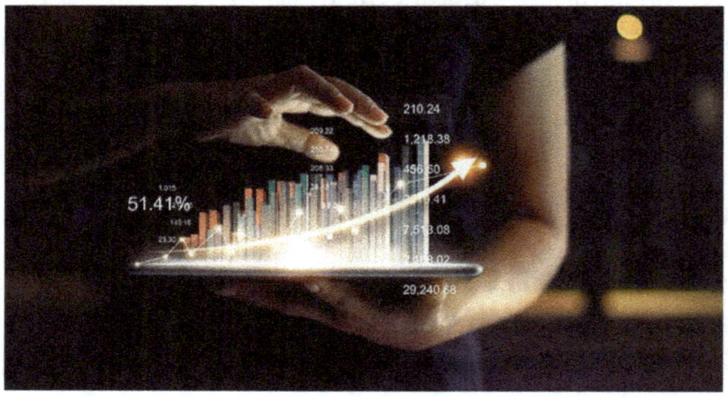


Almost all businesses use data mining, and it's important to understand the data mining process and how it can help a business make decisions.

- Business understanding: The first step to successful data mining is to understand the overall objectives of the business, then be able to convert this into a data mining problem and a plan. Without an understanding of the ultimate goal of the business, you won't be able to design a good data mining algorithm. For example, a supermarket may want to use data mining to learn more about their customers. The business understanding is that a supermarket is looking to find out what their customers are buying the most.
- Data understanding: After you know what the business is looking for, it's time to collect data. There are many complex ways that data can be obtained from an organization, organized, stored, and managed. Data mining involves getting familiar with the data, identifying any issues, getting insights, or observing subsets. For example, the supermarket may use a rewards program where customers can input their phone number when they purchase, giving the supermarket access to their shopping data.
- Data Preparation: Data preparation involves getting the information production ready. This is the biggest part of data mining. It is taking the computer-language data, and converting it into a form that people can understand and quantify. Transforming and cleaning the data for modeling is a key for this step.
- Modeling: In the modeling phase, mathematical models are used to search for patterns in the data. There are usually several techniques that can be used for the same set of data. There is a lot of trial and error involved in modeling.
- Evaluation: When the model is complete, it needs to be carefully evaluated and the steps to make the model need to be reviewed, to ensure it meets the business objectives. At the end of this phase, a decision about the data mining results will be made. In the supermarket example, the data mining results will provide a list of what the customer has purchased, which is what the business was looking for.

- Deployment: This can be a simple or complex part of data mining, depending on the output of the process. It can be as simple as generating a report, or as complex as creating a repeatable data mining process to happen regularly.

After the data mining process has been completed, a business will be able to make their decisions and implement changes based on what they have learned.

## How does Data Mining Inform Business Analytics?

So why is data mining important for businesses? Businesses that utilize data mining are able to have a competitive advantage, better understanding of their customers, and good oversight of business operations, improved customer acquisition, and new business opportunities. Different industries will have different benefits from their data analytics. Some industries are looking for the best ways to get new customers, others are looking for new marketing techniques, and others are working to improve their systems. The data mining process is what gives businesses the opportunities and understanding for how to make their decisions, analyze their information, and move forward.

## Data Mining Techniques in Business Analytics

Now that you understand why data mining is important, it's beneficial to see how data mining works specifically in business settings:

- Classification: This data mining technique is more complex, using attributes of data to move them into discernable categories, helping you draw further conclusions. Supermarket data mining may use classification to group the types of groceries customers are buying, like produce, meat, bakery items, etc. These classifications help the store learn even more about customers, outputs, etc.

- Clustering: This technique is very similar to classification, chunking data together based on their similarities. Cluster groups are less structured than classification groups, making it a more simple option for data mining. In the supermarket example, a simple cluster group could be food and non-food items instead of the specific classes.

- Association rules: Association in data mining is all about tracking patterns, specifically based on linked variables. In the supermarket example, this may mean that many customers who buy a specific item may also buy a second, related item. This is how stores may know how to group certain food items together, or in online shopping they may show "people also bought this" section.

- Regression analysis: Regression is used to plan and model, identifying the likelihood of a specific variable. The supermarket may be able to project price points based on availability, consumer demand, and their competition. Regression helps data mining by identifying the relationship between variables in a set.

- Anomaly/outlier detection: For many data mining cases, just seeing the overarching pattern might not be all you need. Data needs to be able to identify and understand the outliers in your data as well. For example, in the supermarket if most of the shoppers are female, but one week in February is mostly men, you'll want to investigate that outlier and understand what is behind it.

These data mining techniques are a key for businesses to be able to understand the information they have and better their practices.

## Data Warehouse

The Big Data revolution was supposed to be a gold mine for organizations everywhere. As the data piles kept growing, though, the problem quickly became clear: where on earth do you put all that data? That's where data warehouses came in. These allow you to bring in all your data from all the myriad sources it comes from, stick it in one place, organize it in a clear and comprehensive way, and ultimately create a single version of truth.

Major investments were made to make sure the data was stored in a way it could be pulled out quickly and conveniently with all the required aggregations prepared in advance. You could then use this as one source for Business Intelligence and Business Analytics. So, that is where more BI tools are needed. Your data warehouse might be the perfect storage system for all that data, but you still need something on top to extract it from there, and then a way to join the different sources, and then a tool to analyze the data – which means you need different tools, and people to write code and prepare reports that can allow you to work directly with the data stored in your data warehouse. Something that will allow users to dive right in, find what they need, analyze and draw out the key insights to make better business decisions. For example, there are solutions out there that allow you to extract the data you need, manipulate and analyze it quickly and conveniently, and refresh this swiftly whenever your data is updated. With this type of technology, you may even be able to cut straight to the original applications without having to load everything into your data warehouse first.

### How Data Warehouses Work

Data Warehouse:

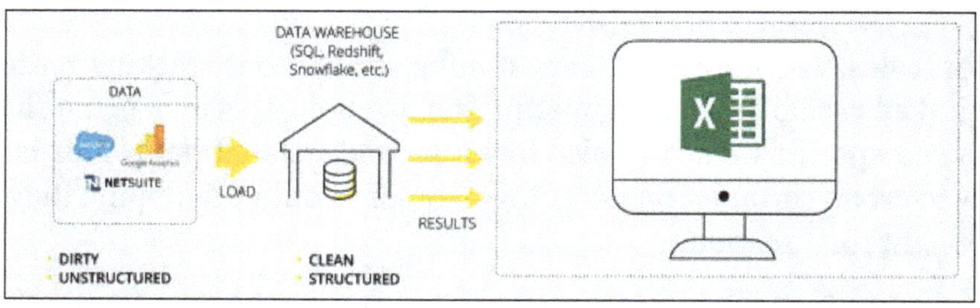


No Data Warehouse:

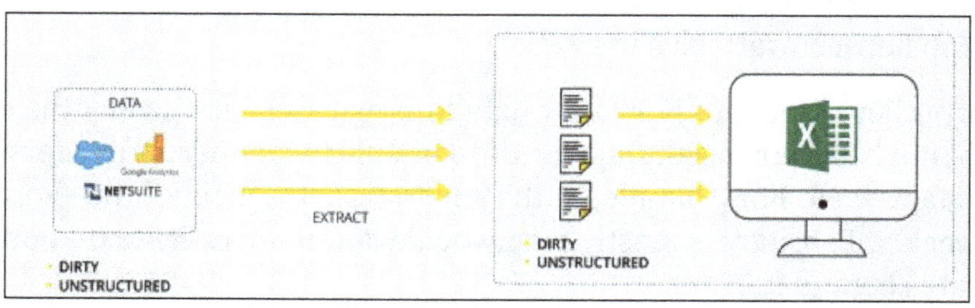

In the past, businesses without a data warehouse were stuck with masses of highly detailed, but messy and unstructured data, from which end users on the business side of the organization struggled to get anything useful out of. A data warehouse takes all that scattered data and lays it out nice and tidy in a huge relational database, through a process of Extract-Transform-Load (ETL). This takes a huge load off transactional systems, as well as improving data quality and helping to prepare it for analysis.

This also makes sure that when extracting or adding data the operational systems are not being affected. The trouble with this becomes clear when you try to actually use that data for Business Intelligence (BI). No analytics engine is strong enough to run queries that sift through every fragment of data contained in your database. To do that, you need a phenomenally powerful hardware setup.

To get around this, organizations started using "data marts". These work by giving different groups of people access to one subsection of the whole data warehouse. While this reduces the pressure on an individual's machine when they need to run a query, it also means no one person can ever get the full picture from the data the company collects. Hardly an ideal outcome.

Traditional BI didn't have a way around this, though. It couldn't tap into the raw data in the data warehouse, or pick and choose what it wanted to see within the database. As a result, the BI solutions of the past used either data marts or OLAP cubes to connect to the data. The latter cuts down query times by pre-summarizing certain elements of the data before it starts searching through the database.

Both options are speedier than working with complete, giant datasets, but they mean you lose either scope or detail in your data, as well as decentralizing it which partly defeats the point of having a comprehensive data warehouse in the first place.

## What Can't a Data Warehouse Do?

Data warehouses offer an excellent way to clean up and store your data in a way that can be easily searched and organized. That's what they are for. The important thing to understand, though, is that this is all they are for. They don't have any analytical function, so you need that on top. The fact that data warehouses are so good at tidying up your data can also be a drawback. This is because they are relational databases, which makes them highly restrictive in terms of the kind of data you can store and how you store it.

You only have a certain number of columns and ways to sort and identify each item, so anything that doesn't fit neatly into this poses a challenge—for example, photo or video content, language analysis, and so on. It also means that data warehouses only store past/historical data, also referred to as analytical data. You can't store current real-time (i.e. transactional) data.

This limits the kind of insights you can get out of the data stored in your warehouse, even with an analytics engine attached. Depending on what sources you use, getting a complete and accurate picture might mean drawing data directly from other applications or types of databases into your BI platform.

Then there's the issue of getting enough support from IT. If you're moving with the times and embracing new ways of engaging with customers or collecting information about your business and processes, that means you either need to add new data streams and types to your warehouse constantly, or you'll need to work with multiple systems.

The former can feel frustrating if you've already invested heavily in building a data warehouse, while the latter is far from a simple task—you'll almost certainly need plenty of help from your IT department to keep on top of it. If you do, and this creates a delay in accessing and analyzing all the data available to you, you could find that your data warehouse ends up slowing you down instead of speeding you up. This situation simply means that you have to keep investing in your data warehouse to make room for more data and to be able to load data from new data sources that did not exist originally when the data warehouse was built. A good example is a service provider that stores billing information regularly. When a new service is added, the data from this new service is not uploaded to the data warehouse until it is configured to do so by programmers. Until then, the data cannot be analyzed, leaving management in the dark about adoption and success.

## Does Everyone Need a Data Warehouse?

As explained that your data warehouse's limitations could mean you need to use other data streams alongside the warehouse for analysis. However, if you have a sophisticated enough BI system that you can connect to those original data sources directly, and can guarantee your access to clean and complete data well, you might not need a data warehouse at all.

ElastiCubes use an in-memory columnar database approach, meaning that a) rather than having to load all the data in the database into the BI platform for analysis, it whips through and loads just the bits you need, and b) it optimizes use of your computer's disk, RAM and CPU, so that you can use a single commodity server to crunch terabytes of data on a standard machine, even if there are a high number of concurrent users.

## Traditional BI Without DW

Without Data Warehouse:

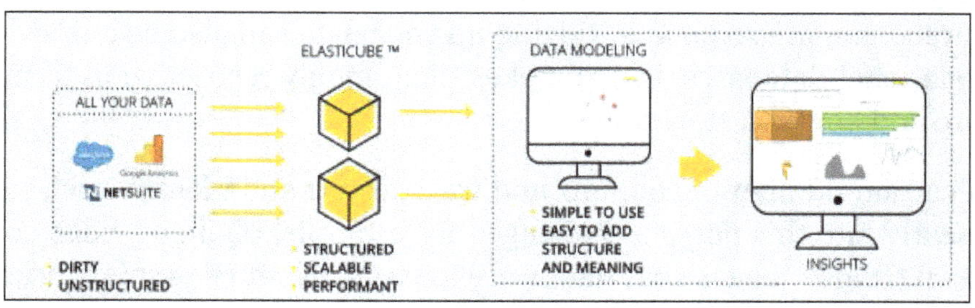


It also cleans, centralizes and structures this detailed data for you, performs ETL functions within the ElastiCube server, and presents the results in an intuitive dashboard so that it's optimized for use by business users of BI. This dashboard can easily be shared across your company.

As a result, you can access all the data you have for any given analytics task, in a neat and tidy format, without having to invest heavily in hardware or lean on IT for support. If you don't yet have a data warehouse, you may find that this system makes one redundant.

If you've already committed to a data warehouse, there's no reason you can't continue to connect this to a BI system for analysis. In fact, the right BI solution can actually help you to get more out of your existing data warehouse, to maximize your investment.

In this setup you can connect ElastiCubes to the raw data in your data warehouse, allowing you to retain the granular detail of this clean, centralized, structured data. Compare this to traditional systems which use data marts or OLAP cubes to connect to this raw data, summarizing it and decentralizing it in the process. New, sophisticated BI technologies aren't here to render your database obsolete (unless you want them to). More commonly, they help you get the most out of the system you already have.

## BI with Data Warehouse

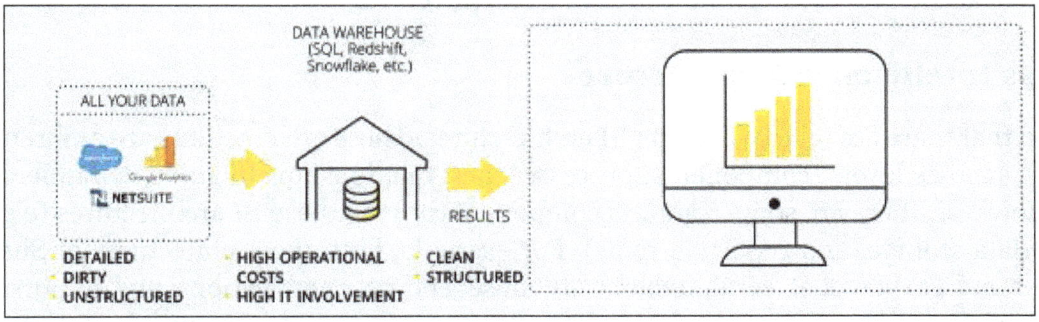


With Data Warehouse:

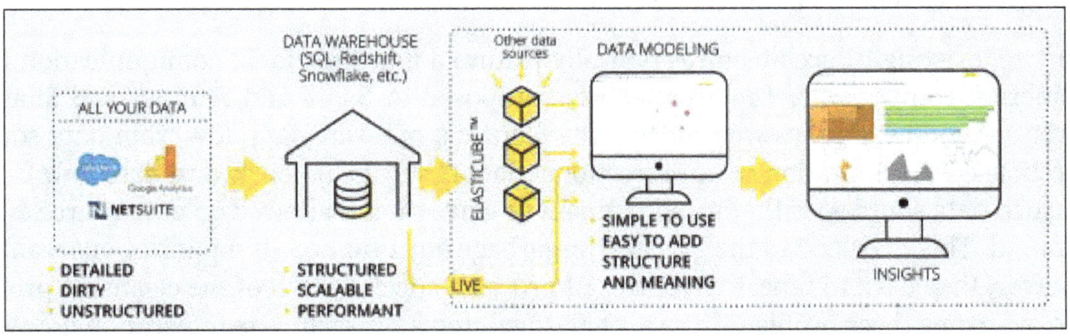


It does all this while future-proofing your data strategy. You don't need to establish additional ways to import new or difficult data streams into your database because you'll be able to connect to them directly. You don't need to worry that your store of data is growing all the time, because it's not going to bottleneck when you try to get it from your warehouse and into your analytics tools. You can scale.

# Data Presentation Architecture

As organizations begin to adopt BI, one very important task is to make sure that they follow a good BI architectural plan in their implementation process so as to ascertain the success of their BI investment. BI architecture is a framework detailing different components of BI (i.e., data, people, processes, technology, and the management) and how these components need to come together to ensure smooth functioning of a BI system. Examples of information contained in a BI architecture are the types of data that need to be collected, the methods to be used to analyze data, and the way to present certain information. Having a solid BI architecture is critical. If the underlying architecture is not designed properly, inconsistencies that arise among the different components may lead to problems such as inability to share information among the components, inability to meet business requirements, and poor business performance. In the worst case, a bad BI architecture may lead to the scenario where wrong information is delivered to the wrong person at the wrong time.

Even in the case where BI systems are functional despite bad architecture, organizations will not be able to maximize the value they should have gotten from their BI investments. Even though the importance of a good BI architecture is non-arguable, a review of the literature shows that there is still a lack of academic research in the area of BI architecture.

## Business Intelligence Architecture

It is found that there are several existing BI architectures. These architectures are different in their structures such as layers, components, processes, and relationships to guide BI implementation efforts. However, there are some common components among these BI architectures (e.g., source systems, data storage, and reporting tools). For example, both the architectures of Shariat and Hightower and Turban et al. contain data warehouse, end user applications, and BI portal. Nonetheless, one important component missing from these existing BI architectures is that of analytical and reporting such as data mining, predictive analytics, and data visualization. These features are new BI capabilities that are important and should be included in a BI architecture.

Furthermore, existing BI architectures typically feature a uni-directional communication flow between different components. The architectures proposed in Baars and Kemper and Shariat and Hightower are good examples where they only feature a one-way data flow from data sources to data warehouse. The limitation of uni-directional data flow (i.e., no backward data flow from data warehouse to data sources) is that no adjustment or correction is allowed on data source even if an error is found. This may lead to the garbage-in-garbage out situation. If organizations want to correct the error, they have to repeat the entire BI process especially that of the cleansing procedures again. To overcome these problems, Dayal et al. suggested a two-way data integration flow whereby the cleansed data can be sent back to data sources to improve accuracy and reduce cleansing work.

Another issue with existing BI architectures is the lack of support on metadata management. A good BI architecture should include the layer of metadata. A metadata repository is essential for business users to store and standardize metadata across different systems. By having a well-structured metadata, organizations will be able to track and monitor data flows within their BI environment. In addition, they will be able to ensure the consistency of definitions and descriptions of data that support BI components and thus avoid misunderstanding and misinterpretation of data.

Aside from that, some of the architectures do not include operational data store (ODS) within the BI environment. For instance, Watson's BI architecture contains only data warehouse and data marts whereas Baars and Kemper and Turban et al. include only data warehouse. In order to address operational data needs of an organization, it is essential to implement ODS to provide current or near current integrated information that can be accessed or updated directly by users.

Through this way, decision makers will be able to react faster to changing business environment and requirements. Furthermore, it is necessary to consider data staging area in the ETL (Extract-Transform-Load) process. As most of the data from data source require cleansing and transformation, it is important to create a temporary storage for data to reside prior to loading into ODS or data warehouse. Without building this staging area, the process of working on the data from data source and the process of loading the data into data warehouse can be very time consuming and resource-intensive.

## The Proposed Framework of Business Intelligence Architecture

The five layers are data source, ETL (Extract-Transform-Load), data warehouse, end user, and metadata layers.

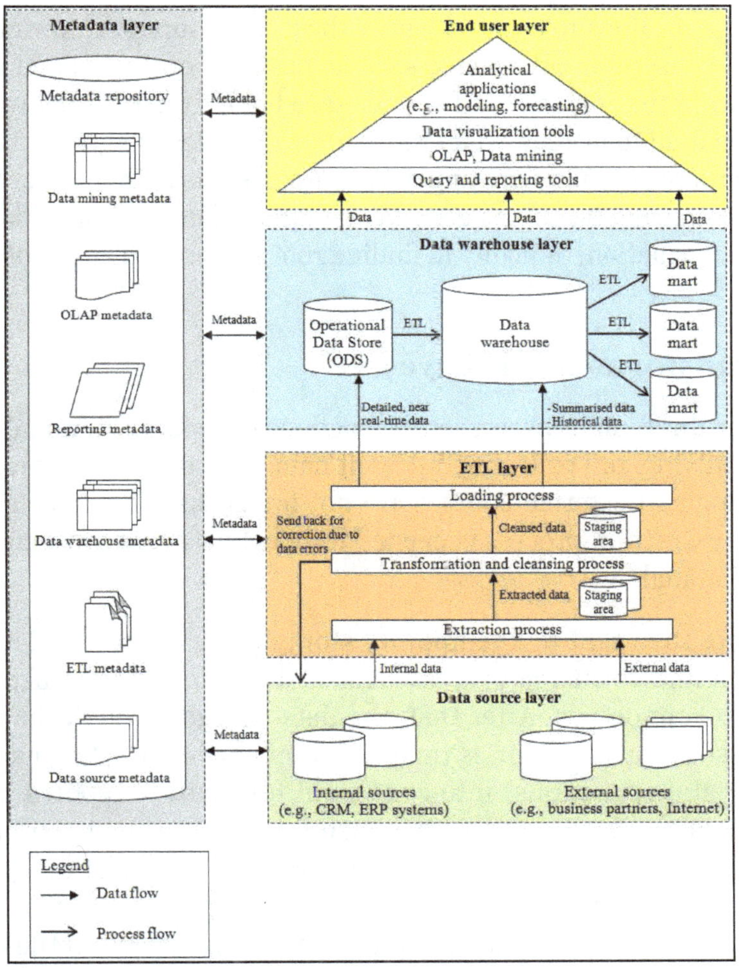


Proposed BI Architecture.

## Data Source Layer

Nowadays, many application domains require the use of structured data as well as unstructured and semi-structured data to make effective and timely decision. All these data can be acquired from two types of sources: internal and external. Internal data source refers to data that is captured and maintained by operational systems inside an organization such as Customer

Relationship Management and Enterprise Resource Planning systems. Internal data sources include the data related to business operations (i.e., customers, products, and sales data). These operational systems are also known as online transaction processing systems because they process large amount of transactions in real time and update data whenever it is needed. Operational systems contain only current data that is used to support daily business operations of an organization. Generally, operational systems are process-oriented as they focus mainly on specific business operations such as sales, accounting, and purchasing.

External data source refers to those that originate outside an organization. This type of data can be collected from external sources such as business partners, syndicate data suppliers, the Internet, governments, and market research organizations. These data are often related to competitors, market, environment (e.g., customer demographic and economic), and technology.

It is important for organizations to clearly identify their data sources. Knowing where the required data can be obtained is useful in addressing specific business questions and requirements, thereby resulting in significant time savings and greater speed of information delivery. Furthermore, the knowledge can also be used to facilitate data replication, data cleansing, and data extraction. This is because even though there are many existing data sources, some of them might be inaccessible, unreliable or irrelevant to current business needs. With correct identification of data sources, problems such as inconsistent information, difficulty in finding root causes, and issues of data isolation can be avoided.

## ETL (Extract-Transform-Load) Layer

This layer focuses on three main processes: extraction, transformation and loading. Extraction is the process of identifying and collecting relevant data from different sources. Usually, the data collected from internal and external sources are not integrated, incomplete, and may be duplicated. Therefore, the extraction process is needed to select data that are significant in supporting organizational decision making.

The extracted data are then sent to a temporary storage area called the data staging area prior to the transformation and cleansing process. This is done to avoid the need of extracting data again should any problem occurs. After that, the data will go through the transformation and the cleansing process. Transformation is the process of converting data using a set of business rules (such as aggregation functions) into consistent formats for reporting and analysis. Data transformation process also includes defining business logic for data mapping and standardizing data definitions in order to ensure consistency across an organization. As for data cleansing, it refers to the process of identifying and correcting data errors based on pre-specified rules. If there is an error found on the extracted data, then it is sent back to the data source for correction. Once data have been transformed and cleansed, they are stored in the staging area. This can prevent the need of transforming data again if the loading processes fail or terminate. Loading is the last phase of the ETL process. The data in staging area are loaded into target repository.

## Data Warehouse Layer

There are three components in the data warehouse layer, namely operational data store, data warehouse, and data marts. Data flows from operational data store to data warehouse and subsequently to data mart.

## Operational Data Store

An operational data store (ODS) is used to integrate all data from the ETL layer and load them into data warehouses. ODS is a database that stores subject-oriented, detailed, and current data from multiple sources to support tactical decision making. It provides an integrated view of near real-time data such as transactions and prices. In addition, the data stored in ODS is volatile, which means it can be over-written or updated with new data that flow into ODS. As such, ODS does not store any historical data. Generally, ODS is designed to support operational processing and reporting needs of a specific application by providing an integrated view of data across many different business applications. It is normally used by middle management level for daily management and short-term decision making. Since the data stored in ODS are updated frequently (i.e., in minutes or hours), it is useful for reporting types that require real time (within 15 minutes) or near time (updated in 15 minutes to 1 hour) information.

## Data Warehouse

Data warehouse is one of the most important components in BI architecture. Inmon defines data warehouse as "a subject-oriented, integrated, time-variant, and non-volatile collection of data in support of management's decision making process". The characteristics of a data warehouse are described as follows:

- Subject-oriented: Data from various sources are organized into groups based on common subject areas that an organization would like to focus on, such as customers, sales, and products.
- Integrated: Data warehouse gathers data from various sources. All of these data must be consistent in terms of naming conventions, formats, and other related characteristics.
- Time-variant: Each data stored in the data warehouse has time dimension to keep track of the changes or trends on the data. In other words, data warehouse will store historical changes on each piece of data.
- Non-volatile: New data can be added into data warehouse regularly. But, all the data stored in data warehouse are read-only. This means users are not allowed to update, over-write or delete the stored data.

Data warehouse is a central storage that collects and stores data from internal and external sources for strategic decision making, queries, and analysis. Data warehouse stores aggregated or summarized data. In addition, it also stores large amount of historical data for the purpose of long term analysis. Data are stored in data warehouse longer (5 to 10 years) than in ODS (60 to 90 days). Data in a data warehouse is updated regularly, for instance weekly or sometimes daily. As a result, it does not contain the latest data as in operational systems and ODS. Aside from that, data warehouses are designed to support OLAP (Online Analytical Processing) applications by storing and maintaining data in multi-dimensional structures for query, reporting, and analysis.

## Data Mart

While the data in a data warehouse is mainly used to support various needs across the whole organization, it is not equipped to support the needs and requirements of specific departments. Consequently, it is necessary to have data marts to support them. A data mart is a subset of the data warehouse that is used to support analytical needs of a particular business function or department. Like data warehouses, it contains historical data that can help users to access and analyze different data trends. However, it can only keep data for 60 to 90 days. Therefore, the amount of data stored in a data mart is much lesser than the data stored in a data warehouse. There can be many data marts inside an organization. Data warehouses and data marts are built based on multi-dimensional data model which consists of fact and dimension tables. Fact table contains quantitative data about business entities such as sales amount, quantity, and price. Dimension table contains data (such as product, customer, data, and location) that describes facts.

## Metadata Layer

Metadata refers to data about data. It describes where data are being used and stored, the source of data, what changes have been made to the data, and how one piece of data relates to other information. Metadata repository is used to store technical and business information about data as well as business rules and data definitions. Good management and use of metadata can reduce development time, simplify on-going maintenance, and provide users with information about data source. For instance, users do not have to re-design data structure (such as table name and data types) for data modeling since the data structures needed have been stored as metadata. Users can just query and retrieve these metadata from repositories. Therefore, it is essential to ensure that metadata in repositories are maintained and updated regularly.

There are many different types of metadata to support a BI architecture such as data source, ETL, reporting, OLAP, and data mining metadata. Data source metadata consists of information about access mode, structure of data sets (e.g., relational tables, views, stored procedures), and referential integrity constraints. As data are integrated into the data warehouse layer using ETL tools, an extraction log is maintained to record the changes made to data element during the extraction process to ensure the quality of data. This log is ETL metadata and it is stored in metadata repository. ETL metadata generally contains information about sources, targets, transformation rules, and mapping. Metadata repository is also used to document the information about data contained in the data warehouse layer. It includes description of data structure (schema, dimensions, and hierarchies) and definitions of conformed dimensions and conformed facts. These metadata guide the process of extracting, transforming, and loading data into target repository. OLAP metadata provides descriptions about structure of cubes, dimensions, hierarchies, levels, and the type of drill paths being taken. Data mining metadata include descriptions about algorithms and queries. Reporting metadata are XML-based and are used to store report templates and reporting descriptions such as report name, start date, and end date. These metadata also contain information about structures of charts and queries.

## End User Layer

The end user layer consists of tools that display information in different formats to different users. These tools can be grouped hierarchically in a pyramid shape. As one moves from the bottom to the top of the pyramid, the degree of comprehensiveness at which data are being processed and presented increases. This is to tailor to increasing complexity in decision-making as one move up organizational hierarchy. For instance, the highest level of pyramid consists of analytical applications which are usually used by top management while the lowest level consists of query and reporting tools which are used mostly by operational management level.

## Query and Reporting Tools

Query and reporting tools are very useful tools which allow end users to access and query data quickly, and to produce reports for decision making and management purposes. There are many different types of reports including standard reports, ad-hoc reports, budgeting and planning reports, and metadata reports. Both internal and external users can manage reports and other information easier and faster through BI portals. BI portal is a popular end user tool to deliver information. It is a single, secure interface that integrates data and information from various sources so that users can have a one-stop access to different types of information.

## OLAP (Online Analytical Processing)

One or more OLAP servers can manage data in the data warehouse layer for reporting, analysis, modelling, and planning to optimize business. OLAP server is a "data manipulation engine that is designed to support multi-dimensional data structures". OLAP server can provide multi-dimensional and summarized views of aggregated data. OLAP is a user-friendly graphical tool that allows users to quickly view and analyze business data from different perspectives. Besides that, OLAP also allows users to easily compare different types of data and complex computations.

In order to reduce query time, data in OLAP server are organized in the form of data cubes instead of tables (rows and columns) as in relational data model. Data cubes are dimensional models stored in multi-dimensional OLAP structures. They contain fact and dimensional tables to store and manage multi-dimensional data so that users can analyze data easily and in a faster manner. Four basic OLAP operations used in analyzing multi-dimensional data are:

- Roll-up or drill-up: It increases the level of aggregation, either by moving up to a higher level (more detailed data) along a dimensional hierarchy or by reducing one or more dimensions from a given data cube.
- Drill-down: It is the opposite of roll-up. It decreases the level of aggregation by moving down to a lower level (less detailed data) along a dimensional hierarchy or by adding one or more dimensions to a data cube.
- Slice and dice: The slice operation can be performed by selecting a specific value on a single dimension, resulting in a sub-cube. The dice operation performs a projection on a data cube by selecting a range of values on two or more dimensions.
- Pivot: It enables users to rotate the axes of the data cube, meaning swapping the dimensions to get different views of data.

## Data Mining

Data mining process can be achieved with the integration of data warehouses and OLAP servers by performing further data analysis in OLAP cubes. Since the amount of data in an organization is growing rapidly, it is necessary to have data mining to make decisions faster. Basically, data mining is a process that automatically identifies useful information such as unusual patterns, trends, and relationships that are hidden within large amount of data. This can be achieved by applying statistical techniques such as classification, time-series analysis or clustering. Data mining techniques have been used in many application areas such as marketing, financial, medical, and manufacturing to predict future results and summarize details of data.

## Data Visualisation Tools

Data visualisation tools such as dashboard and scorecards can be provided to managers and executives who need an overall view of their business performance. Dashboard is a useful tool that allows users to visualize data using charts, coloured metrics or tables. Users can also view more detailed information about key performance indicators across their organizations. By doing so, managers can closely and more effectively monitor their business performance and progress toward defined goals.

## Analytical Applications

Analytical applications provide functionalities such as modeling, forecasting, sales analysis, and what-if scenarios. These applications can be used to support both internal and external business processes. Applications that are equipped with analytical capabilities allow users to gain insights into improving the performance of business operations. By employing analytical applications, decision makers can also identify and understand what factors drive their business value, and thus able to leverage opportunities faster than their competitors.

For a BI system to work smoothly, all five layers described above have to be linked together in a systematic manner. Data originating from internal and external sources have to be extracted, transformed, and loaded into the data warehouse layer. When the data passes through the ETL layer, it can flow to both directions, either to ODS (and then to data warehouse) or to data warehouse directly. Since data warehouse is developed for the usage of the entire organization, data from the warehouse is sent to data marts to fulfill specific operational needs. At end user layer, data in the ODS, data warehouse, and data marts can be accessed by using a variety of tools such as query and reporting tools, data visualisation tools, and analytical applications. Finally, there is a centralized metadata repository that is connected with various components such as the ETL layer, the data warehouse layer, and the end user layer.

The data flows among the components as proposed in the framework for this paper are multi-directional. Such consideration overcomes limitations of uni-directional data flow in many existing BI architectures. A multi-directional flow can enhance query performance and improve accuracy because data error at one layer can be returned to the previous layer for clarification if error occurs. For instance, if an error data is found in the ETL layer, that particular piece of data can be sent back to the data source layer (i.e., internal sources) for modification. Nevertheless, data flow from external sources to ETL layer is only uni-directional. No correction or adjustment is feasible to external source since it originates from the outside of an organization.

## Data Sampling

Sampling is a common statistics technique used, for instance, for political or opinion polls. If a researcher wants to determine the most popular way of commuting to work in the US, they will not need to talk to every American citizen. Instead, they can select a representative group of 1,000 members, hoping it will be enough to make the results accurate.

In web analytics, sampling works in a very similar way. Only a subset of your traffic data is selected and analyzed, and that sample is used to estimate the overall results. But can you really be sure that your software will choose a representative set of your traffic? Unfortunately most of web analytics tools automatically start sampling data when you reach a particular limit of actions tracked on your website.

### What are Data Sampling Methods?

Samples come in different shapes and sizes as there are various data sampling methods. You can basically divide them into probability and non-probability sampling.

Probability sampling is an approach in which samples from a larger population are chosen using a method based on various statistical methods. So you select random numbers that correspond to points (users) in data set and ensure that everyone in your set has equal chance of getting selected.

This particular method provides the best chance to create a truly representative sample of the population. On the other hand, non-probabilistic sampling is an approach where a data sample is determined based on the subjective judgment of an analyst. It means that not all points of the population will have a chance to be selected.

Applying this method gives you a smaller chance to create a sample that accurately illustrates the larger population.

### Issues with Sampled Data

Web-data sampling may result in far less accurate reports. The best way to understand it is to get some first-hand experience. Have you ever tried to compare reports based on sampled and complete traffic? It is a good idea to see what kind of discrepancies you may be facing and then decide if the issue is serious or not. Even if your discrepancy is less than 10%, which is not bad at all, it may not stay this way forever.

It is better to take proper steps to get full and clean reports. Note that 5% discrepancy between different tools is acceptable and depends on numerous factors. In tools such as Google Analytics, your data is aggregated and delivered to you as a random data set, which means you cannot be sure if your reports are displaying the overall traffic and meaningful trends, or if the selected set is missing the point. When you invest a substantial amount of money and time into analyzing your reports, they should be accurate.

After all, you decide on the direction and next steps of development of your business based on this information. If you do not have this knowledge, you could just go with your gut, which may actually be a better idea than working with unreliable data. Always make sure your analytics tool provides solid data and try to avoid sampling. Otherwise, you may be missing out some crucial information.

## Data Preparation

Data preparation is a pre-processing step that involves cleansing, transforming, and consolidating data. In other words, it is a process that involves connecting to one or many different data sources, cleaning dirty data, reformatting or restructuring data, and finally merging this data to be consumed for analysis. More often than not, this is the most time consuming step of the entire analysis life cycle and the speed and efficiency of the data prep process directly impacts the time it takes to discover insights.

## Importance of Data Preparation

### Self-Service Analytics

As businesses demand faster and more flexible access to data, self-service analytics plays a key part in enabling business users to quickly prepare their own data for exploratory analysis thereby accelerating the time-to-insight by allowing an organization to bypass the IT bottleneck (as projects can take months or years to deliver) and ultimately driving better business decision making. Data sources are prepared on the fly for analysis, thus eliminating the need for complex ETL processes for data discovery.

### Predictive Modeling

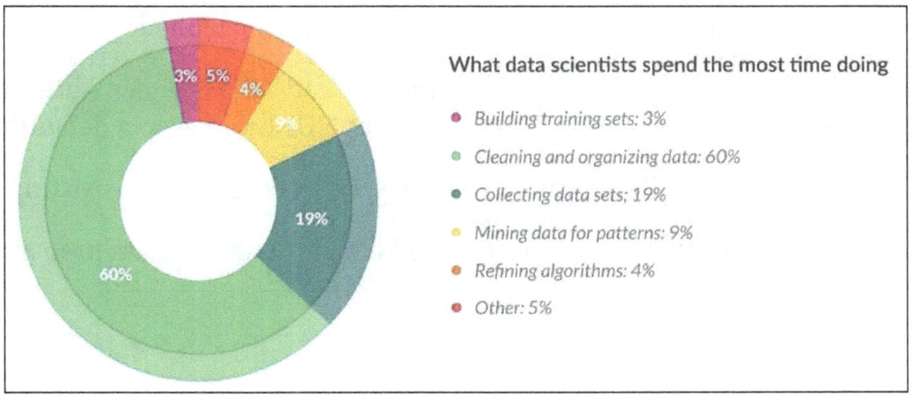


Data scientists spend almost 80% of their time on data preparation. Most data scientists spend the majority of their time on collecting different types of data and then preparing that data to make feature (meaning fields/attributes) engineering decisions prior to actually building, testing, and training the model.

Feature Engineering is a process where features are changed or new ones are derived to improve the model performance in terms of accuracy. This is where the business domain expertise is needed and involves adding new data sources, applying business rules, and reshaping or restructuring the data to interpret it correctly. For example, if we want to predict retail sales for a specific time period – the holiday season for instance – it is important to understand the seasonal nature of the business and add a feature that identifies the shopping period, as this may be when the highest sales are expected.

## What Does Data Preparation Entail?

### Data Access

Since data is stored differently based on the type of data, different sets of tools are needed to connect to the respective data sources. For example, structured data is stored in relational databases and uses SQL to query the data, unstructured data stored in Hadoop would use Hive, Spark or Pig, data extracts for file formats like CSV, TXT, JSON, XML, etc., and for other formats tools like Python and R are used. In other words, to be able to connect to all different sources is a cumbersome and difficult task, especially for analysts and data scientists.

## Data Profiling

Perform an analysis to check data quality and identify fields with no information value that could skew the model for predictive analysis. This might include contents, blanks, and duplicates and take an informed decision on how to address such issues or ignore such fields.

Cleaning up messy data involves tasks such as:

- Merging: Combine/enrich relevant data from different datasets into a new dataset.
- Appending: Combine two smaller (but similar) datasets into a larger dataset.
- Filtering: Rule-based narrowing of a larger dataset into a smaller dataset.
- Deduping: Remove duplicates based on specific criteria as defined.
- Cleansing: Edit or replace values, i.e. some records had "F" as gender while others had "Female"; alter to have "Female" for all records or set NULL values to a default value.
- Transforming: Convert missing values or derive a new column from existing column(s).
- Aggregating: Roll up data to have summarized data for analysis data preparation.

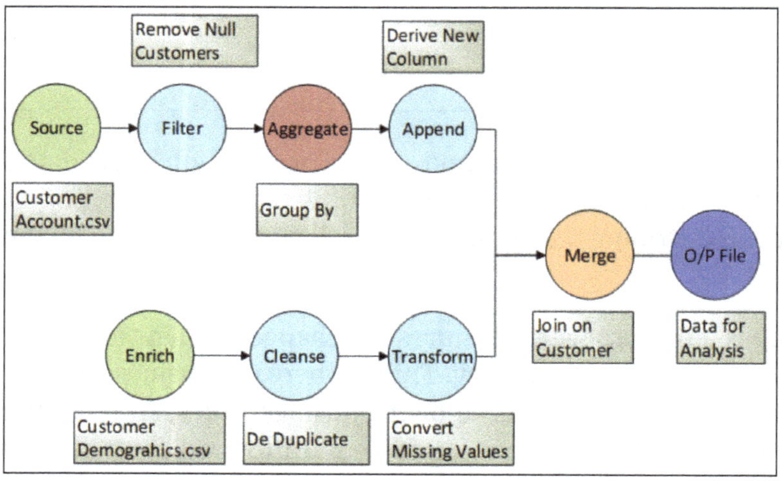


## Sampling and Partitioning

This involves breaking down the entire dataset into a smaller set of sample data to reduce the size of the training data. These samples are then used for training, testing, and validating the model. It is important to ensure that the sample set includes data covering various scenarios to ensure the model is trained accordingly and not end up with a biased or inaccurate model.

## What Tool(s) do you Need?

There are many tools available in the market like Trifacta, Alteryx, Datawatch, Paxata, and others that offer features like visual profiling & transformations, build & schedule pipelines, data mashup & blending, and enable self-service discovery. Each one has their respective strengths and I recommend that you spend some time identifying the right one for your specific business needs.

Whichever tools you choose to use, the overall objective is the same:

- Help improve the efficiency and productivity of analysis.
- Assist with agile development of new data pipelines.
- Enable collaboration between lines of business, analysts, and IT.

It is important to understand that data preparation tools are not intended to replace existing ETL/ELT processes, are not an enterprise solution, and offer minimal governance. Self-service analytics offers complete democratization of data management tasks in the hands of business users and thus poses a serious risk to data quality and data privacy. So unless data governance policies take these risks into consideration through clearly defined rules, procedures, and access controls, the intended gains from self-service analytics may not be achieved.

## Data Visualization

Data visualization is the technique to assist people in understanding the significance of data by arranging it in the visual context. When text-based data is exposed in any data visualization tool, a viewer can easily recognize any patterns, trends, and correlations in data. The images used in data visualization have interactive and dynamic capabilities that allow users to manipulate them, extract data for querying and deep analysis.

Data visualization is not limited to standard charts and graphs made in Microsoft Excel spreadsheet, the number of ways is available to display data such as dials and gauges, geographic maps, info graphics, heat maps, bar and pie charts, etc. Suppose a data scientist looks for writing advanced predictive analytics or machine learning algorithms, it is necessary for him to visualize the outcomes to direct the results and ensure that algorithms work fine.

In short to craft good data visualization, a well-sourced, complete and clean data is required to visualize, then a right chart is chosen, now design and customize visualization according to simple preferences, there is no requirement to add any elements that distract from the data, and the last visualization is complete and ready to publish in front of viewers.

### Features and Importance of Data Visualization

If you talk about the main objective or need of data visualization, it is to understand the consequence of data available and to communicate this information precisely, coherently and efficiently. Data visualization turns large and small datasets into a pictorial form that visualizes in a simple manner and that is more comfortable for the human brain to interpret and process.

It comprises of some specific features due to which it is used versatile, are described below:

- It is interactive and exposed trends.
- It contributes a viewpoint, narrates a story and describes the process.
- It applies animation and real images.

- It fixes data into meaning and conserves time.
- It grants access to raw data and extracts meaningful, knowledgeable insights.

There are multiple ways to process information inside the human brain, charts and graphs might be a decent tool to visualize large amounts of complex data in a more accessible way, it is far better than to peruse over spreadsheets or reports. In simple words, data visualization is a smart, easy way to communicate concepts in a specific manner and can be experimented with different situations by doing slight manipulations and adjustments.

It helps in identifying areas that lack concentration and development, analysing which factors impact consumer behavior, direct in understanding the right place for a product, estimating sales and volumes, etc. Some examples of Data Visualization tools include FusionCharts, Highcharts, Tableau and Qlikview.

## Five Common Types of Data Visualization

We have data or sort of information in the form of numbers, or statistics, there is always a story lying behind numbers, visualizing that statistics brings creation in them. Presenting and visualizing data accurately establish trust between you and your viewers, let's discuss how to select the most authentic and likable approach to visualize data.

## Bar Graphs

If you want to analyze data over time or the data is assembled in multiple categories such as various industries, variety of food, the progress of a company in the past 5 years, etc. a Bar Graph is the best choice with some characteristics or some kinds of careful suggestions, in order to make bar graph more effectively and easy to read, outline includes orders of the bars should be chronological, fix time frames label at one axis and label other quantities on other axes, data should not be placed from most to least or least to most but must be in chronology.

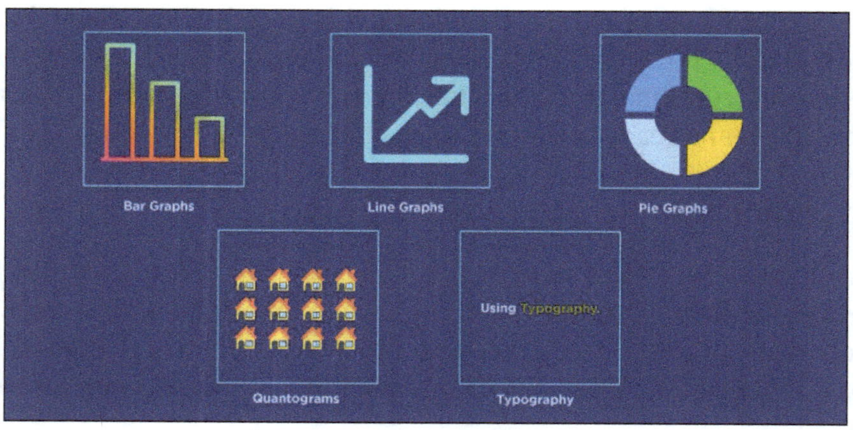


Various types of data visualization tools.

Bar graphs include data in the form of multiple categories; we can either make individual graphs for each and every category or keep it in a single form through including multiple bars as one for each category at each time label. These bars could be assigned side by side or accumulated on top of each other. If the dataset is arranged into multiple categories but isn't confined in time, we could use the bars' order from most to least or least to most. This arrangement helps the viewers to get a conclusion easily.

## Line Chart

Line graphs are also used for presenting data over time or classified data by category as bar graphs. The only difference is that line graphs allow for refinement. If you want to present data over very long time periods or continuously changing data, the line graph could be a solid choice to consider.

Most of the time it happens, we clearly don't know how to fill data accurately in the time duration for which data is available, in that condition we are drawing nothing other than a straight line, though the rate of progress or decay between time duration is not linear up to a remarkable extent, so line graphs must be used very delicately to avoid malformation of data.

## Pie Chart

It is a presentation of data visualization in the circular form or circular chart. It is one of the most popular forms of data visualization, it can only be used when a smart portion of data add up to a whole. For example, 40 % of the marks are considered to pass in an exam, which could be displayed in the pie chart as it is indicating to 40 % out of the total 100 % of the marks.

We can convert the percentage to proportions or proportions to the percentage for this aim, additionally; circle charts cannot be used to show an increase or decrease on their own. In case, if a pie chart could be used to present the data over time, there is a need to make a new chart for each time period and every measurement and display them together for comparison.

## Quantagrams

The repeated pictogram or icon representation to show quantity is termed as Quantagrams, A very common example to show the multi-character quantities using Quantagrams is the number of people. You must have seen Quantagrams as classic male and female icons at the doors of the restroom. This technique is suitable for small numbers, small percentages or proportions.

If we talk about pictograms, they are so simple and feel sound or reductive if they get used for any severe issues or a large quantity. It would appear as minimized if a severe issue is represented with simple sorted icons. We can opt Typography if we need to visualize data for large statistics.

## Typography

It is limited to certain cases where it can be accepted as the best solution provider, it is not restricted to provide an old text-only solution, and instead, it is intelligently used to achieve a successful and effective piece of content. The data would be fit for typography if it is large or greater than 100, never be a percentage of a whole or increase or decrease in percentage, and can't be compared to another number.

In order to improve typography visualization, it can be combined with a pictogram or icon that gives the viewer a clear visual picture with the context of the subject matter of data and numbers.

# Data Profiling

The quality of data is measured by various types of data profiling. "Profiling is a systematic analysis of the content of a data source." In simple terms, data profiling is examining the data available in the source and collecting statistics and information about that data. These profiling and quality statistics have a large effect on your business analytics.

## Importance of Data Profiling

- With more data comes greater emphasis on data quality, for optimal results from any analysis.
- If the quality of your data is poor, it could affect your company's success more than you think. It was reported by the Data Warehouse Institute that it costs $600 billion a year to American businesses to recover from data quality problems. Moreover, it also leads to delay and failure of large and important IT projects and goals.
- High-quality data allows for companies in the retail industry to increase sales and customer retention rates.
- Error-free decision making is the goal of any company in any industry. Proper profiling of data leads to just that.

## Types of Data Profiling in Business Analytics

There are three main types of profiling:

- Structure discovery: Verifying the data is reliable, consistent, and has been arranged correctly based on a specific format – for example, if US phone numbers have all 10-digits.
- Content discovery: The discovery of errors by looking at individual data records – i.e. which phone numbers are missing a digit.
- Relationship discovery: How the parts of data are interconnected. For example, key relationships between tables or references between cells or tables. Understanding relationships is imperative to reusing data. Related data sources should be combined into one or collected in a way that protects crucial relationships.

## Best Practices for Data Profiling

Before you begin you data profiling journey, it is important to know and understand some proven best practices:

- First, identifies natural keys: These are specific and distinct values in each column that can help process updates and inserts. This is useful for tables without headers.
- Second, identify missing or unknown data: This helps ETL architects setup the correct default values.
- Third, select appropriate data types and sizes in your target database: This enables setting

column widths just wide enough for the data, to improve visibility and performance of the profiling.

Following these best practices will ensure your data to be improved to the highest quality, preparing it for further in depth analysis. The higher the quality of your data, the more precise the results produced by any analysis will be. It is extremely worth any analysts time and money to conduct data profiling steps before proceeding to calculate any information.

## Data Filtering

Data filtering is the process of choosing a smaller part of your data set and using that subset for viewing or analysis. Filtering is generally (but not always) temporary – the complete data set is kept, but only part of it is used for the calculation.

Filtering may be used to:

- Look at results for a particular period of time.
- Calculate results for particular groups of interest.
- Exclude erroneous or "bad" observations from an analysis.
- Train and validate statistical models.

Filtering requires you to specify a rule or logic to identify the cases you want to include in your analysis. Filtering can also be referred to as "sub setting" data, or a data "drill-down".

### Example of Filtering

The table below shows some of the rows of a data set from a survey about peoples' preferred Cola. The survey data contains demographic information about the respondents as well as each person's preferred cola and that person's rating (out of 5) for each of six varieties of cola.

| | | | | Brand Ratings | | | | | |
|---|---|---|---|---|---|---|---|---|---|
| ID | Age | Gender | Preferred cola | Coca-Cola | Diet Coke | Coke Zero | Pepsi | Diet Pepsi | Pepsi Max |
| 1 | 25 to 29 | Female | Pepsi Max | 2 | 5 | 2 | 3 | 1 | 4 |
| 2 | 45 to 49 | Male | Pepsi Max | 5 | 1 | 5 | 5 | 3 | 4 |
| 3 | 25 to 29 | Female | Diet Coke | 5 | 4 | 2 | 3 | 1 | 1 |
| 4 | 25 to 29 | Female | Coca-Cola | 4 | 2 | 2 | 2 | 2 | 2 |
| 5 | 55 to 64 | Female | Diet Coke | 3 | 4 | 3 | 3 | 4 | 2 |
| 6 | 55 to 64 | Female | Diet Pepsi | 3 | 3 | 3 | 3 | 4 | 4 |
| 7 | 50 to 54 | Female | Coke Zero | 2 | 3 | 5 | 2 | 2 | 2 |
| 8 | 35 to 39 | Female | Coca-Cola | 4 | 2 | 5 | 3 | 2 | 5 |
| 9 | 65 or more | Male | Diet Pepsi | 5 | 5 | 3 | 5 | 5 | 3 |
| 10 | 45 to 49 | Female | Coke Zero | 4 | 4 | 4 | 5 | 5 | 3 |
| 11 | 45 to 49 | Male | Coca-Cola | 4 | 1 | 1 | 4 | 1 | 1 |
| 12 | 55 to 64 | Male | Coca-Cola | 5 | 2 | 2 | 5 | 2 | 2 |
| 13 | 55 to 64 | Male | Coca-Cola | 5 | 2 | 2 | 3 | 2 | 2 |
| 14 | 30 to 34 | Male | Pepsi Max | 3 | 2 | 5 | 3 | 3 | 5 |
| 15 | 65 or more | Female | Diet Pepsi | 2 | 4 | 2 | 5 | 4 | 2 |

Filtering this data involves:

- Coming up with a rule for the observations needed.
- Selecting the observations that fit the rule.
- Conducting the analysis using only the information contained in those selected observations.

For example, the table below show the data filtered for Males only. The darker colored rows are kept in the analysis while the remaining rows are excluded. Results computed for Males are then calculated based on the highlighted rows (ID's 2, 9, 11, 12, 13, 14). If we want to know the average rating for Coca-Cola among males, we would compute that as (5 + 5 + 4 + 5 + 5 + 3) / 6 = 4.5.

| | | | | Brand Ratings | | | | | |
|---|---|---|---|---|---|---|---|---|---|
| ID | Age | Gender | Preferred cola | Coca-Cola | Diet Coke | Coke Zero | Pepsi | Diet Pepsi | Pepsi Max |
| 1 | 25 to 29 | Female | Pepsi Max | 2 | 5 | 2 | 3 | 1 | 4 |
| 2 | 45 to 49 | Male | Pepsi Max | 5 | 1 | 5 | 5 | 3 | 4 |
| 3 | 25 to 29 | Female | Diet Coke | 5 | 4 | 2 | 3 | 1 | 1 |
| 4 | 25 to 29 | Female | Coca-Cola | 4 | 2 | 2 | 2 | 2 | 2 |
| 5 | 55 to 64 | Female | Diet Coke | 3 | 4 | 3 | 3 | 4 | 2 |
| 6 | 55 to 64 | Female | Diet Pepsi | 3 | 3 | 3 | 3 | 4 | 4 |
| 7 | 50 to 54 | Female | Coke Zero | 2 | 3 | 5 | 2 | 2 | 2 |
| 8 | 35 to 39 | Female | Coca-Cola | 4 | 2 | 5 | 3 | 2 | 5 |
| 9 | 65 or more | Male | Diet Pepsi | 5 | 5 | 3 | 5 | 5 | 3 |
| 10 | 45 to 49 | Female | Coke Zero | 4 | 4 | 4 | 5 | 5 | 3 |
| 11 | 45 to 49 | Male | Coca-Cola | 4 | 1 | 1 | 4 | 1 | 1 |
| 12 | 55 to 64 | Male | Coca-Cola | 5 | 2 | 2 | 5 | 2 | 2 |
| 13 | 55 to 64 | Male | Coca-Cola | 5 | 2 | 2 | 3 | 2 | 2 |
| 14 | 30 to 34 | Male | Pepsi Max | 3 | 2 | 5 | 3 | 3 | 5 |
| 15 | 65 or more | Female | Diet Pepsi | 2 | 4 | 2 | 5 | 4 | 2 |

## Results for Different Groups

A basic need for most research is to obtain results for different groups in the data. One may want to ask about the prevalence of a disease within a demographic segment of the overall population, understand sales figures for the past 3 months, or view feedback given by customers who gave your restaurant 1 star on Yelp. In each case, a logical rule defines whether each case in the sample is excluded or included.

From the example above, we may wish to compute the average rating for each beverage within for the Males in the sample. Such filtering transforms the results like this:

| | Unfiltered | | | Filtered to Males | |
|---|---|---|---|---|---|
| | Average | Sample size | | Average | Sample size |
| Coca-Cola | 3.73 | 15 | Coca-Cola | 4.50 | 6 |
| Diet Coke | 2.93 | 15 | Diet Coke | 2.17 | 6 |
| Coke Zero | 3.07 | 15 | Coke Zero | 3.00 | 6 |
| Pepsi | 3.60 | 15 | Pepsi | 4.17 | 6 |
| Diet Pepsi | 2.73 | 15 | Diet Pepsi | 2.67 | 6 |
| Pepsi Max | 2.80 | 15 | Pepsi Max | 2.83 | 6 |

Sometimes filtering is carried out implicitly. For example, in survey research, the columns of a crosstab correspond to a special case of filtering, where filtered results are computed separately for each column, and the results are displayed side-by-side.

# Data Cleansing

Small businesses can get away with a few Excel spreadsheets for tracking their operations. However, as these companies continue to grow, they can no longer keep up the speed using this simple method. At one point or another, data begins to pour in and a single-page spreadsheet transforms into a database that later grows into a data warehouse.

Without proper investment in data science projects, these companies will never unlock the potential of this data to accelerate their growth and increase their operational efficiency (for example, in building better products or delivering better services).

Organizations that want to win on their markets need to know where to find the data they need and how it all ties together. But before setting out to analyze data, they need to make sure that their data sets are clean. Smart companies are definitely aware of the importance of data cleaning.

Datasets usually contain large volumes of data that may be stored in formats that are not easy to use. That's why data scientists need first to make sure that data is correctly formatted and conforms to the set of rules. Moreover, combining data from different sources can be tricky, and another job of data scientists is making sure that the resulting combination of information makes sense.

Data sparseness and formatting inconsistencies are the biggest challenges – and that's what data cleansing is all about. Data cleaning is a task that identifies incorrect, incomplete, inaccurate, or irrelevant data, fixes the problems, and makes sure that all such issues will be fixed automatically in the future.

## What are the Steps of Data Cleaning?

Here are some of the most common steps and methods of data cleansing experienced development teams swear by:

- Dealing with missing data,
- Standardizing the process,
- Validating data accuracy,
- Removing duplicate data,
- Handling structural errors,
- Getting rid of unwanted observations.

Let's delve into the details of three selected methods:

- Dealing with missing data: Ignoring missing values in a data set is a huge mistake as most algorithms simply don't accept them. Some companies deal with this problem by imputing the missing values based on other observations or dropping the observations with missing values altogether. But these strategies lead to loss of information (note that "no value" also tells us something. If companies miss categorical data, they can label them as "Missing." Missing numeric data should be flagged and filled with 0 to allow the algorithm estimate the optimal constant for such a situation.

- Structural errors: These are mistakes that arise during measurement, transferring data, and other issues that arise of out of poor data management. Inconsistent punctuation, typos, and mislabeled classes are the most common problems here. Such errors illustrate data cleaning importance really well.
- Unwanted observations: Companies dealing with data science often encounter unwanted observations in the data sets. These can be duplicate observations or ones that are irrelevant for the specific problem they're trying to solve. Checking for irrelevant observations is a great strategy for streamline the process of engineering features – the development team will have a much easier time building models.

## Here's why Data Cleaning is so Important

Data quality is of central importance to enterprises that rely on data for maintaining their operations. To give you an example, businesses need to make sure that accurate invoices are emailed to the right customers. To make the most of customer data and to boost the value of the brand businesses need to focus on data quality.

Here are some more benefits data cleansing brings to enterprises:

- Avoid costly errors: Data cleansing is the single best solution for steering clear of the costs that crop up when organizations are busy processing errors, correcting incorrect data, or troubleshooting.
- Boost customer acquisition: Organizations that maintain their databases in shape can develop lists of prospects using accurate and updated data. As a result, they increase the efficiency of their customer acquisition and reduce its cost.
- Make sense of data across different channels: Data cleaning clears the way to managing multichannel customer data seamlessly, allowing organizations to find opportunities for successful marketing campaigns and new ways for reaching their target audiences.
- Improve the decision-making process: Nothing helps to boost a decision-making process like clean data. Accurate and updated data supports analytics and business intelligence that in turn provide organizations with resources for better decision-making and execution.
- Increase employee productivity: Clean and well-maintained databases ensure high productivity of employees who can take advantage of that information in a broad range of areas, starting from customer acquisition to resource planning. Businesses that actively improve their data consistency and accuracy also improve their response rate and boost revenue.

## Does Outsourcing Data Cleaning Make Sense?

A company that is busy growing its volume of operations often struggles to keep its databases in shape. And cleaning data is a necessary step t creating high-quality algorithms, especially in demanding areas such as machine learning. Only properly cleansed data can generate valuable business insights and actions. Outsourcing data set cleaning and management is a smart move. That way, businesses can take advantage of extra resources in a low-cost and low-risk way, without adding new data scientists to their team.

Data cleansing outsourcing is a flexible solution – the resources are available right when companies need them. Moreover, they can also experiment with new ideas without having to invest a lost up front.

## Cleaning your Data is a must

Businesses that take proper care of their databases are rewarded with these and many more benefits. Organizations that keep business critical information at a high-quality gain a significant competitive advantage in their markets because they're able to adjust their operations to the changing circumstances quickly.

## References


- Role-data-business-20405: smallbusiness.chron.com, Retrieved 22, July 2020
- How-big-data-can-help-do-wonders-in-business: simplilearn.com, Retrieved 03, August 2020
- Using-big-data-in-business: bigdataanalyticsnews.com, Retrieved 11, August 2020
- Data-mining-business-analytics: wgu.edu, Retrieved 20, August 2020
- Data-warehouses-live-long-prosper-ba-bi: sisense.com, Retrieved 01, May 2020
- A-five-layered-business-Intelligence-architecture-267990779: researchgate.net, Retrieved 17, July 2020
- Common-types-data-visualization-business-analytics: analyticssteps.com, Retrieved 30, June 2020
- Why-is-clean-data-so-important-for-analytics-and-business-intelligence: sunscrapers.com, Retrieved 27, August 2020
- What-is-data-profiling-why-is-it-important-in-business-analytics: inzata.com, Retrieved 27, June 2020

# 4

# Operational Intelligence

Operational intelligence is an approach to data analysis that enables decisions and actions in business operations to be based on real-time data as it is generated or collected by companies. Business activity monitoring, complex event processing, business process management, metadata, root cause analysis, etc. are some of its concepts. This chapter closely examines the technical components of operational intelligence to provide an extensive understanding of the subject.

## Operational Intelligence

Operational intelligence (OI) is a category of real-time dynamic, business analytics that delivers visibility and insight into data, streaming events and business operations. Operational Intelligence solutions run queries against streaming data feeds and event data to deliver real-time analytic results as operational instructions. Operational Intelligence provides organizations the ability to make decisions and immediately act on these analytic insights, through manual or automated actions.

### Purpose

The purpose of OI is to monitor business activities and identify and detect situations relating to inefficiencies, opportunities, and threats and provide operational solutions. Some definitions define operational intelligence an event-centric approach to delivering information that empowers people to make better decisions.

In addition, these metrics act as the starting point for further analysis (drilling down into details, performing root cause analysis — tying anomalies to specific transactions and of the business activity).

Sophisticated OI systems also provide the ability to associate metadata with metrics, process steps, channels, etc. With this, it becomes easy to get related information, e.g., "retrieve the contact information of the person that manages the application that executed the step in the business transaction that took 60% more time than the norm," or "view the acceptance/rejection trend for the customer who was denied approval in this transaction," or "Launch the application that this process step interacted with."

### Features

Different operational intelligence solutions may use many different technologies and be implemented in different ways. This section lists the common features of an operational intelligence solution.

- Real-time monitoring.
- Real-time situation detection.
- Real-time dashboards for different user roles.
- Correlation of events.
- Industry-specific dashboards.
- Multidimensional analysis.
- Root cause analysis.
- Time Series and trend analysis.
- Big Data Analytics: Operational Intelligence is well suited to address the inherent challenges of Big Data. Operational Intelligence continuously monitors and analyzes the variety of high velocity, high volume Big Data sources. Often performed in memory, OI platforms and solutions then present the incremental calculations and changes, in real-time, to the end-user.

## Technology Components

Operational intelligence solutions share many features, and therefore many also share technology components. This is a list of some of the commonly found technology components, and the features they enable:

- Business activity monitoring (BAM) - Dashboard customization and personalization.
- Complex event processing (CEP) - Advanced, continuous analysis of real-time information and historical data.
- Business process management (BPM) - To perform model-driven execution of policies and processes defined as Business Process Model and Notation (BPMN) models.
- Metadata framework to model and link events to resources.
- Multi-channel publishing and notification.
- Dimensional database.
- Root cause analysis.
- Multi-protocol event collection.

Operational intelligence is a relatively new market segment (compared to the more mature business intelligence and business process management segments). In addition to companies that produce dedicated and focussed products in this area, there are numerous companies in adjacent areas that provide solutions with some OI components.

Operational intelligence places complete information at one's fingertips, enabling one to make smarter decisions in time to maximize impact. By correlating a wide variety of events and data from both streaming feeds and historical data silos, operational intelligence helps organizations gain real-time visibility of information, in context, through advanced dashboards, real-time insight into business performance, health and status so that immediate action based on business policies and processes can be taken. Operational intelligence applies the benefits of real-time analytics, alerts, and actions to a broad spectrum of use cases across and beyond the enterprise.

One specific technology segment is AIDC (Automatic Identification and Data Capture) represented by barcodes, RFID and voice recognition.

## Comparison with Other Technologies or Solutions

### Business Intelligence

OI is often linked to or compared with business intelligence (BI) or real time business intelligence, in the sense that both help make sense out of large amounts of information. But there are some basic differences: OI is primarily activity-centric, whereas BI is primarily data-centric. As with most technologies, each of these could be sub-optimally coerced to perform the other's task. OI is, by definition, real-time, unlike BI or "On-Demand" BI, which are traditionally after-the-fact and report-based approaches to identifying patterns. Real-time BI (i.e., On-Demand BI) relies on the database as the sole source of events.

OI provides continuous, real-time analytics on data at rest and data in-flight, whereas BI typically looks only at historical data at rest. OI and BI can be complementary. OI is best used for short-term planning, such as deciding on the "next best action," while BI is best used for longer-term planning (over the next days to weeks). BI requires a more reactive approach, often reacting to events that have already taken place.

If all that is needed is a glimpse at historical performance over a very specific period of time, existing BI solutions should meet the requirement. However, historical data needs to be analyzed with events that are happening now, or to reduce the time between when intelligence is received and when action is taken, then Operational Intelligence is the more appropriate approach.

### Systems Management

System Management mainly refers to the availability and capability monitoring of IT infrastructure. Availability monitoring refers to monitoring the status of IT infrastructure components such as servers, routers, networks, etc. This usually entails pinging or polling the component and waiting to receive a response. Capability monitoring usually refers to synthetic transactions where user activity is mimicked by a special software program, and the responses received are checked for correctness.

### Complex Event Processing

There is a strong relationship between complex event processing companies and operational intelligence, especially since CEP is regarded by many OI companies as a core component of their OI solutions. CEP companies tend to focus solely on development of a CEP framework for other companies to use within their organisations as a pure CEP engine.

### Business Activity Monitoring

Business activity monitoring (BAM) is software that aids in monitoring of business processes, as those processes are implemented in computer systems. BAM is an enterprise solution primarily intended to provide a real-time summary of business processes to operations managers and upper management. The main difference between BAM and OI appears to be in the implementation details — real-time situation detection appears in BAM and OI and is often implemented using CEP. Furthermore, BAM focuses on high-level process models whereas OI instead relies on correlation to infer a relationship between different events.

### Business Process Management

A business process management suite is the runtime environment where one can perform model-driven execution of policies and processes defined as BPMN models. As part of an operational intelligence suite, a BPM suite can provide the capability to define and manage policies across the enterprise, apply the policies to events, and then take action according to the predefined policies. A BPM suite also provides the capability to define policies as if/then statements and apply them to events.

## Business Activity Monitoring

Business activity monitoring (BAM) is software that aids in monitoring of business activities, as those activities are implemented in computer systems.

The term was originally coined by analysts at Gartner, Inc. and refers to the aggregation, analysis, and presentation of real-time information about activities inside organizations and involving customers and partners. A business activity can either be a business process that is orchestrated by business process management (BPM) software, or a business process that is a series of activities spanning multiple systems and applications. BAM is an enterprise solution primarily intended to provide a real-time summary of business activities to operations managers and upper management.

### Goals and Benefits

The goals of business activity monitoring is to provide real time information about the status and results of various operations, processes, and transactions. The main benefits of BAM are to enable an enterprise to make better informed business decisions, quickly address problem areas, and re-position organizations to take full advantage of emerging opportunities.

### Key Features

One of the most visible features of BAM solutions is the presentation of information on dashboards containing the key performance indicators (KPIs) used to provide assurance and visibility of activity and performance. This information is used by technical and business operations to provide visibility, measurement, and assurance of key business activities. It is also exploited by event correlation to detect and warn of impending problems.

Although BAM systems usually use a computer dashboard display to present data, BAM is distinct from the dashboards used by business intelligence (BI) insofar as events are processed in real-time or near real-time and pushed to the dashboard in BAM systems, whereas BI dashboards refresh at predetermined intervals by polling or querying databases. Depending on the refresh interval selected, BAM and BI dashboards can be similar or vary considerably.

Some BAM solutions additionally provide trouble notification functions, which allows them to interact automatically with the issue tracking system. For example, whole groups of people can be sent e-mails, voice or text messages, according to the nature of the problem. Automated problem solving, where feasible, can correct and restart failed processes.

## Deployment Effort

In nearly all BAM deployments extensive tailoring to specific enterprises is required. Many BAM solutions seek to reduce extensive customization and may offer templates that are written to solve common problems in specific sectors, for example banking, manufacturing, and stockbroking. Due to the high degree of system integration required for initial deployment, many enterprises use experts that specialize in BAM to implement solutions.

BAM is now considered a critical component of Operational Intelligence (OI) solutions to deliver visibility into business operations. Multiple sources of data can be combined from different organizational silos to provide a common operating picture that uses current information. Wherever real-time insight has the greatest value, OI solutions can be applied to deliver the needed information.

## Processing Events

All BAM solutions process events. While most of the first BAM solutions were closely linked to BPM solutions and therefore processed events emitted as the process was being orchestrated, this had the disadvantage of requiring enterprises to invest in BPM before being able to acquire and use BAM. The newer generation of BAM solutions are based on complex event processing (CEP) technology, and can process high volumes of underlying technical events to derive higher level business events, therefore reducing the dependency on BPM, and providing BAM to a wider audience of customers.

## Examples

A bank might be interested in minimizing the amount of money it borrows overnight from a central bank. Interbank transfers must be communicated and arranged through automation by a set time each business day. The failure of any vital communication could cost the bank large sums in interest charged by the central bank. A BAM solution would be programmed to become aware of each message and await confirmation. Failure to receive confirmation within a reasonable amount of time would be grounds for the BAM solution to raise an alarm that would set in motion manual intervention to investigate the cause of the delay and to push the problem toward resolution before it becomes costly.

Another example involves a mobile telecommunications company interested in detecting a situation whereby new customers are not set up promptly and correctly on their network and within the various CRM and billing solutions. Low-level technical events such as messages passing from one application to another over a middleware system, or transactions detected within a database logfile, are processed by a CEP engine. All events relating to an individual customer are correlated in order to detect an anomalous situation whereby an individual customer has not been promptly or correctly provisioned, or set up. An alert can be generated to notify technical operations or to notify business operations, and the failed provisioning step may be restarted automatically.

## Complex Event Processing

Event processing is a method of tracking and analyzing (processing) streams of information (data) about things that happen (events), and deriving a conclusion from them. Complex event processing, or CEP, is event processing that combines data from multiple sources to infer events or patterns that suggest more complicated circumstances. The goal of complex event processing is to identify meaningful events (such as opportunities or threats) and respond to them as quickly as possible.

These events may be happening across the various layers of an organization as sales leads, orders or customer service calls. Or, they may be news items, text messages, social media posts, stock market feeds, traffic reports, weather reports, or other kinds of data. An event may also be defined as a "change of state," when a measurement exceeds a predefined threshold of time, temperature, or other value. Analysts suggest that CEP will give organizations a new way to analyze patterns in real-time and help the business side communicate better with IT and service departments.

The vast amount of information available about events is sometimes referred to as the event cloud.

### Conceptual Description

Among thousands of incoming events, a monitoring system may for instance receive the following three from the same source:

- Church bells ringing.
- The appearance of a man in a tuxedo with a woman in a flowing white gown.
- Rice flying through the air.

From these events the monitoring system may infer a *complex event*: a wedding. CEP as a technique helps discover complex events by analyzing and correlating other events: the bells, the man and woman in wedding attire and the rice flying through the air.

CEP relies on a number of techniques, including:

- Event-pattern detection.
- Event abstraction.
- Event filtering.
- Event aggregation and transformation.

- Modeling event hierarchies.
- Detecting relationships (such as causality, membership or timing) between events.
- Abstracting event-driven processes.

Commercial applications of CEP exist in variety of industries and include algorithmic stock-trading, the detection of credit-card fraud, business activity monitoring, and security monitoring.

## History

The CEP area has roots in discrete event simulation, the active database area and some programming languages. The activity in the industry was preceded by a wave of research projects in the 1990s. According to the first project that paved the way to a generic CEP language and execution model was the Rapide project in Stanford University, directed by David Luckham. In parallel there have been two other research projects: Infospheres in California Institute of Technology, directed by K. Mani Chandy, and Apama in University of Cambridge directed by John Bates. The commercial products were dependents of the concepts developed in these and some later research projects. Community efforts started in a series of event processing symposiums organized by the Event Processing Technical Society, and later by the ACM DEBS conference series. One of the community efforts was to produce the event processing manifesto.

## Related Concepts

CEP is used in Operational Intelligence (OI) solutions to provide insight into business operations by running query analysis against live feeds and event data. OI solutions collect real-time data and correlate against historical data to provide insight into and analysis of the current situation. Multiple sources of data can be combined from different organizational silos to provide a common operating picture that uses current information. Wherever real-time insight has the greatest value, OI solutions can be applied to deliver the information needed.

In network management, systems management, application management and service management, people usually refer instead to event correlation. As CEP engines, event correlation engines (*event correlators*) analyze a mass of events, pinpoint the most significant ones, and trigger actions. However, most of them do not produce new inferred events. Instead, they relate high-level events with low-level events.

Inference engines, e.g. rule-based reasoning engines typically produce inferred information in artificial intelligence. However, they do not usually produce new information in the form of complex (i.e., inferred) events.

## Example

A more systemic example of CEP involves a car, some sensors and various events and reactions. Imagine that a car has several sensors—one that measures tire pressure, one that measures speed, and one that detects if someone sits on a seat or leaves a seat.

In the first situation, the car is moving and the pressure of one of the tires moves from 45 psi to 41 psi over 15 minutes. As the pressure in the tire is decreasing, a series of events containing the tire pressure is generated. In addition, a series of events containing the speed of the car is generated. The car's Event Processor may detect a situation whereby a loss of tire pressure over a relatively long period of time results in the creation of the "lossOfTirePressure" event. This new event may trigger a reaction process to note the pressure loss into the car's maintenance log, and alert the driver via the car's portal that the tire pressure has reduced.

In the second situation, the car is moving and the pressure of one of the tires drops from 45 psi to 20 psi in 5 seconds. A different situation is detected—perhaps because the loss of pressure occurred over a shorter period of time, or perhaps because the difference in values between each event were larger than a predefined limit. The different situation results in a new event "blowOutTire" being generated. This new event triggers a different reaction process to immediately alert the driver and to initiate onboard computer routines to assist the driver in bringing the car to a stop without losing control through skidding.

In addition, events that represent detected situations can also be combined with other events in order to detect more complex situations. For example, in the final situation the car is moving normally and suffers a blown tire which results in the car leaving the road and striking a tree, and the driver is thrown from the car. A series of different situations are rapidly detected. The combination of "blowOutTire", "zeroSpeed" and "driverLeftSeat" within a very short period of time results in a new situation being detected: "occupantThrownAccident". Even though there is no direct measurement that can determine conclusively that the driver was thrown, or that there was an accident, the combination of events allows the situation to be detected and a new event to be created to signify the detected situation. This is the essence of a complex (or composite) event. It is complex because one cannot directly detect the situation; one has to infer or deduce that the situation has occurred from a combination of other events.

## Types

Most CEP solutions and concepts can be classified into two main categories:

- Aggregation-oriented CEP.
- Detection-oriented CEP.

An aggregation-oriented CEP solution is focused on executing on-line algorithms as a response to event data entering the system. A simple example is to continuously calculate an average based on data in the inbound events.

Detection-oriented CEP is focused on detecting combinations of events called events patterns or situations. A simple example of detecting a situation is to look for a specific sequence of events.

There also exist hybrid approaches.

## Integration with Business Process Management

A natural fit for CEP has been with Business Process Management, or BPM. BPM focuses on end-to-end business processes, in order to continuously optimize and align for its operational environment.

However, the optimization of a business does not rely solely upon its individual, end-to-end processes. Seemingly disparate processes can affect each other significantly. Consider this scenario: In the aerospace industry, it is good practice to monitor breakdowns of vehicles to look for trends (determine potential weaknesses in manufacturing processes, material, etc.). Another separate process monitors current operational vehicles' life cycles and decommissions them when appropriate. One use for CEP is to link these separate processes, so that in the case of the initial process (breakdown monitoring) discovering a malfunction based on metal fatigue (a significant event), an action can be created to exploit the second process (life cycle) to issue a recall on vehicles using the same batch of metal discovered as faulty in the initial process.

The integration of CEP and BPM must exist at two levels, both at the business awareness level (users must understand the potential holistic benefits of their individual processes) and also at the technological level (there needs to be a method by which CEP can interact with BPM implementation). For a recent state of the art review on the integration of CEP with BPM, which is frequently labeled as Event-Driven Business Process Management, refer to.

Computation-oriented CEP's role can arguably be seen to overlap with Business Rule technology.

For example, customer service centers are using CEP for click-stream analysis and customer experience management. CEP software can factor real-time information about millions of events (clicks or other interactions) per second into business intelligence and other decision-support applications. These "recommendation applications" help agents provide personalized service based on each customer's experience. The CEP application may collect data about what customers on the phone are currently doing, or how they have recently interacted with the company in other various channels, including in-branch, or on the Web via self-service features, instant messaging and email. The application then analyzes the total customer experience and recommends scripts or next steps that guide the agent on the phone, and hopefully keep the customer happy.

## In Financial Services

The financial services industry was an early adopter of CEP technology, using complex event processing to structure and contextualize available data so that it could inform trading behavior, specifically algorithmic trading, by identifying opportunities or threats that indicate traders (or automatic trading systems) should buy or sell. For example, if a trader wants to track stocks that have five up movements followed by four down movements, CEP technology can track such an event. CEP technology can also track drastic rise and fall in number of trades. Algorithmic trading is already a practice in stock trading. It is estimated that around 60% of Equity trading in the United States is by way of algorithmic trades. CEP is expected to continue to help financial institutions improve their algorithms and be more efficient.

Recent improvements in CEP technologies have made it more affordable, helping smaller firms to create trading algorithms of their own and compete with larger firms. CEP has evolved from an emerging technology to an essential platform of many capital markets. The technology's most consistent growth has been in banking, serving fraud detection, online banking, and multichannel marketing initiatives.

Today, a wide variety of financial applications use CEP, including profit, loss, and risk management systems, order and liquidity analysis, quantitative trading and signal generation systems, and others.

Integration with time series databases.

A time series database is a software system that is optimized for the handling of data organized by time. Time series are finite or infinite sequences of data items, where each item has an associated timestamp and the sequence of timestamps is non-decreasing. Elements of a time series are often called ticks. The timestamps are not required to be ascending (merely non-decreasing) because in practice the time resolution of some systems such as financial data sources can be quite low (milliseconds, microseconds or even nanoseconds), so consecutive events may carry equal timestamps.

Time series data provides a historical context to the analysis typically associated with complex event processing. This can apply to any vertical industry such as finance and cooperatively with other technologies such as BPM.

Consider the scenario in finance where there is a need to understand historic price volatility to determine statistical thresholds of future price movements. This is helpful for both trade models and transaction cost analysis.

The ideal case for CEP analysis is to view historical time series and real-time streaming data as a single time continuum. What happened yesterday, last week or last month is simply an extension of what is occurring today and what may occur in the future. An example may involve comparing current market volumes to historic volumes, prices and volatility for trade execution logic. Or the need to act upon live market prices may involve comparisons to benchmarks that include sector and index movements, whose intra-day and historic trends gauge volatility and smooth outliers.

## Business Process Management

Business process management (BPM) is a field in operations management that focuses on improving corporate performance by managing and optimizing a company's business processes. It can therefore be described as a "process optimization process." It is argued that BPM enables organizations to be more efficient, more effective and more capable of change than a functionally focused, traditional hierarchical management approach. These processes can impact the cost and revenue generation of an organization.

As a policy-making approach, BPM sees processes as important assets of an organization that must be understood, managed, and developed to announce value-added products and services to clients or customers. This approach closely resembles other total quality management or continual improvement process methodologies and BPM proponents also claim that this approach can be supported, or enabled, through technology. As such, many BPM articles and scholars frequently discuss BPM from one of two viewpoints: people and/or technology.

## Definitions

BPMInstitute.org defines Business Process Management as:

> "The definition, improvement and management of a firm's end-to-end enterprise business processes in order to achieve three outcomes crucial to a performance-based, customer-driven firm: 1) clarity on strategic direction, 2) alignment of the firm's resources, and 3) increased discipline in daily operations."

The Workflow Management Coalition, BPM.com and several other sources have come to agreement on the following definition:

> Business Process Management (BPM) is a discipline involving any combination of modeling, automation, execution, control, measurement and optimization of business activity flows, in support of enterprise goals, spanning systems, employees, customers and partners within and beyond the enterprise boundaries.

The Association Of Business Process Management Professionals defines BPM as:

> Business Process Management (BPM) is a disciplined approach to identify, design, execute, document, measure, monitor, and control both automated and non-automated business processes to achieve consistent, targeted results aligned with an organization's strategic goals. BPM involves the deliberate, collaborative and increasingly technology-aided definition, improvement, innovation, and management of end-to-end business processes that drive business results, create value, and enable an organization to meet its business objectives with more agility. BPM enables an enterprise to align its business processes to its business strategy, leading to effective overall company performance through improvements of specific work activities either within a specific department, across the enterprise, or between organizations.

Gartner defines Business process management (BPM) as:

> "The discipline of managing processes (rather than tasks) as the means for improving business performance outcomes and operational agility. Processes span organizational boundaries, linking together people, information flows, systems and other assets to create and deliver value to customers and constituents."

It is common to confuse BPM with a BPM Suite (BPMS). BPM is a professional discipline done by people, whereas a BPMS is a technological suite of tools designed to help the BPM professionals accomplish their goals. BPM should also not be confused with an application or solution developed to support a particular process. Suites and solutions represent ways of automating business processes, but automation is only one aspect of BPM.

## Changes in Business Process Management

The concept of business process may be as traditional as concepts of tasks, department, production, and outputs, arising from job shop scheduling problems in the early 20th Century. The management and improvement approach as of 2010, with formal definitions and technical modeling, has been around since the early 1990s. Note that the term "business process" is sometimes used by IT practitioners as synonymous with the management of middleware processes or with integrating application software tasks.

Although BPM initially focused on the automation of business processes with the use of information technology, it has since been extended to integrate human-driven processes in which human interaction takes place in series or parallel with the use of technology. For example, workflow management systems can assign individual steps requiring deploying human intuition or judgment to relevant humans and other tasks in a workflow to a relevant automated system.

More recent variations such as "human interaction management" are concerned with the interaction between human workers performing a task.

As of 2010 technology has allowed the coupling of BPM with other methodologies, such as Six Sigma. Some BPM tools such as SIPOCs, process flows, RACIs, CTQs and histograms allow users to:

- Visualize - functions and processes.
- Measure - determine the appropriate measure to determine success.
- Analyze - compare the various simulations to determine an optimal improvement.
- Improve - select and implement the improvement.
- Control - deploy this implementation and by use of user-defined dashboards monitor the improvement in real time and feed the performance information back into the simulation model in preparation for the next improvement iteration.
- Re-engineer - revamp the processes from scratch for better results.

This brings with it the benefit of being able to simulate changes to business processes based on real-world data (not just on assumed knowledge). Also, the coupling of BPM to industry methodologies allows users to continually streamline and optimize the process to ensure that it is tuned to its market need.

As of 2012 research on BPM has paid increasing attention to the compliance of business processes. Although a key aspect of business processes is flexibility, as business processes continuously need to adapt to changes in the environment, compliance with business strategy, policies and government regulations should also be ensured. The compliance aspect in BPM is highly important for governmental organizations. As of 2010 BPM approaches in a governmental context largely focus on operational processes and knowledge representation. Although there have been many technical studies on operational business processes in both the public and private sectors, researchers have rarely taken legal compliance activities into account, for instance the legal implementation processes in public-administration bodies.

## BPM Life-cycle

Business process management activities can be arbitrarily grouped into categories such as design, modeling, execution, monitoring, and optimization.

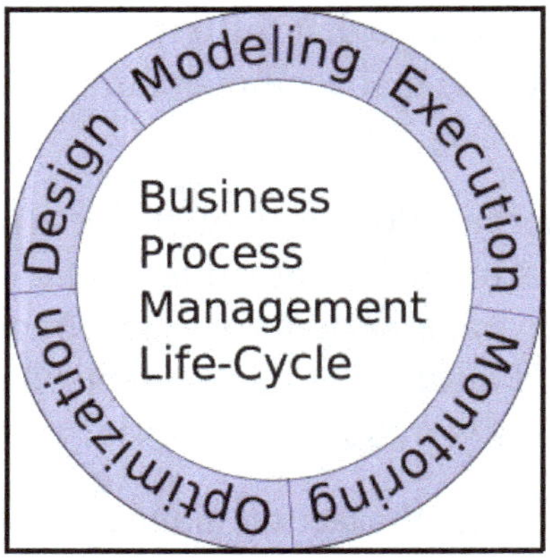


## Design

Process design encompasses both the identification of existing processes and the design of "to-be" processes. Areas of focus include representation of the process flow, the factors within it, alerts and notifications, escalations, standard operating procedures, service level agreements, and task hand-over mechanisms.

Whether or not existing processes are considered, the aim of this step is to ensure that a correct and efficient theoretical design is prepared.

The proposed improvement could be in human-to-human, human-to-system or system-to-system workflows, and might target regulatory, market, or competitive challenges faced by the businesses.

The existing process and the design of new process for various applications will have to synchronise and not cause major outage or process interruption.

## Modeling

Modeling takes the theoretical design and introduces combinations of variables (e.g., changes in rent or materials costs, which determine how the process might operate under different circumstances).

It may also involve running "what-if analysis"(Conditions-when, if, else) on the processes: *"What if I have 75% of resources to do the same task?" "What if I want to do the same job for 80% of the current cost?"*.

## Execution

One of the ways to automate processes is to develop or purchase an application that executes the required steps of the process; however, in practice, these applications rarely execute all the steps of the process accurately or completely. Another approach is to use a combination of software and human intervention; however this approach is more complex, making the documentation process difficult.

As a response to these problems, software has been developed that enables the full business process (as developed in the process design activity) to be defined in a computer language which can be directly executed by the computer. The process models can be run through execution engines that automate the processes directly from the model (*e.g.* calculating a repayment plan for a loan) or, when a step is too complex to automate, Business Process Modeling Notation (BPMN) provides front-end capability for human input. Compared to either of the previous approaches, directly executing a process definition can be more straightforward and therefore easier to improve. However, automating a process definition requires flexible and comprehensive infrastructure, which typically rules out implementing these systems in a legacy IT environment.

Business rules have been used by systems to provide definitions for governing behavior, and a business rule engine can be used to drive process execution and resolution.

## Monitoring

Monitoring encompasses the tracking of individual processes, so that information on their state can be easily seen, and statistics on the performance of one or more processes can be provided. An example of this tracking is being able to determine the state of a customer order (*e.g.* order arrived, awaiting delivery, invoice paid) so that problems in its operation can be identified and corrected.

In addition, this information can be used to work with customers and suppliers to improve their connected processes. Examples are the generation of measures on how quickly a customer order is processed or how many orders were processed in the last month. These measures tend to fit into three categories: cycle time, defect rate and productivity.

The degree of monitoring depends on what information the business wants to evaluate and analyze and how business wants it to be monitored, in real-time, near real-time or ad hoc. Here, business activity monitoring (BAM) extends and expands the monitoring tools generally provided by BPMS.

Process mining is a collection of methods and tools related to process monitoring. The aim of process mining is to analyze event logs extracted through process monitoring and to compare them with an *a priori* process model. Process mining allows process analysts to detect discrepancies between the actual process execution and the *a priori* model as well as to analyze bottlenecks.

## Optimization

Process optimization includes retrieving process performance information from modeling or monitoring phase; identifying the potential or actual bottlenecks and the potential opportunities for cost savings or other improvements; and then, applying those enhancements in the design of the process. Process mining tools are able to discover critical activities and bottlenecks, creating greater business value.

## Re-engineering

When the process becomes too complex or inefficient, and optimization is not fetching the desired output, it is usually recommended by a company steering committee chaired by the president / CEO to re-engineer the entire process cycle. Business process reengineering (BPR) has been used by organizations to attempt to achieve efficiency and productivity at work.

## BPM Suites

A market has developed for Enterprise software leveraging the Business Process Management concepts to organize and automate processes. The recent convergence of these software from distinct pieces such as Business rules engine, Business Process Modelling, Business Activity Monitoring and Human Workflow has given birth to integrated Business Process Management Suites. Forrester Research, Inc recognize the BPM suite space through three different lenses:

- Human-centric BPM.
- Integration-centric BPM (Enterprise Service Bus).
- Document-centric BPM (Dynamic Case Management).

However, standalone integration-centric and document-centric offerings have matured into separate, standalone markets.

## Practice

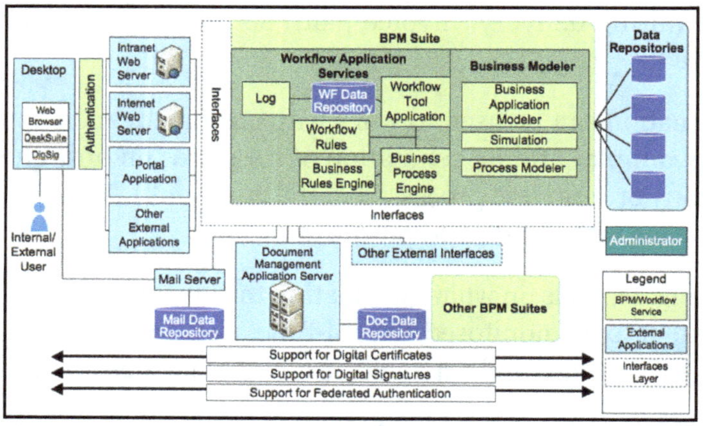


Example of Business Process Management (BPM) Service Pattern: This pattern shows how business process management (BPM) tools can be used to implement business processes through the orchestration of activities between people and systems.

While the steps can be viewed as a cycle, economic or time constraints are likely to limit the process to only a few iterations. This is often the case when an organization uses the approach for short to medium term objectives rather than trying to transform the organizational culture. True iterations are only possible through the collaborative efforts of process participants. In a majority of organizations, complexity will require enabling technology to support the process participants in these daily process management challenges.

To date, many organizations often start a BPM project or program with the objective of optimizing an area that has been identified as an area for improvement.

Currently, the international standards for the task have limited BPM to the application in the IT sector, and ISO/IEC 15944 covers the operational aspects of the business. However, some corporations with the culture of best practices do use standard operating procedures to regulate their operational process. Other standards are currently being worked upon to assist in BPM implementation (BPMN, Enterprise Architecture, Business Motivation Model).

## BPM Technology

BPM is now considered a critical component of operational intelligence (OI) solutions to deliver real-time, actionable information. This real-time information can be acted upon in a variety of ways - alerts can be sent or executive decisions can be made using real-time dashboards. OI solutions use real-time information to take automated action based on pre-defined rules so that security measures and or exception management processes can be initiated.

As such, some people view BPM as "the bridge between Information Technology (IT) and Business.". In fact, an argument can be made that this "holistic approach" bridges organizational and technological silos.

There are four critical components of a BPM Suite:

- Process engine — a robust platform for modeling and executing process-based applications, including business rules.
- Business analytics — enable managers to identify business issues, trends, and opportunities with reports and dashboards and react accordingly.
- Content management — provides a system for storing and securing electronic documents, images, and other files.
- Collaboration tools — remove intra- and interdepartmental communication barriers through discussion forums, dynamic workspaces, and message boards.

BPM also addresses many of the critical IT issues underpinning these business drivers, including:

- Managing end-to-end, customer-facing processes.
- Consolidating data and increasing visibility into and access to associated data and information.
- Increasing the flexibility and functionality of current infrastructure and data.
- Integrating with existing systems and leveraging service oriented architecture (SOA).
- Establishing a common language for business-IT alignment.

Validation of BPMS is another technical issue that vendors and users need to be aware of, if regulatory compliance is mandatory. The validation task could be performed either by an authenticated third party or by the users themselves. Either way, validation documentation will need to be generated. The validation document usually can either be published officially or retained by users.

## Cloud Computing BPM

Cloud computing business process management is the use of (BPM) tools that are delivered as software services (SaaS) over a network. Cloud BPM business logic is deployed on an application server and the business data resides in cloud storage.

### Market

According to Gartner, 20% of all the "shadow business processes" will be supported by BPM cloud platforms. Gartner refers to all the hidden organizational processes that are supported by IT departments as part of legacy business processes such as Excel spreadsheets, routing of emails using rules, phone calls routing, etc. These can, of course also be replaced by other technologies such as workflow software.

### Benefits

The benefits of using cloud BPM services include removing the need and cost of maintaining specialized technical skill sets in-house and reducing distractions from an enterprise's main focus. It offers controlled IT budgeting and enables geographical mobility.

### Internet of Things

The emerging Internet of Things poses a significant challenge to control and manage the flow of information through large numbers of devices. To cope with this, a new direction known as BPM Everywhere shows promise as way of blending traditional process techniques, with additional capabilities to automate the handling of all the independent devices.

## Metadata

In the 2010s, metadata typically refers to digital forms; however, even traditional card catalogues from the 1960s and 1970s are an example of metadata, as the cards contain information about the books in the library (author, title, subject, etc.).

Metadata is "data [information] that provides information about other data". Three distinct types of metadata exist: structural metadata, descriptive metadata, and administrative metadata.

Structural metadata is data about the containers of data. For instance a "book" contains data, and data about the book is metadata about that container of data.

Descriptive metadata uses individual instances of application data or the data content.

In many countries, the metadata relating to emails, telephone calls, web pages, video traffic, IP connections and cell phone locations are routinely stored by government organizations.

## History

Metadata was traditionally used in the card catalogs of libraries until the 1980s, when libraries converted their catalog data to digital databases. In the 2000s, as digital formats are becoming the prevalent way of storing data and information, metadata is also used to describe digital data using metadata standards.

There are different metadata standards for each different discipline (e.g., museum collections, digital audio files, websites, etc.). Describing the contents and context of data or data files increases its usefulness. For example, a web page may include metadata specifying what software language the page is written in (e.g., HTML), what tools were used to create it, what subjects the page is about, and where to find more information about the subject. This metadata can automatically improve the reader's experience and make it easier for users to find the web page online. A CD may include metadata providing information about the musicians, singers and songwriters whose work appears on the disc.

A principal purpose of metadata is to help users find relevant information and discover resources. Metadata also helps to organize electronic resources, provide digital identification, and support the archiving and preservation of resources. Metadata assists users in resource discovery by "allowing resources to be found by relevant criteria, identifying resources, bringing similar resources together, distinguishing dissimilar resources, and giving location information." Metadata of telecommunication activities including Internet traffic is very widely collected by various national governmental organizations. This data is used for the purposes of traffic analysis and can be used for mass surveillance.

## Definition

Metadata means "data about data". Although the "meta" prefix means «after» or «beyond», it is used to mean «about» in epistemology. Metadata is defined as the data providing information about one or more aspects of the data; it is used to summarize basic information about data which can make tracking and working with specific data easier. Some examples include:

- Means of creation of the data.
- Purpose of the data.
- Time and date of creation.
- Creator or author of the data.
- Location on a computer network where the data was created.
- Standards used.
- File size.

For example, a digital image may include metadata that describes how large the picture is, the color depth, the image resolution, when the image was created, the shutter speed, and other data. A text document's metadata may contain information about how long the document is, who the author is, when the document was written, and a short summary of the document. Metadata within web pages can also contain descriptions of page content, as well as key words linked to the content. These links are often called "Metatags", which were used as the primary factor in determining order for a web search until the late 1990s. The reliance of metatags in web searches was decreased in the late 1990s because of "keyword stuffing". Metatags were being largely misused to trick search engines into thinking some websites had more relevance in the search than they really did.

Metadata can be stored and managed in a database, often called a metadata registry or metadata repository. However, without context and a point of reference, it might be impossible to identify metadata just by looking at it. For example: by itself, a database containing several numbers, all 13 digits long could be the results of calculations or a list of numbers to plug into an equation - without any other context, the numbers themselves can be perceived as the data. But if given the context that this database is a log of a book collection, those 13-digit numbers may now be identified as ISBNs - information that refers to the book, but is not itself the information within the book. The term "metadata" was coined in 1968 by Philip Bagley, in his book "Extension of Programming Language Concepts" where it is clear that he uses the term in the ISO 11179 "traditional" sense, which is "structural metadata" i.e. "data about the containers of data"; rather than the alternate sense "content about individual instances of data content" or metacontent, the type of data usually found in library catalogues. Since then the fields of information management, information science, information technology, librarianship, and GIS have widely adopted the term. In these fields the word *metadata* is defined as "data about data". While this is the generally accepted definition, various disciplines have adopted their own more specific explanation and uses of the term.

## Types

While the metadata application is manifold, covering a large variety of fields, there are specialized and well-accepted models to specify types of metadata. Bretherton & Singley (1994) distinguish between two distinct classes: structural/control metadata and guide metadata. *Structural metadata* describes the structure of database objects such as tables, columns, keys and indexes. *Guide metadata* helps humans find specific items and are usually expressed as a set of keywords in a natural language. According to Ralph Kimball metadata can be divided into 2 similar categories: technical metadata and business metadata. *Technical metadata* corresponds to internal metadata, and *business metadata* corresponds to external metadata. Kimball adds a third category, *process metadata*. On the other hand, NISO distinguishes among three types of metadata: descriptive, structural, and administrative.

*Descriptive metadata* is typically used for discovery and identification, as information to search and locate an object, such as title, author, subjects, keywords, publisher. *Structural metadata* describes how the components of an object are organized. An example of structural metadata would be how pages are ordered to form chapters of a book. Finally, *administrative metadata* gives information to help manage the source. Administrative metadata refers to the technical information, including file type, or when and how the file was created. Two sub-types of administrative metadata are rights management metadata and preservation metadata. *Rights management metadata* explains intellectual property rights, while *preservation metadata* contains information to preserve and save a resource.

## Structures

Metadata (metacontent) or, more correctly, the vocabularies used to assemble metadata (metacontent) statements, is typically structured according to a standardized concept using a well-defined metadata scheme, including: metadata standards and metadata models. Tools such as controlled vocabularies, taxonomies, thesauri, data dictionaries, and metadata registries can be used to apply further standardization to the metadata. Structural metadata commonality is also of paramount importance in data model development and in database design.

## Syntax

Metadata (metacontent) syntax refers to the rules created to structure the fields or elements of metadata (metacontent). A single metadata scheme may be expressed in a number of different markup or programming languages, each of which requires a different syntax. For example, Dublin Core may be expressed in plain text, HTML, XML, and RDF.

A common example of (guide) metacontent is the bibliographic classification, the subject, the Dewey Decimal class number. There is always an implied statement in any "classification" of some object. To classify an object as, for example, Dewey class number 514 (Topology) (i.e. books having the number 514 on their spine) the implied statement is: "<book><subject heading><514>. This is a subject-predicate-object triple, or more importantly, a class-attribute-value triple. The first two elements of the triple (class, attribute) are pieces of some structural metadata having a defined semantic. The third element is a value, preferably from some controlled vocabulary, some reference (master) data. The combination of the metadata and master data elements results in a statement which is a metacontent statement i.e. "metacontent = metadata + master data". All of these elements can be thought of as "vocabulary". Both metadata and master data are vocabularies which can be assembled into metacontent statements. There are many sources of these vocabularies, both meta and master data: UML, EDIFACT, XSD, Dewey/UDC/LoC, SKOS, ISO-25964, Pantone, Linnaean Binomial Nomenclature, etc. Using controlled vocabularies for the components of metacontent statements, whether for indexing or finding, is endorsed by ISO 25964: "If both the indexer and the searcher are guided to choose the same term for the same concept, then relevant documents will be retrieved." This is particularly relevant when considering search engines of the internet, such as Google. The process indexes pages then matches text strings using its complex algorithm; there is no intelligence or "inferencing" occurring, just the illusion thereof.

## Hierarchical, Linear and Planar Schemata

Metadata schemata can be hierarchical in nature where relationships exist between metadata elements and elements are nested so that parent-child relationships exist between the elements. An example of a hierarchical metadata schema is the IEEE LOM schema, in which metadata elements may belong to a parent metadata element. Metadata schemata can also be one-dimensional, or linear, where each element is completely discrete from other elements and classified according to one dimension only. An example of a linear metadata schema is the Dublin Core schema, which is one dimensional. Metadata schemata are often two dimensional, or planar, where each element is completely discrete from other elements but classified according to two orthogonal dimensions.

## Hypermapping

In all cases where the metadata schemata exceed the planar depiction, some type of hypermapping is required to enable display and view of metadata according to chosen aspect and to serve special views. Hypermapping frequently applies to layering of geographical and geological information overlays.

## Granularity

The degree to which the data or metadata is structured is referred to as its "granularity". "Granularity" refers to how much detail is provided. Metadata with a high granularity allows for deeper, more detailed, and more structured information and enables greater levels of technical manipulation. A lower level of granularity means that metadata can be created for considerably lower costs but will not provide as detailed information. The major impact of granularity is not only on creation and capture, but moreover on maintenance costs. As soon as the metadata structures become outdated, so too is the access to the referred data. Hence granularity must take into account the effort to create the metadata as well as the effort to maintain it.

## Standards

International standards apply to metadata. Much work is being accomplished in the national and international standards communities, especially ANSI (American National Standards Institute) and ISO (International Organization for Standardization) to reach consensus on standardizing metadata and registries. The core metadata registry standard is ISO/IEC 11179 Metadata Registries (MDR), the framework for the standard is described in ISO/IEC 11179-1:2004. A new edition of Part 1 is in its final stage for publication in 2015 or early 2016. It has been revised to align with the current edition of Part 3, ISO/IEC 11179-3:2013 which extends the MDR to support registration of Concept Systems. This standard specifies a schema for recording both the meaning and technical structure of the data for unambiguous usage by humans and computers. ISO/IEC 11179 standard refers to metadata as information objects about data, or "data about data". In ISO/IEC 11179 Part-3, the information objects are data about Data Elements, Value Domains, and other reusable semantic and representational information objects that describe the meaning and technical details of a data item. This standard also prescribes the details for a metadata registry, and for registering and administering the information objects within a Metadata Registry. ISO/IEC 11179 Part 3 also has provisions for describing compound structures that are derivations of other data elements, for example through calculations, collections of one or more data elements, or other forms of derived data. While this standard describes itself originally as a "data element" registry, its purpose is to support describing and registering metadata content independently of any particular application, lending the descriptions to being discovered and reused by humans or computers in developing new applications, databases, or for analysis of data collected in accordance with the registered metadata content. This standard has become the general basis for other kinds of metadata registries, reusing and extending the registration and administration portion of the standard.

The Dublin Core metadata terms are a set of vocabulary terms which can be used to describe resources for the purposes of discovery. The original set of 15 classic metadata terms, known as the Dublin Core Metadata Element Set are endorsed in the following standards documents:

- IETF RFC 5013.
- ISO Standard 15836-2009.
- NISO Standard Z39.85.

Although not a standard, Microformat (also mentioned in the section metadata on the internet below) is a web-based approach to semantic markup which seeks to re-use existing HTML/XHTML tags to convey metadata. Microformat follows XHTML and HTML standards but is not a standard in itself. One advocate of microformats, Tantek Çelik, characterized a problem with alternative approaches:

> "Here's a new language we want you to learn, and now you need to output these additional files on your server. It's a hassle. (Microformats) lower the barrier to entry."

## Use

### Photographs

Metadata may be written into a digital photo file that will identify who owns it, copyright and contact information, what brand or model of camera created the file, along with exposure information (shutter speed, f-stop, etc.) and descriptive information, such as keywords about the photo, making the file or image searchable on a computer and/or the Internet. Some metadata is created by the camera and some is input by the photographer and/or software after downloading to a computer. Most digital cameras write metadata about model number, shutter speed, etc., and some enable you to edit it; this functionality has been available on most Nikon DSLRs since the Nikon D3, on most new Canon cameras since the Canon EOS 7D, and on most Pentax DSLRs since the Pentax K-3. Metadata can be used to make organizing in post-production easier with the use of key-wording. Filters can be used to analyze a specific set of photographs and create selections on criteria like rating or capture time.

Photographic Metadata Standards are governed by organizations that develop the following standards. They include, but are not limited to:

- IPTC Information Interchange Model IIM (International Press Telecommunications Council).
- IPTC Core Schema for XMP.
- XMP – Extensible Metadata Platform (an ISO standard).
- Exif – Exchangeable image file format, Maintained by CIPA (Camera & Imaging Products Association) and published by JEITA (Japan Electronics and Information Technology Industries Association).

- Dublin Core (Dublin Core Metadata Initiative – DCMI).
- PLUS (Picture Licensing Universal System).
- VRA Core (Visual Resource Association).

## Telecommunications

Information on the times, origins and destinations of phone calls, electronic messages, instant messages and other modes of telecommunication, as opposed to message content, is another form of metadata. Bulk collection of this call detail record metadata by intelligence agencies has proven controversial after disclosures by Edward Snowden Intelligence agencies such as the NSA are keeping online metadata of millions of internet user for up to a year, regardless of whether or not they are persons of interest to the agency.

## Video

Metadata is particularly useful in video, where information about its contents (such as transcripts of conversations and text descriptions of its scenes) is not directly understandable by a computer, but where efficient search of the content is desirable. There are two sources in which video metadata is derived: (1) operational gathered metadata, that is information about the content produced, such as the type of equipment, software, date, and location; (2) human-authored metadata, to improve search engine visibility, discoverability, audience engagement, and providing advertising opportunities to video publishers. In today's society most professional video editing software has access to metadata. Avid's MetaSync and Adobe's Bridge are two prime examples of this.

## Web Pages

Web pages often include metadata in the form of meta tags. Description and keywords in meta tags are commonly used to describe the Web page's content. Meta elements also specify page description, key words, authors of the document, and when the document was last modified. Web page metadata helps search engines and users to find the types of web pages they are looking for.

## Creation

Metadata can be created either by automated information processing or by manual work. Elementary metadata captured by computers can include information about when an object was created, who created it, when it was last updated, file size, and file extension. In this context an *object* refers to any of the following:

- A physical item such as a book, CD, DVD, a paper map, chair, table, flower pot, etc.
- An electronic file such as a digital image, digital photo, electronic document, program file, database table, etc.

Data virtualization has emerged in the 2000s as the new software technology to complete the virtualization "stack" in the enterprise. Metadata is used in data virtualization servers which are enterprise infrastructure components, alongside database and application servers. Metadata in these servers is saved as persistent repository and describe business objects in various enterprise systems and applications. Structural metadata commonality is also important to support data virtualization.

## Statistics and Census Services

Standardization work has had a large impact on efforts to build metadata systems in the statistical community. Several metadata standards are described, and their importance to statistical agencies is discussed. Applications of the standards at the Census Bureau, Environmental Protection Agency, Bureau of Labor Statistics, Statistics Canada, and many others are described. Emphasis is on the impact a metadata registry can have in a statistical agency.

## Library and Information Science

Metadata has been used in various ways as a means of cataloging items in libraries in both digital and analog format. Such data helps classify, aggregate, identify, and locate a particular book, DVD, magazine or any object a library might hold in its collection. Until the 1980s, many library catalogues used 3x5 inch cards in file drawers to display a book's title, author, subject matter, and an abbreviated alpha-numeric string (call number) which indicated the physical location of the book within the library's shelves. The Dewey Decimal System employed by libraries for the classification of library materials by subject is an early example of metadata usage. Beginning in the 1980s and 1990s, many libraries replaced these paper file cards with computer databases. These computer databases make it much easier and faster for users to do keyword searches. Another form of older metadata collection is the use by US Census Bureau of what is known as the "Long Form." The Long Form asks questions that are used to create demographic data to find patterns of distribution. Libraries employ metadata in library catalogues, most commonly as part of an Integrated Library Management System. Metadata is obtained by cataloguing resources such as books, periodicals, DVDs, web pages or digital images. This data is stored in the integrated library management system, ILMS, using the MARC metadata standard. The purpose is to direct patrons to the physical or electronic location of items or areas they seek as well as to provide a description of the item/s in question.

More recent and specialized instances of library metadata include the establishment of digital libraries including e-print repositories and digital image libraries. While often based on library principles, the focus on non-librarian use, especially in providing metadata, means they do not follow traditional or common cataloging approaches. Given the custom nature of included materials, metadata fields are often specially created e.g. taxonomic classification fields, location fields, keywords or copyright statement. Standard file information such as file size and format are usually automatically included. Library operation has for decades been a key topic in efforts toward international standardization. Standards for metadata in digital libraries include Dublin Core, METS, MODS, DDI, DOI, URN, PREMIS schema, EML, and OAI-PMH. Leading libraries in the world give hints on their metadata standards strategies.

## In Museums

Metadata in a museum context is the information that trained cultural documentation specialists, such as archivists, librarians, museum registrars and curators, create to index, structure, describe, identify, or otherwise specify works of art, architecture, cultural objects and their images. Descriptive metadata is most commonly used in museum contexts for object identification and resource recovery purposes.

## Usage

Metadata is developed and applied within collecting institutions and museums in order to:

- Facilitate resource discovery and execute search queries.
- Create digital archives that store information relating to various aspects of museum collections and cultural objects, and serves for archival and managerial purposes.
- Provide public audiences access to cultural objects through publishing digital content online.

## Standards

Many museums and cultural heritage centers recognize that given the diversity of art works and cultural objects, no single model or standard suffices to describe and catalogue cultural works. For example, a sculpted Indigenous artifact could be classified as an artwork, an archaeological artifact, or an Indigenous heritage item. The early stages of standardization in archiving, description and cataloging within the museum community began in the late 1990s with the development of standards such as Categories for the Description of Works of Art (CDWA), Spectrum, the Conceptual Reference Model (CIDOC), Cataloging Cultural Objects (CCO) and the CDWA Lite XML schema. These standards use HTML and XML markup languages for machine processing, publication and implementation. The Anglo-American Cataloguing Rules (AACR), originally developed for characterizing books, have also been applied to cultural objects, works of art and architecture. Standards, such as the CCO, are integrated within a Museum's Collection Management System (CMS), a database through which museums are able to manage their collections, acquisitions, loans and conservation. Scholars and professionals in the field note that the "quickly evolving landscape of standards and technologies" create challenges for cultural documentarians, specifically non-technically trained professionals. Most collecting institutions and museums use a relational database to categorize cultural works and their images. Relational databases and metadata work to document and describe the complex relationships amongst cultural objects and multi-faceted works of art, as well as between objects and places, people and artistic movements. Relational database structures are also beneficial within collecting institutions and museums because they allow for archivists to make a clear distinction between cultural objects and their images; an unclear distinction could lead to confusing and inaccurate searches.

## Cultural Objects and Art Works

An object's materiality, function and purpose, as well as the size (e.g., measurements, such as height, width, weight), storage requirements (e.g., climate-controlled environment) and focus of the museum and collection, influence the descriptive depth of the data attributed to the object by cultural documentarians. The established institutional cataloging practices, goals and expertise of cultural documentarians and database structure also influence the information ascribed to cultural objects, and the ways in which cultural objects are categorized. Additionally, museums often employ standardized commercial collection management software that prescribes and limits the ways in which archivists can describe artworks and cultural objects. As well, collecting institutions and museums use Controlled Vocabularies to describe cultural objects and artworks in their collections. Getty Vocabularies and the Library of Congress Controlled Vocabularies are reputable within the museum community and are recommended by CCO standards. Museums are encouraged to use controlled vocabularies that are contextual and relevant to their collections and enhance the functionality of their digital information systems. Controlled Vocabularies are beneficial within databases because they provide a high level of consistency, improving resource retrieval. Metadata structures, including controlled vocabularies, reflect the ontologies of the systems from which they were created. Often the processes through which cultural objects are described and categorized through metadata in museums do not reflect the perspectives of the maker communities.

## Museums and The Internet

Metadata has been instrumental in the creation of digital information systems and archives within museums, and has made it easier for museums to publish digital content online. This has enabled audiences who might not have had access to cultural objects due to geographic or economic barriers to have access to them. In the 2000s, as more museums have adopted archival standards and created intricate databases, discussions about Linked Data between museum databases have come up in the museum, archival and library science communities. Collection Management Systems (CMS) and Digital Asset Management tools can be local or shared systems. Digital Humanities scholars note many benefits of interoperability between museum databases and collections, while also acknowledging the difficulties achieving such interoperability.

## Law

## United States of America

Problems involving metadata in litigation in the United States are becoming widespread. Courts have looked at various questions involving metadata, including the discoverability of metadata by parties. Although the Federal Rules of Civil Procedure have only specified rules about electronic documents, subsequent case law has elaborated on the requirement of parties to reveal metadata. In October 2009, the Arizona Supreme Court has ruled that metadata records are public record. Document metadata have proven particularly important in legal environments in which litigation has requested metadata, which can include sensitive information detrimental to a certain party in court. Using metadata removal tools to "clean" or redact documents can mitigate the risks of unwittingly sending sensitive data. This process partially protects law firms from potentially damaging leaking of sensitive data through electronic discovery.

## Australia

In Australia the need to strengthen national security has resulted in the introduction of a new metadata storage law. This new law means that both security and policing agencies will be allowed to access up to two years of an individual's metadata, supposedly to make it easier to stop any terrorist attacks and serious crimes from happening. In the 2000s, the law does not allow access to content of people's messages, phone calls or email and web-browsing history, but these provisions could be changed by the government.

## In Healthcare

Australian medical research pioneered the definition of metadata for applications in health care. That approach offers the first recognized attempt to adhere to international standards in medical sciences instead of defining a proprietary standard under the World Health Organization (WHO) umbrella. The medical community yet did not approve the need to follow metadata standards despite research that supported these standards.

## Data Warehousing

Data warehouse (DW) is a repository of an organization's electronically stored data. Data warehouses are designed to manage and store the data. Data warehouses differ from business intelligence (BI) systems, because BI systems are designed to use data to create reports and analyze the information, to provide strategic guidance to management. Metadata is an important tool in how data is stored in data warehouses. The purpose of a data warehouse is to house standardized, structured, consistent, integrated, correct, "cleaned" and timely data, extracted from various operational systems in an organization. The extracted data are integrated in the data warehouse environment to provide an enterprise-wide perspective. Data are structured in a way to serve the reporting and analytic requirements. The design of structural metadata commonality using a data modeling method such as entity relationship model diagramming is important in any data warehouse development effort. They detail metadata on each piece of data in the data warehouse. An essential component of a data warehouse/business intelligence system is the metadata and tools to manage and retrieve the metadata. Ralph Kimball describes metadata as the DNA of the data warehouse as metadata defines the elements of the data warehouse and how they work together.

Kimball et al. refers to three main categories of metadata: Technical metadata, business metadata and process metadata. Technical metadata is primarily definitional, while business metadata and process metadata is primarily descriptive. The categories sometimes overlap.

- Technical metadata defines the objects and processes in a DW/BI system, as seen from a technical point of view. The technical metadata includes the system metadata, which defines the data structures such as tables, fields, data types, indexes and partitions in the relational engine, as well as databases, dimensions, measures, and data mining models. Technical metadata defines the data model and the way it is displayed for the users, with the reports, schedules, distribution lists, and user security rights.
- Business metadata is content from the data warehouse described in more user-friendly terms. The business metadata tells you what data you have, where they come from, what they mean and what their relationship is to other data in the data warehouse. Business metadata may also serve as a documentation for the DW/BI system. Users who browse the data warehouse are primarily viewing the business metadata.
- Process metadata is used to describe the results of various operations in the data warehouse. Within the ETL process, all key data from tasks is logged on execution. This includes start time, end time, CPU seconds used, disk reads, disk writes, and rows processed.

When troubleshooting the ETL or query process, this sort of data becomes valuable. Process metadata is the fact measurement when building and using a DW/BI system. Some organizations make a living out of collecting and selling this sort of data to companies - in that case the process metadata becomes the business metadata for the fact and dimension tables. Collecting process metadata is in the interest of business people who can use the data to identify the users of their products, which products they are using, and what level of service they are receiving.

## On The Internet

The HTML format used to define web pages allows for the inclusion of a variety of types of metadata, from basic descriptive text, dates and keywords to further advanced metadata schemes such as the Dublin Core, e-GMS, and AGLS standards. Pages can also be geotagged with coordinates. Metadata may be included in the page's header or in a separate file. Microformats allow metadata to be added to on-page data in a way that regular web users do not see, but computers, web crawlers and search engines can readily access. Many search engines are cautious about using metadata in their ranking algorithms due to exploitation of metadata and the practice of search engine optimization, SEO, to improve rankings. See Meta element article for further discussion. This cautious attitude may be justified as people, according to Doctorow, are not executing care and diligence when creating their own metadata and that metadata is part of a competitive environment where the metadata is used to promote the metadata creators own purposes. Studies show that search engines respond to web pages with metadata implementations, and Google has an announcement on its site showing the meta tags that its search engine understands. Enterprise search startup Swiftype recognizes metadata as a relevance signal that webmasters can implement for their website-specific search engine, even releasing their own extension, known as Meta Tags 2.

## In Broadcast Industry

In broadcast industry, metadata is linked to audio and video broadcast media to:

- *Identify* the media: clip or playlist names, duration, timecode, etc.
- *Describe* the content: notes regarding the quality of video content, rating, description (for example, during a sport event, keywords like *goal, red card* will be associated to some clips).
- *Classify* media: metadata allows to sort the media or to easily and quickly find a video content (a TV news could urgently need some archive content for a subject). For example, the BBC have a large subject classification system, Lonclass, a customized version of the more general-purpose Universal Decimal Classification.

This metadata can be linked to the video media thanks to the video servers. Most major broadcast sport events like FIFA World Cup or the Olympic Games use this metadata to distribute their video content to TV stations through keywords. It is often the host broadcaster who is in charge of organizing metadata through its *International Broadcast Centre* and its video servers. This metadata is recorded with the images and are entered by metadata operators (*loggers*) who associate in live metadata available in *metadata grids* through software (such as Multicam(LSM) or IPDirector used during the FIFA World Cup or Olympic Games).

## Geospatial

Metadata that describes geographic objects in electronic storage or format (such as datasets, maps, features, or documents with a geospatial component) has a history dating back to at least 1994 (refer MIT Library page on FGDC Metadata). This class of metadata is described more fully on the geospatial metadata article.

## Ecological and Environmental

Ecological and environmental metadata is intended to document the "who, what, when, where, why, and how" of data collection for a particular study. This typically means which organization or institution collected the data, what type of data, which date(s) the data was collected, the rationale for the data collection, and the methodology used for the data collection. Metadata should be generated in a format commonly used by the most relevant science community, such as Darwin Core, Ecological Metadata Language, or Dublin Core. Metadata editing tools exist to facilitate metadata generation (e.g. Metavist, Mercury: Metadata Search System, Morpho). Metadata should describe provenance of the data (where they originated, as well as any transformations the data underwent) and how to give credit for (cite) the data products.

## Digital Music

When first released in 1982, Compact Discs only contained a Table Of Contents (TOC) with the number of tracks on the disc and their length in samples. Fourteen years later in 1996, a revision of the CD Red Book standard added CD-Text to carry additional metadata. But CD-Text was not widely adopted. Shortly thereafter, it became common for personal computers to retrieve metadata from external sources (e.g. CDDB, Gracenote) based on the TOC.

Digital audio formats such as digital audio files superseded music formats such as cassette tapes and CDs in the 2000s. Digital audio files could be labelled with more information than could be contained in just the file name. That descriptive information is called the audio tag or audio metadata in general. Computer programs specializing in adding or modifying this information are called tag editors. Metadata can be used to name, describe, catalogue and indicate ownership or copyright for a digital audio file, and its presence makes it much easier to locate a specific audio file within a group, typically through use of a search engine that accesses the metadata. As different digital audio formats were developed, attempts were made to standardize a specific location within the digital files where this information could be stored.

As a result, almost all digital audio formats, including mp3, broadcast wav and AIFF files, have similar standardized locations that can be populated with metadata. The metadata for compressed and uncompressed digital music is often encoded in the ID3 tag. Common editors such as TagLib support MP3, Ogg Vorbis, FLAC, MPC, Speex, WavPack TrueAudio, WAV, AIFF, MP4, and ASF file formats.

## Cloud Applications

With the availability of Cloud applications, which include those to add metadata to content, metadata is increasingly available over the Internet.

## Administration and Management

### Storage

Metadata can be stored either *internally*, in the same file or structure as the data (this is also called *embedded metadata*), or *externally*, in a separate file or field from the described data. A data repository typically stores the metadata *detached* from the data, but can be designed to support embedded metadata approaches. Each option has advantages and disadvantages:

- Internal storage means metadata always travels as part of the data they describe; thus, metadata is always available with the data, and can be manipulated locally. This method creates redundancy (precluding normalization), and does not allow managing all of a system's metadata in one place. It arguably increases consistency, since the metadata is readily changed whenever the data is changed.
- External storage allows collocating metadata for all the contents, for example in a database, for more efficient searching and management. Redundancy can be avoided by normalizing the metadata's organization. In this approach, metadata can be united with the content when information is transferred, for example in Streaming media; or can be referenced (for example, as a web link) from the transferred content. On the down side, the division of the metadata from the data content, especially in standalone files that refer to their source metadata elsewhere, increases the opportunity for misalignments between the two, as changes to either may not be reflected in the other.

Metadata can be stored in either human-readable or binary form. Storing metadata in a human-readable format such as XML can be useful because users can understand and edit it without specialized tools. On the other hand, these formats are rarely optimized for storage capacity, communication time, and processing speed. A binary metadata format enables efficiency in all these respects, but requires special libraries to convert the binary information into human-readable content.

### Database Management

Each relational database system has its own mechanisms for storing metadata. Examples of relational-database metadata include:

- Tables of all tables in a database, their names, sizes, and number of rows in each table.
- Tables of columns in each database, what tables they are used in, and the type of data stored in each column.

In database terminology, this set of metadata is referred to as the catalog. The SQL standard specifies a uniform means to access the catalog, called the information schema, but not all databases implement it, even if they implement other aspects of the SQL standard. For an example of database-specific metadata access methods, see Oracle metadata. Programmatic access to metadata is possible using APIs such as JDBC, or SchemaCrawler.

## Root Cause Analysis

Root cause analysis (RCA) is a method of problem solving used for identifying the root causes of faults or problems. A factor is considered a root cause if removal thereof from the problem-fault-sequence prevents the final undesirable event from recurring; whereas a causal factor is one that affects an event's outcome, but is not a root cause. Though removing a causal factor can benefit an outcome, it does not prevent its recurrence with certainty.

For example, imagine a fictional segment of students who received poor testing scores. After initial investigation, it was verified that students taking tests in the final period of the school day got lower scores. Further investigation revealed that late in the day, the students lacked ability to focus. Even further investigation revealed that the reason for the lack of focus was hunger. So, the root cause of the poor testing scores was hunger, remedied by moving the testing time to soon after lunch.

As another example, imagine an investigation into a machine that stopped because it overloaded and the fuse blew. Investigation shows that the machine overloaded because it had a bearing that wasn't being sufficiently lubricated. The investigation proceeds further and finds that the automatic lubrication mechanism had a pump which was not pumping sufficiently, hence the lack of lubrication. Investigation of the pump shows that it has a worn shaft. Investigation of why the shaft was worn discovers that there isn't an adequate mechanism to prevent metal scrap getting into the pump. This enabled scrap to get into the pump, and damage it. The root cause of the problem is therefore that metal scrap can contaminate the lubrication system. Fixing this problem ought to prevent the whole sequence of events recurring. Compare this with an investigation that does not find the root cause: replacing the fuse, the bearing, or the lubrication pump will probably allow the machine to go back into operation for a while. But there is a risk that the problem will simply recur, until the root cause is dealt with.

Following the introduction of Kepner–Tregoe analysis—which had limitations in the highly complex arena of rocket design, development and launch—RCA arose in the 1950s as a formal study by the National Aeronautics and Space Administration (NASA) in the United States. New methods of problem analysis developed by NASA included a high level assessment practice called MORT (Management Oversight Risk Tree). MORT differed from RCA by assigning causes to common classes of cause shortcomings that could be summarized into a short list. These included work practice, procedures, management, fatigue, time pressure, along with several others. For example: if an aircraft accident occurred as a result of adverse weather conditions augmented by pressure to leave on time; failure to observe weather precautions could indicate a management or training problem; and lack of appropriate weather concern might indict work practices. Because several measures (methods) may effectively address the root causes of a problem, RCA is an iterative process and a tool of continuous improvement.

RCA is applied to methodically identify and correct the root causes of events, rather than to simply address the symptomatic result. Focusing correction on root causes has the goal of entirely preventing problem recurrence. Conversely, RCFA (Root Cause Failure Analysis) recognizes that complete prevention of recurrence by one corrective action is not always possible.

RCA is typically used as a reactive method of identifying event(s) causes, revealing problems and solving them. Analysis is done *after* an event has occurred. Insights in RCA make it potentially useful as a preemptive method. In that event, RCA can be used to *forecast* or predict probable events even *before* they occur. While one follows the other, RCA is a completely separate process to incident management.

Rather than one sharply defined methodology, RCA comprises many different tools, processes, and philosophies. However, several very-broadly defined approaches or "schools" can be identified by their basic approach or field of origin: safety-based, production-based, assembly-based, process-based, failure-based, and systems-based.

1. Safety-based RCA arose from the fields of accident analysis and occupational safety and health.
2. Production-based RCA has roots in the field of quality control for industrial manufacturing.
3. Process-based RCA, a follow-on to production-based RCA, broadens the scope of RCA to include business processes.
4. Failure-based RCA originates in the practice of failure analysis as employed in engineering and maintenance.
5. Systems-based RCA has emerged as an amalgam of the preceding schools, incorporating elements from other fields such as change management, risk management and systems analysis.

Despite the different approaches among the various schools of root cause analysis, all share some common principles. Several general processes for performing RCA can also be defined.

## General Principles

1. The primary aim of root cause analysis is: to identify the factors that resulted in the nature, the magnitude, the location, and the timing of the harmful outcomes (consequences) of one or more past events; to determine what behaviors, actions, inactions, or conditions need to be changed; to prevent recurrence of similar harmful outcomes; and to identify lessons that may promote the achievement of better consequences. ("Success" is defined as the near-certain prevention of recurrence.)
2. To be effective, root cause analysis must be performed systematically, usually as part of an investigation, with conclusions and root causes that are identified backed up by documented evidence. A team effort is typically required.
3. There may be more than one root cause for an event or a problem, wherefore the difficult part is demonstrating the persistence and sustaining the effort required to determine them.

4. The purpose of identifying all solutions to a problem is to prevent recurrence at lowest cost in the simplest way. If there are alternatives that are equally effective, then the simplest or lowest cost approach is preferred.
5. The root causes identified will depend on the way in which the problem or event is defined. Effective problem statements and event descriptions (as failures, for example) are helpful and usually required to ensure the execution of appropriate analyses.
6. One logical way to trace down root causes is by utilizing hierarchical clustering data-mining solutions (such as graph-theory-based data mining). A root cause is defined in that context as "the conditions that enable one or more causes". Root causes can be deductively sorted out from upper groups of which the groups include a specific cause.
7. To be effective, the analysis should establish a sequence of events or timeline for understanding the relationships between contributory (causal) factors, root cause(s) and the defined problem or event to be prevented.
8. Root cause analysis can help transform a reactive culture (one that reacts to problems) into a forward-looking culture (one that solves problems before they occur or escalate). More importantly, RCA reduces the frequency of problems occurring over time within the environment where the process is used.
9. Root cause analysis as a force for change is a threat to many cultures and environments. Threats to cultures are often met with resistance. Other forms of management support may be required to achieve effectiveness and success with root cause analysis. For example, a "non-punitive" policy toward problem identifiers may be required.

## General Process for Performing and Documenting an RCA-based Corrective Action

RCA (in steps 3, 4 and 5) forms the most critical part of successful corrective action, directing the corrective action at the true root cause of the problem. Knowing the root cause is secondary to the goal of prevention, as it is not possible to determine an absolutely effective corrective action for the defined problem without knowing the root cause.

1. Define the problem or describe the event to prevent in the future. Include the qualitative and quantitative attributes (properties) of the undesirable outcomes. Usually this includes specifying the natures, the magnitudes, the locations, and the timing of events. In some cases, "lowering the risks of reoccurrences" may be a reasonable target. For example, "lowering the risks" of future automobile accidents is certainly a more economically attainable goal than "preventing all" future automobile accidents.
2. Gather data and evidence, classifying it along a timeline of events to the final failure or crisis. For every behavior, condition, action and inaction, specify in the "timeline" what should have been done when it differs from what was done.
3. In data mining Hierarchical Clustering models, use the clustering groups instead of classifying: (a) peak the groups that exhibit the specific cause; (b) find their upper-groups; (c) find group characteristics that are consistent; (d) check with experts and validate.

4. Ask "why" and identify the causes associated with each sequential step towards the defined problem or event. "Why" is taken to mean "What were the factors that directly resulted in the effect?"
5. Classify causes into two categories: causal factors that relate to an event in the sequence; and root causes that interrupted that step of the sequence chain when eliminated.
6. Identify all other harmful factors that have equal or better claim to be called "root causes." If there are multiple root causes, which is often the case, reveal those clearly for later optimum selection.
7. Identify corrective action(s) that will, with certainty, prevent recurrence of each harmful effect and related outcomes or factors. Check that each corrective action would, if pre-implemented before the event, have reduced or prevented specific harmful effects.
8. Identify solutions that, when effective and with consensus agreement of the group: prevent recurrence with reasonable certainty; are within the institution's control; meet its goals and objectives; and do not cause or introduce other new, unforeseen problems.
9. Implement the recommended root cause correction(s).
10. Ensure effectiveness by observing the implemented solutions in operation.
11. Identify other possibly useful methodologies for problem solving and problem avoidance.
12. Identify and address the other instances of each harmful outcome and harmful factor.

## References


- Luckham, David C. (2012). Event Processing for Business: Organizing the Real-Time Enterprise. Hoboken, New Jersey: John Wiley & Sons, Inc.,. p. 3. ISBN 978-0-470-53485-4
- "VRA Core Support Pages". Visual Resource Association Foundation. Visual Resource Association Foundation. Retrieved 06, March 2020
- Hooland, Seth Van; Verborgh, Ruben (2014). Linked Data for Libraries, Archives and Museums: How to Clean, Link and Publish Your Metadata. London: Facet
- Kimball, Ralph (2008). The Data Warehouse Lifecycle Toolkit (Second ed.). New York: Wiley. pp. 10, 115–117, 131–132, 140, 154–155. ISBN 978-0-470-14977-5
- National Information Standards Organization; Rebecca Guenther; Jaqueline Radebaugh (2004). Understanding Metadata (PDF). Bethesda, MD: NISO Press. ISBN 1-880124-62-9. Retrieved 16, May 2020

5

# Role of Analytics in Business Decision Making

Business analytics makes use of data and models to expedite decision making processes or solve various kinds of decision problems. Business performance management, customer analytics, diamond model, funnel analytics, uplift modeling, win-loss analytics, etc. are included in its domain. This chapter covers the subject matter in a comprehensive manner.

## Business Decision Making

Decision making is a vital component of small business success. Decisions based on a foundation of knowledge and sound reasoning can lead the company into long-term prosperity; conversely, decisions made on the basis of flawed logic, emotionalism, or incomplete information can quickly put a small business out of commission (indeed, bad decisions can cripple even big, capital-rich corporations over time). All business people recognize the painful necessity of choice. Furthermore, making these choices must be done in a timely fashion, for as most people recognize, indecision is in essence a choice in and of itself—a choice to take no action. Ultimately, what drives business success is the quality of decisions and their implementation. Good decisions mean good business.

The concept of decision making has a long history; choosing among alternatives has always been a part of life. But sustained research attention to business decision making has developed only in recent years. Contemporary advances in the field include progress in such elements of decision making as the problem context; the processes of problem finding, problem solving, and legitimation; and procedural and technical aids.

## Steps of the Decision Making Process

The following are the seven key steps of the decision making process.

- Identify the decision. The first step in making the right decision is recognizing the problem or opportunity and deciding to address it. Determine why this decision will make a difference to your customers or fellow employees.
- Gather information. Next, it's time to gather information so that you can make a decision based on facts and data. This requires making a value judgment, determining what information is relevant to the decision at hand, along with how you can get it. Ask yourself what you need to know in order to make the right decision, and then actively seek out anyone who needs to be involved.
- Identify alternatives. Once you have a clear understanding of the issue, it's time to identify the various solutions at your disposal. It's likely that you have many different options when it comes to making your decision, so it is important to come up with a range of options. This helps you determine which course of action is the best way to achieve your objective.
- Weigh the evidence. In this step, you'll need to "evaluate for feasibility, acceptability and desirability" to know which alternative is best, according to management experts Phil Higson and Anthony Sturgess. Managers need to be able to weigh pros and cons, then select the option that has the highest chances of success. It may be helpful to seek out a trusted second opinion to gain a new perspective on the issue at hand.
- Choose among alternatives. When it's time to make your decision, be sure that you understand the risks involved with your chosen route. You may also choose a combination of alternatives now that you fully grasp all relevant information and potential risks.
- Take action. Next, you'll need to create a plan for implementation. This involves identifying what resources are required and gaining support from employees and stakeholders. Getting others onboard with your decision is a key component of executing your plan effectively, so be prepared to address any questions or concerns that may arise.
- Review your decision. An often-overlooked but important step in the decision making process is evaluating your decision for effectiveness. Ask yourself what you did well and what can be improved next time.

## The Elements of Decision Making

## The Problem Context

All decisions are about problems, and problems shape context at three levels.

The macrocontext draws attention to global issues (exchange rates, for example), national concerns (the cultural orientations toward decision processes of different countries), and provincial and state laws and cultures within nations. The meso context attends to organizational cultures and structure. The microcontext addresses the immediate decision environment—the organization's employees, board, or office.

Decision processes differ from company to company. But all companies need to take these three context levels into consideration when a decision needs to be made. Fortunately, economical ways to obtain this information are available and keep the cost of preparing for decisions from becoming prohibitive.

## Problem Finding and Agenda Setting

An important difficulty in decision making is failure to act until one is too close to the decision point—when information and options are greatly limited. Organizations usually work in a "reactive" mode. Problems are "found" only after the issue has begun to have a negative impact on the business. Nevertheless, processes of environmental scanning and strategic planning are designed to perform problem reconnaissance to alert business people to problems that will need attention down the line. Proactivity can be a great strength in decision making, but it requires a decision intelligence process that is absent from many organizations.

Moreover, problem identification is of limited use if the business is slow to heed or resolve the issue. Once a problem has been identified, information is needed about the exact nature of the problem and potential actions that can be taken to rectify it. Unfortunately, small business owners and other key decision makers too often rely on information sources that "edit" the data—either intentionally or unintentionally—in misleading fashion. Information from business managers and other employees, vendors, and customers alike has to be regarded with a discerning eye, then.

Another kind of information gathering reflects the array and priority of solution preferences. What is selected as possible or not possible, acceptable or unacceptable, negotiable or non-negotiable depends upon the culture of the firm itself and its environment. A third area of information gathering involves determining the possible scope and impact that the problem and its consequent decision might have. Knowledge about impact may alter the decision preferences. To some extent, knowledge about scope dictates who will need to be involved in the decision process.

## Problem Solving

Problem solving—also sometimes referred to as problem management—can be divided into two parts—process and decision. The process of problem solving is predicated on the existence of a system designed to address issues as they crop up. In many organizations, there does not seem to be any system. In such businesses, owners, executives, and managers are apparently content to operate with an ultimately fatalistic philosophy—what happens, happens. Business experts contend that such an attitude is simply unacceptable, especially for smaller businesses that wish to expand, let alone survive. The second part of the problem management equation is the decision, or choice, itself. Several sets of elements need to be considered in looking at the decision process. One set refers to the rationales used for decisions. Others emphasize the setting, the scope and level of the decision, and the use of procedural and technical aids.

## Rationales

Organizational decision makers have adopted a variety of styles in their decision making processes. For example, some business leaders embrace processes wherein every conceivable response to an issue is examined before settling on a final response, while others adopt more flexible philosophies. The legitimacy of each style varies in accordance with individual business realities in such realms as market competitiveness, business owner personality, acuteness of the problem, etc.

## Settings

Certainly, some entrepreneurs/owners make business decisions without a significant amount of input or feedback from others. Home-based business owners without any employees, for example, are likely to take a far different approach to problem-solving than will business owners who have dozens of employees and/or several distinct internal departments. The latter owners will be much more likely to include findings of meetings, task forces, and other information gathering efforts in their decision making process. Of course, even a business owner who has no partners or employees may find it useful to seek information from outside sources (accountants, fellow businesspeople, attorneys, etc.) before making important business decisions. "Since the owner makes all the key decisions for the small business, he or she is responsible for its success or failure," wrote David Karlson in Avoiding Mistakes in Your Small Business. "Marketing and finance are two of several areas in which small business owners frequently lack sufficient experience, since they previously worked as specialists for other people before they started their own businesses. As a result, they generally do not have the experience needed to make well-informed decisions in the areas with which they are unfamiliar. The demands of running and growing a small business will soon expose any Achilles heel in a president/owner. It is best to find out your weaknesses early, so you can develop expertise or get help in these areas."

## Scope and Level

Finally, attention must be paid to problem scope and organizational level. Problems of large scope need to be dealt with by top levels of the organization. Similarly, problems of smaller scope can be handled by lower levels of the organization. This is a failing of many organizations, large and small. Typically, top level groups spend much too much time deciding low-level, low-impact problems, while issues of high importance and organizational impact linger on without being addressed or resolved.

## Procedural and Technical Aids

In recent years, a number of procedural and technical aids have been developed to help business managers in their decision making processes. Most of these have taken the form of software programs that guide individuals or groups through the various elements of the decision making process in a wide variety of operational areas (budgeting, marketing, inventory control, etc.). Leadership seminars and management training offer guidance in the decision making process as well.

## Outcome

Whatever decision making process is utilized, those involved in making the decision need to make sure that a response has actually been arrived at. All too often, meetings and other efforts to resolve outstanding business issues adjourn under an atmosphere of uncertainty. Participants in decision making meetings are sometimes unsure about various facets of the decision arrived at. Some meeting participants, for example, may leave a meeting still unsure about how the agreed-upon response to a problem is going to be implemented, while others may not even be sure what the agreed-upon response is. Indeed, business researchers indicate that on many occasions, meeting participants depart with fundamentally different understandings of what took place. It is up to the small business owner to make sure that all participants in the decision making process fully understand all aspects of the final decision.

## Implementation

The final step in the decision making process is the implementation of the decision. This is an extremely important element of decision making; after all, the benefits associated with even the most intelligent decision can be severely compromised if implementation is slow or flawed.

## Factors in Poor Decision Making

Several factors in flawed decision making are commonly cited by business experts, including the following: limited organizational capacity; limited information; the costliness of analysis; interdependencies between fact and value; the openness of the system(s) to be analyzed; and the diversity of forms on which business decisions actually arise. Moreover, time constraints, personal distractions, low levels of decision making skill, conflict over business goals, and interpersonal factors can also have a deleterious impact on the decision making capacities of a small (or large) business.

A second category of difficulties is captured in a number of common pitfalls of the decision procedure. One such pitfall is "decision avoidance psychosis," which occurs when organizations put off making decisions that need to be made until the very last minute. A second problem is decision randomness. This process was outlined in the famous paper called "A Garbage Can Model of Organizational Choice" by Cohen, March and Olsen. They argued that organizations have four roles or vectors within them: problem knowers (people who know the difficulties the organization faces): solution providers (people who can provide solutions but do not know the problems); resource controllers (people who do not know problems and do not have solutions but control the allocation of people and money in the organization) and a group of "decision makers looking for work" (or decision opportunities). For effective decision making, all these elements must be in the same room at the same time. In reality, most organizations combine them at random, as if tossing them into a garbage can.

Decision drift is another malady that can strike at a business with potentially crippling results. This term, also sometimes known as the Abilene Paradox in recognition of a famous model of this behavior, refers to group actions that take place under the impression that the action is the will of the majority, when in reality; there never really was a decision to take that action.

Decision coercion, also known as groupthink, is another very well-known decision problem. In this flawed decision making process, decisions are actually coerced by figures in power. This phenomenon can most commonly be seen in instances where a business owner or top executive creates an atmosphere where objections or concerns about a decision favored by the owner/executive are muted because of fears about owner/executive reaction.

## Improving Decision Making

Business consultants and experts agree that small business owners and managers can take several basic steps to improve the decision making process at their establishments.

- Improve the setting: Organizing better meetings (focused agenda, clear questions, current and detailed information, necessary personnel) can be a very helpful step in effective decision making. Avoid the garbage can; get the relevant people in the same room at the same time. Pay attention to planning and seek closure.
- Use Logical Techniques: Decision making is a simple process when approached in a logical and purposeful manner. Small businesses that are able to perceive the problem, gather and present data, intelligently discuss the data, and implement the decision without succumbing to emotionalism are apt to make good ones that will launch the firm on a prosperous course.
- Evaluate decisions and decision making patterns: Evaluation tends to focus the attention, and make individuals and teams more sensitive to what they are actually doing in their decision making tasks. Evaluation is especially helpful in

today's business environment because of the interdependency of individuals and departments in executing tasks and addressing goals.

- Determine appropriate levels of decision making: Business enterprises need to make sure that operational decisions are being made at the right level. Keys to avoiding micromanagement and other decision making pitfalls include: giving problems their proper level of importance and context; addressing problems in an appropriate time frame; and establishing and shifting decision criteria in accordance with business goals.

## Business Performance Management

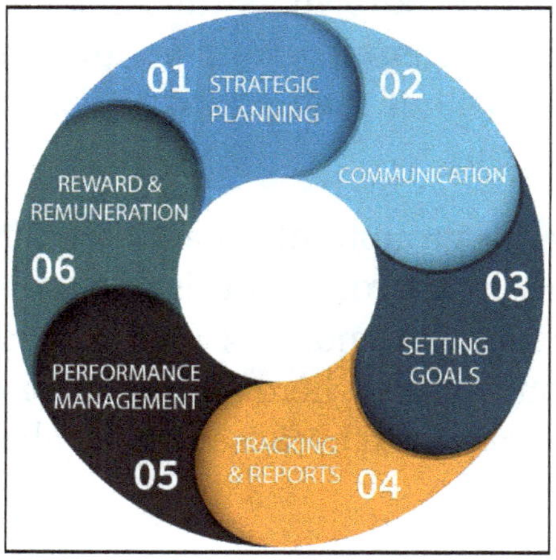


The business world is constantly evaluating its methods to find business processes that are more efficient in terms of cost and the achievement of goals. The practice of creating metrics to measure performance is just one of the ways that business owners and managers attempt to get a better return on investment for their business processes. Business performance management is a way of monitoring the methods a company uses to reach its goals and then using data to find better methods. The idea of monitoring management procedures to develop effective methods for reaching goals has been around since business first began. Even the great warriors of ancient China understood the need to monitor processes and adjust based on the results. Business performance management was developed as a way to streamline this monitoring process and develop a more efficient way of achieving corporate goals.

Business performance management is the act of setting corporate goals, monitoring the methods used to achieve those goals, and then creating ways for managers to more effectively achieve those goals. By collecting and analyzing data, a company can determine what effects managerial changes had on performance and then alter those changes to help create a more effective process. The idea of business performance management is a broad concept, but it is best used to analyze specific goals and help a company to save on operating costs, while generating more revenue at the same time. The important thing to remember about business performance management is that it is used to improve the performance of personnel and management. The use of metrics is just a means to an end, with that end being higher profitability.

## The Three Main Activities

Each business performance management monitoring program utilizes three primary activities: selection of goals, consolidation, and intervention. Each activity works with the other to help create a more efficient process. This is an extremely dynamic system where each activity affects the other and they are all working together to help develop better business processes.

## Selection of Goals

The selection of goals is actually an ongoing process that can be altered by the results that are achieved through intervention. The best place to start with any business performance management program is to set corporate goals and then determine the policies and methods that will be used to achieve those goals. Once the program is underway, the effects that changes have on the process will start to alter the goals. If a managerial decision helped to increase productivity, then it may be necessary to enhance the goal. The point of the goal is to give management a measuring stick to use when it comes to determining success.

## Information Monitoring

The second activity involved in business performance management is information monitoring, also known as information consolidation. This is the part of the process where the data is gathered and the pertinent data is analyzed and used to develop a better way to do business. The list of metrics used to create the data varies by company and by project, but the data becomes a critical part of the performance management process.

## Managerial Adjustments

Once the data has been reviewed, the management staff decides which measures to take to increase efficiency and profitability. These changes are charted and the effects they have go back into the information monitoring activity. It is critical that the adjustments made reflect the goals of the company. This can be tricky because the goals are not always financial. For example, if the goal is to improve employee job satisfaction by 20 percent, then the actions taken by management would not necessarily require a financial consideration.

## The Considerations of Implementation

When a company designs a business performance management program, there are several considerations that have to be made. Not only is company productivity a consideration, but there is also concern for:

- Investors.
- Vendors.
- Partners.
- Competition.

## Most Implemented BPM Framework

Performance measurement frameworks need to be balanced, multidimensional, comprehensive and integrated into the organizational performance measurement framework. Performance measurement frameworks include metrics and a budgeting approach. To implement Business Performance Measurement systems, various frameworks are used. The framework helps the top management to align enterprise objectives with strategy, planning, and execution. Some of the most commonly used frameworks include balanced scorecard, economic value add, quality management, activity-based costing, customer value analysis and action profit linkage model.

Undoubtedly Balanced Scorecard is the most used framework for businesses globally. This framework, strings together the organization's mission and vision with strategic objectives, strategy, and actions. Through strategy mapping, the logical and cause-and-effect between the strategic goals are showcased in a simple graph. For each objective, one KPI (Key Performance Indicator) or measure is identified. The same is also regularly tracked to ensure progress is made towards the aimed outcome. KPIs are an excellent means of organizational efficiency. It helps to bring out the gaps between actual and the targeted performance.

Some of the key features of effective KPIs are:

- Eliminate intangible uncertainties.
- Facilitate a common communication platform.
- Measure performance possible, rather than work done.
- Direct the employee's focus to achieve success.
- Provide performance tracking system to gauge the changes in performance in line with strategy.

The Balanced Scorecard lets managers introduce four new processes that help companies make that important link.

- The first process: translating the vision—assists managers in building a consensus concerning a company's strategy and expresses it in terms that can guide action at the local level.

- The second: communicating and linking—calls for communicating a strategy at all levels of the organization and linking it to a unit and individual goals.
- The third: business planning—enables organizations to integrate business plans with financial plans.
- The fourth: feedback and learning–gives companies the capacity for strategic learning, which consists of gathering feedback, testing the hypotheses on which a strategy is based, and making necessary adjustments.

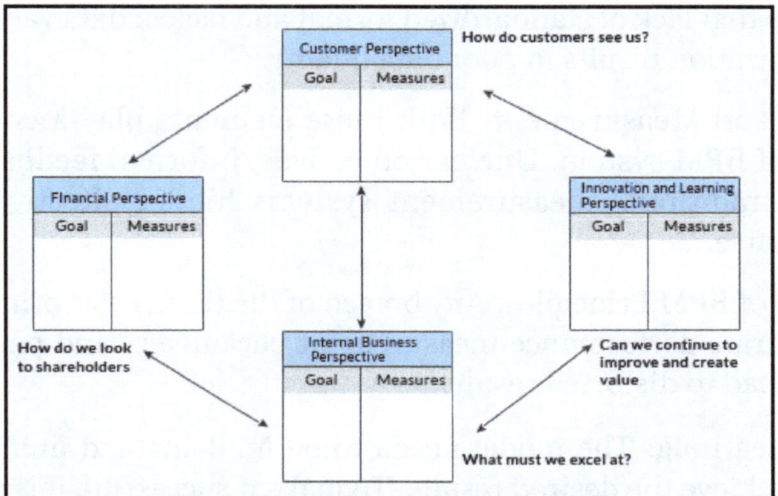


The Balanced Scorecard Links Performance Measures

The Balanced Scorecard links Performance Measures in below dimensions –

- How do customers see us? (customer perspective).
- What must we excel at? (internal perspective).
- Can we continue to improve and create value? (innovation and learning perspective).
- How do we look to shareholders? (financial perspective).

## Impact of BPM on Businesses

Enterprises can maximize their ROI with the help of a well-planned Business Performance Measurement system. Higher levels of efficiency are driven due to the realization of the following factors:

Increased control and visibility:

- Dynamic.
- Cost-effective measurability.
- Precision.

- Relevance.
- Clarity.
- Consistency.

### Limitations of BPM

- Data Quality: BPM systems hugely rely on data. If the data quality is not up to the mark, then it may affect the usefulness of the system. In many cases, it has been seen that lack of standardized format and lack of data validation routine in the organization results in poor data quality.
- Strategy and Measurement: Both these elements play a crucial part in the success of BPM system. Unclear objectives, informal feedback systems, and existing traditional measurement systems hinder effective assessment of performance.
- Violation of BPM Principles: Any breach of the three BPM principles – goal setting, accurate performance measurement parameters and performance tracking may lead to distorted results.

Organizational Learning: The model needs to be implemented uniformly across the organization to achieve the desired results. To make it successful, it is essential that the workforce is trained and conditioned to use the system.

## Customer Analytics

Customer analytics is an activity within of e-commerce whereby customers' online shopping and internet search behavior is examined by software with the results used by teams of marketing professionals looking to increase revenues for online merchants.

Customer analytics uses data collection and subsequent software analysis to zero-in on customers' online order transactions for the purpose of sorting out specific customer demographics, shopping patterns, internet usage and applying predictive analyses to allow marketers to take measures to increase online business profit margins.

Other commonly used terms for customer analytics include Customer Relationship Management analytics, or CRM analytics.

## Why Customer Analytics Matters

Customers have access to information anywhere, anytime including where to shop, what to buy, and how much to pay and so on. This makes it increasingly important to utilize predictive analytics and data to forecast how customers will behave when interacting with brands.

The goal of customer analytics is to create a single, accurate view of a customer to make decisions about how best to acquire and retain customers, identify high-value customers and proactively interact with them. The better the understanding of a customer's buying habits and lifestyle preferences, the more accurate predictive behaviors become and the better the customer journey becomes. Without large amounts of accurate data, any insight derived from analysis could be wildly inaccurate.

## Different Types of Analysis Suit Different Customer Strategies

Organizations that limit their thinking on customer analytics to customer acquisition, growth and retention could be missing out.

We outline six styles of customer analytics to consider for three key objectives.

## Objective: Enable Exceptional Experiences and Advocacy

For organizations seeking to generate social media "buzz", to create "customers for life", and possibly to redefine their industry, there are two styles to consider.

## Style 1: People Make the Difference

Most exceptional customer experiences are driven by exceptional employee behavior. Customer analysis can help by conferring understanding of customers' preferences and behaviors, so that organizations can match them to the right employees in the right circumstances.

## Style 2: Deep Listening

Customers don't always know what they want. Analytics technology provides insight into their wants and needs. Analysis of social media and other customer-created content, as well as monitoring of customers' purchasing and usage data, can yield ideas for new products to develop and new ways to package existing products.

## Objective: Set Expectations and Minimize Problems

Sometimes the objective isn't to delight customers but to stop annoying them. Two further styles can help to reduce or prevent customer dissatisfaction.

### Style 3: Sharing Insights

Organizations fails to use much of the customer data they collect, but they could achieve a variety of benefits from sharing some of it with their customers. Sharing data can establish a company as a trusted element in a customer's decision-making process, and can even lead to opportunities to monetize data. The data may require little analysis, as the emphasis is on openness and sharing, not on providing deep insights.

### Style 4: Ensuring "It Just Works"

An organization's value proposition is often built on a few key attributes, such as product reliability, low cost and service consistency. When these fundamentals go wrong, it can be a long and costly process to regain a customer's trust, especially if his or her needs are met by a competitor in the meantime. Organizations can apply analytics in a variety of ways to determine the key factors for customer satisfaction. In some cases, doing this requires feedback from customers, but in others organizations can use event-monitoring systems to identify issues before they become visible.

## Objective: Do the Usual Things, but Better Every Time

The final two styles should improve the customer relationship the more consistently they are used.

### Style 5: Massive Customization

In an increasingly digital world, it's already surprisingly easy to deliver customized products. It should get even easier as the traditional 4Ps of marketing (price, product, promotion, and place) can be adjusted to suit customers better, which should lead to it becoming commonplace to create and deliver customized products on the basis of analysis.

### Style 6: Changing Behaviors

The most obvious use of analytics is to encourage changes in customers' behavior. One can strive to understand and change behavior at any phase in the customer relationship, and in any context, but most efforts focus on acquisition, cross-selling and retention. In some cases, though, the greatest benefit comes from analysis that is informed by an understanding of customer psychology.

## How to use Customer Analytics

Customer analytics is often managed by an interdisciplinary group made up of business owners from different departments within the company, including marketing, sales, customer service, IT and business analysts.

To be effective and obtain the most meaningful insights, the group must first agree upon which business metrics they need to achieve a single view of the customer experience. Multiple instances of customer relationship management (CRM) applications, disparate enterprise resource planning (ERP) systems and poor customer data integration (CDI) can leave group members with a fragmented view of the customer.

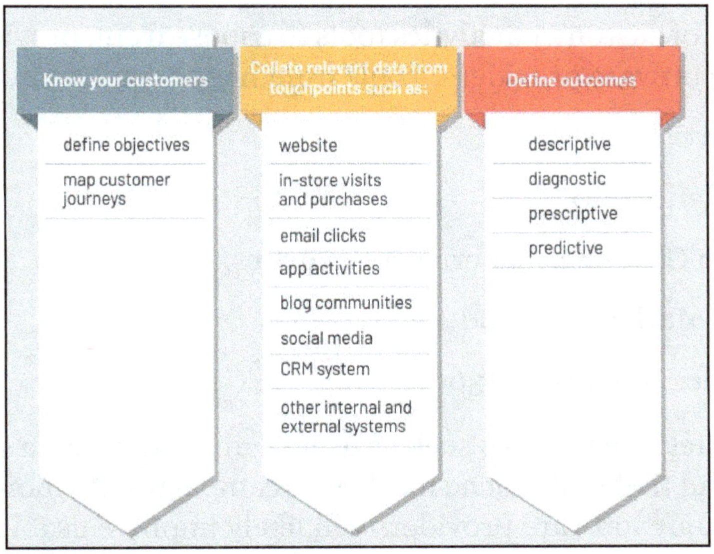


## Customer Analytics Best Practices

By measuring and analyzing data using specific metrics, organizations can create successful customer interactions. Some customer analytics best practices and common metrics that can help drive better business decisions include:

- Targeting customers across all channels and analyzing the various ways a product or service can be distributed.
- Assessing and understanding customers in relation to the brand and whether a customer is satisfied. This can be achieved through a combination of quantitative and qualitative surveys.
- Engaging with customers at the right moment through the right channel.
- Predicting churn rate and taking actions to extend a customer's lifetime value.
- Spotting trends in big data and analyzing online behavior to increase sales.
- Maximizing the customer journey through personalized selling and market segmentation by assessing which customers might buy one type of product versus another.

## Customer Analytics Tools

Customer analytics tools are specialized apps used to gain insight into the customer experience, understand customer behavior and to help tailor marketing campaigns to specific customer segments.

These customer data analysis tools can be part of a CRM suite or sold as stand-alone platforms which do everything from collect customer data from different systems in different locations (data integration) to data analysis and visualization. These tools also connect to popular sales and marketing applications along with web content management systems, email, social platforms and customer loyalty programs.

There are a number of customer analytics tools to choose from, provided by major CRM vendors and niche software providers. Tools from major vendors in this space include:

- Adobe Analytics.
- Google Analytics 360.
- IBM Watson Customer Experience Analytics.
- SAP Hybris Marketing Cloud.
- SAS Customer Intelligence 360.

Some of the tools integrate features such as user segmentation with systems which personalize websites and that build niche marketing campaigns. As more customer analytics tools emerge, major software providers will likely improve usability further so their tools appeal to a wide range of users, and they'll add integration and new services. In addition, advanced features will be built into connected systems, including omnichannel content management platforms.

## Customer Intelligence

The balance of power has shifted from companies to their customers. Your customers now have constant access to a world of information about both your company and your competitors, and they're putting that information to use. Social media and online review sites give them a megaphone to broadcast their feelings about brands—positive and negative. Those voices have an impact. In a 2013 study, 90 percent of people who read online reviews said that their purchasing decisions had been influenced by positive reviews, while 86 percent said they were swayed by negative reviews.

The empowered customer is more demanding and less loyal. "Brands have never been more fragile. "The reason is simple: consumers are supremely well informed and far more likely to investigate the real value of products than to rely on logos." Customers no longer rely on a brand's reputation to gauge the value of a product. According to a 2013 study, 40 percent of retail industry leaders cite millennials' lack of loyalty as their number one concern.

If they're unhappy with a product or an experience, customers will tell you so, and they will expect a response. Companies that neglect to engage with angry customers risk a public relations disaster. Just ask the marketing team at Starbucks, which encountered a backlash to a U.S. campaign that encouraged baristas to have conversations about race with customers who'd rather just pay for a coffee and get on with their day. Or ask Chip Wilson, who stepped down as chairman of athletic wear retailer Lululemon after he prompted public fury by insinuating that overweight customers were to blame for a flaw in a line of yoga pants. As Mark Cuban has said, "Treat your customers like they own you. Because they do."

In the age of the empowered customer, companies must move beyond traditional market research. Their challenge is to harness intelligence about their customers more quickly and comprehensively. By understanding the empowered customer, a company can make effective and intelligent business decisions.

## Customer Intelligence, a Tool to Transform your Brand

Customer intelligence is about producing insight into customers that is both smart and useful. To gather customer intelligence, a company must draw on data from multiple sources and analyze it at the speed of business. This intelligence tells decision-makers not just Who, What, When and Where, but Why. It's the knowledge of why customers behave as they do that allows companies to adapt to meet customer demands. Good customer intelligence not only informs, it guides and advises leaders as they make real-world business decisions. The result is a holistic picture of customers that's more about people than pie charts.

Customer intelligence is also crucially about action. It means using that insight to drive better business decisions and measurable results.

## The Difference between Data, Intelligence and Insight

Data is the raw material of information about customers. It can be biographical information like age and education level, a single response to a survey question or a discrete record of a single purchase. Data is essential but on its own largely useless—it's backward-looking and can't predict how customers will behave. Context gives data meaning. For example, the fact that a customer bought product X twice this month is uninteresting by itself. The fact that a customer bought product X twice this month but only once last month is more interesting. The fact that a 30-year-old customer with a master's degree bought product X once last month and twice this month is more interesting still, and so on.

Intelligence is the holistic and flexible understanding of customers that comes from gathering, contextualizing and analyzing data. Intelligence is data studied and scrutinized at the speed of business— in real time—to produce actionable insight. Customer intelligence means going a step further to place information into context, so we learn that our 30-year-old, grad-school-educated customer has recently moved and has a young family.

"Intelligence is data studied and scrutinized at the speed of business— in real time—to produce actionable insight."

Insight is the deep understanding of customers that comes from gathering, analyzing and synthesizing customer intelligence. Insight goes beyond the Who, What, When and Where to tell us Why customers behave as they do, guiding better business decisions and delivering results. Arriving at insight means learning that our well-educated customer with a young family is shopping with us because Product X is diapers and the young family includes a baby. We learn that the family is also sometimes buying a competitor's diapers because they're a little cheaper and the family is on a tight budget after a move into a new house. Perhaps we decide to build loyalty between this customer and our brand by offering coupons for our diapers to lower their cost and help the family through a financially difficult time.

Marketers who measure the impact of their Customer Intelligence (CI) say that it not only boosts campaign-specific metrics, but also improves customer acquisition, retention, and satisfaction, as well as revenue, profitability, and customer value. Below are his five helpful tips:

## Combine Science and Art

Art comes into play as you discover all the different channels that the voice of your customer can be heard, including open-ended survey questions, and using a flexible feedback tool to capture their valuable comments and insights.

To do this, Qualtrics offers enterprise feedback management solutions to help industry-leaders gather daily survey data, translate customer feedback into action plans, and increases the percentage of satisfied customers.

## Monitor your Customer Experience in Real-time

Schuster suggests finding, "a customer feedback solution that captures transactional data at various touch points in real time." This will indicate where your business processes are working or where they aren't. An important feature your feedback system should be able to do is send alerts when customer responses turn negative, such as an email trigger. This will enable you to identify and take action on problems immediately.

## Close the Loop

While the aforementioned alerts on negative feedback are indispensable, following-up makes an equally substantial difference in improving your customer's experience. Try to set up an action management process where teams or individuals set deadlines to follow up on alerts, identify causes, and track results. The key is to be proactive in resolving potential or current problems.

### Take your Customers' Advice

Businesses should "embrace constructive feedback and engage with your customers by acting on their advice." As a result, "when customers see your business take corrective action, they know they've been heard and are more likely to become stalwart fans."

Make customer satisfaction an integral part of your organization.

A big part of this final step involves being proactive. Don't let customer service slip under the radar as a trivial business objective, and equally fruitless, don't let your feedback disappear into a black hole.

Have a proactive customer service program in play, supported by a customer feedback solution to help your organization use customer intelligence effectively. It will inevitably lead to stronger customer relationships and open up new revenue opportunities.

### The Benefits of Customer Intelligence Done Right

With a well-executed customer intelligence backbone in place, you will be able to shift all of your customer interactions to be data-driven and highly personalized. This, in turn, will generate increased customer satisfaction, loyalty, spend and retention, leading to both short-term and long-term increases in your most important customer KPIs. There is no better way to gain both detailed and holistic views of your customers and how you communicate with them.

Another way of thinking about this is that you will be able to cater to every stage of an infinite number of unique customer journeys. This level of customer understanding will end up delighting each customer and promote very strong brand affinity. There is no better way to build strong relationships and prevent churn than by affirming and acknowledging that you "get" what is important to each and every customer.

An additional aspect of customer intelligence done right is the total visibility it gives you into how your marketing efforts are performing – as a whole, per campaign/offer, per marketing channel, per lifecycle stage, per customer persona, and so forth. There is no substitute for this level of measurement and insight if you succeed at constantly improving and optimizing your customer marketing efforts.

## Diamond Model

The American strategy professor Michael Porter developed an economic diamond model for (small-sized) businesses to help them understand their competitive position in global markets. This Porter Diamond Model, also known as the Porter Diamond theory of National Advantage or Porters double diamond model, has been given this name because all factors that are important in global business competition resemble the points of a diamond. Michael Porter assumes that the competitiveness of businesses is related to the performance of other businesses. Furthermore, other factors are tied together in the value-added chain in a long distance relation or a local or regional context.

## Porter Diamond Model Clusters

Michael Porter uses the concept of clusters of identical product groups in which there is considerable competitive pressure. Businesses within clusters usually stimulate each other to increase productivity, foster innovation and improve business results. Companies operating in such clusters work according to Porter Diamond Model.

In addition, they have the advantage that they can move very well on the international market and that they can maintain their presence and handle international competition. Examples of large clusters are the Swiss watch industry and the Hollywood film industry.

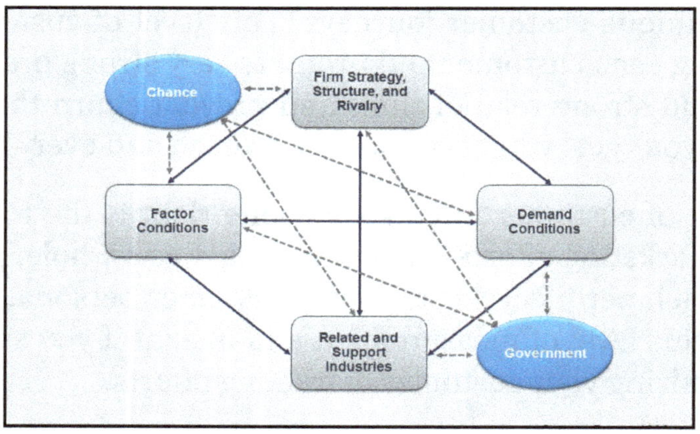


## International Advantage

Organisations can use the Porter's Diamond Model to establish how they can translate national advantages into international advantages. The Porter Diamond Model suggests that the national home base of an organization plays an important role in the creation of advantages on a global scale. This home base provides basic factors that support an organization, including government support but they can also hinder it from building advantages in global competition. The determinants that Michael Porter distinguishes are:

## Factor Conditions

This is the situation in a country relating to production factors like knowledge and infrastructure. These are relevant factors for competitiveness in particular industries. These factors can be grouped into material resources- human resources (labour costs, qualifications and commitment) – knowledge resources and infrastructure. But they also include factors like quality of research or liquidity on stock markets and natural resources like climate, minerals, oil and these could be reasons for creating an international competitive position.

## Related and Supporting Industries

The success of a market also depends on the presence of suppliers and related industries within a region. Competitive suppliers reinforce innovation and internationalization. Besides suppliers, related organizations are of importance too. If an organization is successful this could be beneficial for related or supporting organizations. They can benefit from each other's know-how and encourage each other by producing complementary products.

## Home Demand Conditions

In this determinant the key question is: What reasons are there for a successful market? What is the nature of the market and what is the market size? There always exists an interaction between economies of scale, transportation costs and the size of the home market. If a producer can realize sufficient economies of scale, this will offer advantages to other companies to service the market from a single location. In addition the question can be asked: what impact does this have on the pace and direction of innovation and product development?

## Strategy, Structure and Rivalry

This factor is related to the way in which an organization is organized and managed, its corporate objectives and the measure of rivalry within its own organizational culture. The Furthermore, it focuses on the conditions in a country that determine where a company will be established. Cultural aspects play an important role in this. Regions, provinces and countries may differ greatly from one another and factors like management, working morale and interactions between companies are shaped differently in different cultures. This could provide both advantages and disadvantages for companies in a certain situation when setting up a company in another country. According to Michael Porter domestic rivalry and the continuous search for competitive advantage within a nation can help organizations achieve advantages on an international scale. In addition to the above-mentioned determinants Michael Porter also mentions factors like Government and chance events that influence competition between companies.

## Government

Governments can play a powerful role in encouraging the development of industries and companies both at home and abroad. Governments finance and construct infrastructure (roads, airports) and invest in education and healthcare. Moreover, they can encourage companies to use alternative energy or alternative environmental systems that affect production. This can be effected by granting subsidies or other financial incentives.

## Chance Events

Michael Porter also indicates that in most markets chance plays an important role. This provides opportunities for innovative companies that are not afraid to start up new operations. Entrepreneurs usually start their companies in their homeland, without this having any economic advantages, whereas a similar start abroad would provide more opportunities.

## Porter Diamond Model Example

A few business analysts set-up a case about Mobile telecommunication.

## Demand Conditions

- Evolving mobile possibilities in relation with Internet.
- Growing number of mobile owners. Mobile usage becomes cheaper and cheaper so it accessible for everybody.
- Upcoming online businesses including App builders.
- Government of county x stimulates Mobile Market regulation.

## Factors Endowments

- Government of county x puts continuous efforts in IT policies.
- IT Workforce is developing and growing.
- Level of Education on mobile and Internet technology is high.
- County x has geographical IT advantages.

## Related and Supporting Industry

- This country is leading in the microchip market.
- There are two countries that are trading partners.
- The government is planning to invest in Mobile R&D and IT development.

- County x is leading in all Mobile & IT related production.

Firm strategy and structure.

Venture firms with high IT technology.

Firm and small and medium size IT business companies.

Market competition in Mobile telecommunication.

Target niche market by continuous development and improvement of Mobile technology.

### Advantages

By using the Porter Diamond Model, an organization may identify what factors can build advantages at a national level. The Porter Diamond Model is therefore often used during internationalization efforts. Michael Porter is of the opinion that all factors are decisive for the competitiveness of a company with respect to their foreign competitors. By considering these factors a company will be better able to formulate a strategic goal.

## Funnel Analytics

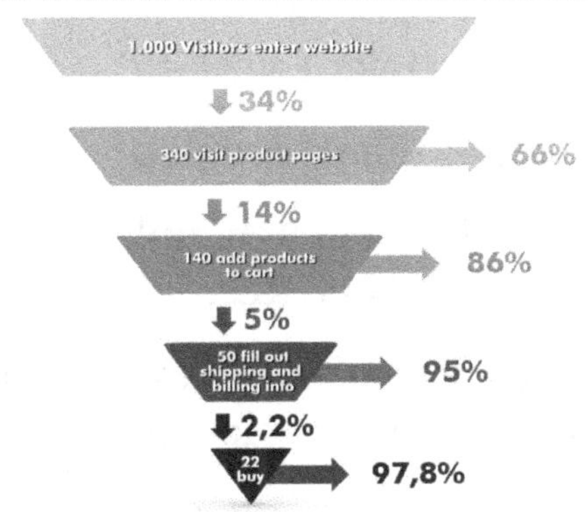


A funnel analysis is a very useful tool for Product Managers to understand the flow of users through their website.

A funnel analysis is a method of understanding the steps required to reach an outcome on a website and how many users get through each of those steps. The set of steps is referred to as a "funnel" because the typical shape visualizing the flow of users is similar to a funnel in your kitchen or garage.

For example, consider a fictional e-commerce company whose ultimate goal (often called a conversion or macro conversion) is to get users who visit the site to make a purchase. The steps required to make a purchase on our site are: visiting the site, adding a product to the shopping cart, clicking to check out and completing the purchase. These steps are sometimes also called goals or micro conversions.

## Funnels Provide Greater Insights than Goals Alone

As essential as goals are in Google Analytics, they serve by themselves more as basic KPIs (key performance indicators) than as actionable starting points for conversion optimization. Most goal pages – such as a purchase receipt or a signup confirmation – are preceded by several other pages designed to drive towards the goal; funnel tracking allows you to begin isolating problems at any point in your visitors' conversion paths so you can take meaningful steps towards optimization.

Let's say that your website, www.nebiketours.com, offers personalized bicycle tours of the New England countryside. You don't actually sell the tours online – the primary call to action for your website visitors is to submit a lead generation form.

## Define the Lead Form Submission as your Goal

You can't create a funnel in Google Analytics without first setting up a goal:

1. Log into Google Analytics, drill down into one of your profiles, and click Admin in the top navigation.
2. Click the Goals tab.
3. Enter a Goal Name, such as Bike Tour Lead.
4. Enter a Goal URL, such as /thank-you.php.
5. Leave the Match Type as Exact Match, unless you need to account for multiple variations of your goal or funnel URLs.
6. It is often useful to enter a Goal Value even for unmonetized lead generation, since it allows Google Analytics to calculate metrics such as Page Value and Per Visit Goal Value.

## Set Up your Funnel

Before you save your goal, you have the option of adding a funnel:

1. Select the Use Funnel checkbox.
2. Enter URLs and names for the funnel steps:

   /catalog.php – Tour Catalog.

   /description.php – Tour Description.

   /inquiry.php – Lead Form.

3. Select the Required Step Checkbox for the First Funnel Step.

Step 3 is often recommended for generating simpler funnel data but is not obligatory. If you do, in fact, want the Funnel Visualization report and the Funnel Conversion Rate to also count entries into the funnel below step 1, keep Required Step unchecked.

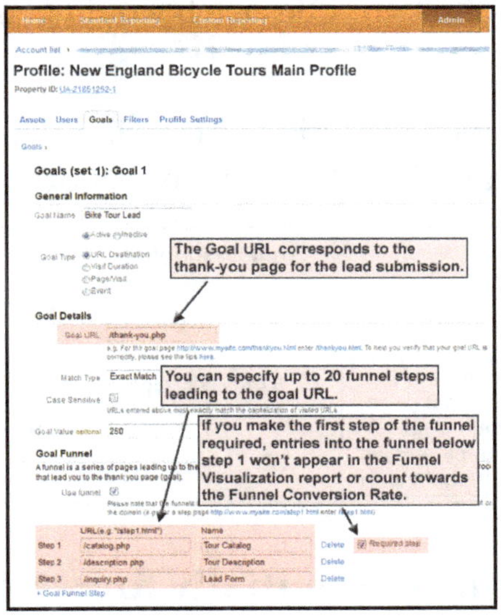


## Funnel Conversion Rate

After you have set up your goal and funnel, and your profile has had some time to collect data, the Funnel Visualization report will display perhaps the single most definitive funnel performance metric in Google Analytics: the Funnel Conversion Rate. If, during funnel setup, you made Step 1 of the funnel required as recommended above, the Funnel Conversion Rate indicates the percentage of visits that included at least one pageview of the first step before at least one pageview of the goal page.

In addition to the overall Funnel Conversion Rate, you can use the report to assess step-to-step drop-off.

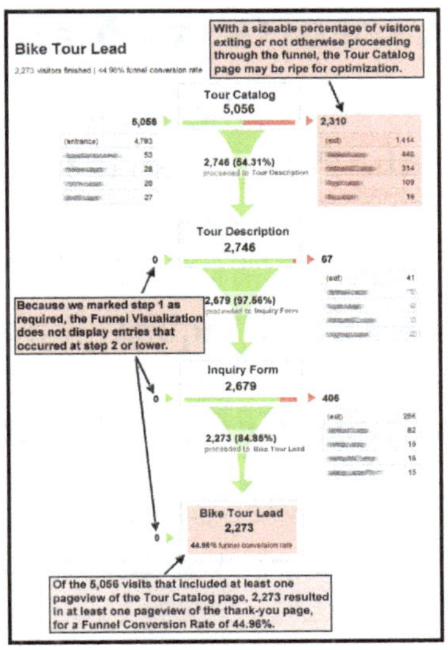

## Multiple Pageviews are Consolidated into Unique Pageviews

The Funnel Visualization report consolidates multiple pageviews that occur for the same page during a single visit into a unique pageview. In our example, a visitor who viewed catalog.php five separate times in a single visit before viewing description.php, inquiry.php, and thank-you.php two times each would generate only a single pageview at each step of the funnel.

This is quite helpful: in conversion analysis, the fact that a visitor has seen the page at least once is generally more significant than the total number of times that the visitor has seen it.

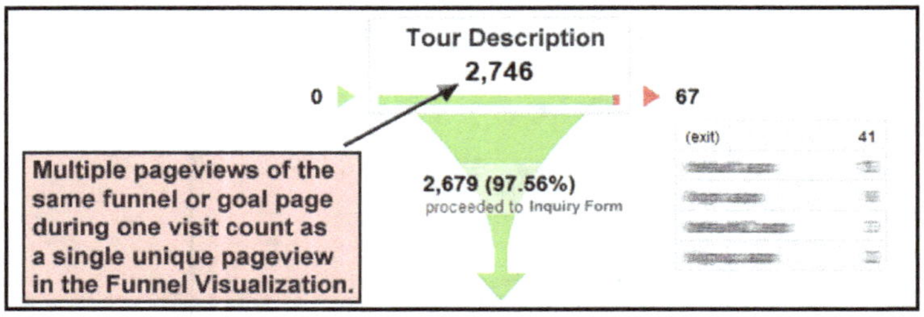


## Pageviews can Occur Nonsequentially for a Funnel Match

Our example funnel and goal pages were defined above as:

catalog.php > description.php > inquiry.php > thank-you.php

The following sequences of pageviews during a visit would match the funnel definition and count towards the Funnel Visualization:

Matching visit: catalog.php > description.php > inquiry.php > thank-you.php

Matching visit: description.php > catalog.php > inquiry.php > thank-you.php

Matching visit: catalog.php > maps.php > description.php > inquiry.php > thank-you.php

## Middle Pageviews don't have to Occur for a Funnel Match

Using the same example funnel as above, the following sequences of pageviews during a visit would also count towards the Funnel Visualization:

Matching visit: catalog.php > inquiry.php > thank-you.php

Matching visit: catalog.php > maps.php > inquiry.php > thank-you.php

## Higher Funnel Steps are Backfilled as Needed

As Brian Clifton explains in Advanced Web Metrics with Google Analytics, steps higher in the funnel are artificially "backfilled" when a lower step has a greater number of pageviews.

You're reading correctly: if there were 2,579 pageviews of description.php and 2,679 pageviews of inquiry.php, the Funnel Visualization will show 2,679 pageviews for description.php as well, even though the page was bypassed and never viewed for 100 of those 2,679 pageviews displayed.

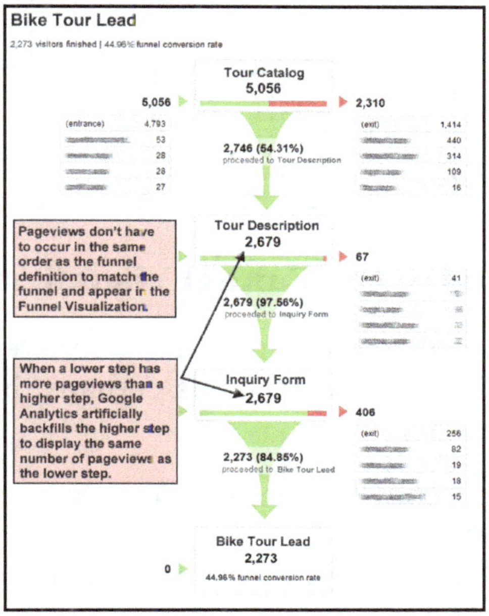


## Abandonment Rate is not Always the Inverse of Conversion Rate

If your Funnel Conversion Rate is 44.96% as above, you might expect the Abandonment Rate to be 55.04% for a total of 100%, but this is not usually the case if your first funnel step is marked as required. While the Funnel Conversion Rate in the Funnel Visualization report respects the first-step requirement, Abandonment Rate does not; hence, the seeming discrepancy.

A visit that included pageviews of description.php and inquiry.php but not catalog.php or thank-you.php:

- Would increase the Abandonment Rate, even though the first page of the funnel wasn't viewed.
- Would not figure into the Funnel Conversion Rate, because the first page of the funnel wasn't viewed.

By the same token, a visit that included pageviews of description.php, inquiry.php and thank-you.php but not catalog.php:

- Would decrease the Abandonment Rate, even though the first page of the funnel wasn't viewed.
- Would not figure into the Funnel Conversion Rate, because the first page of the funnel wasn't viewed.

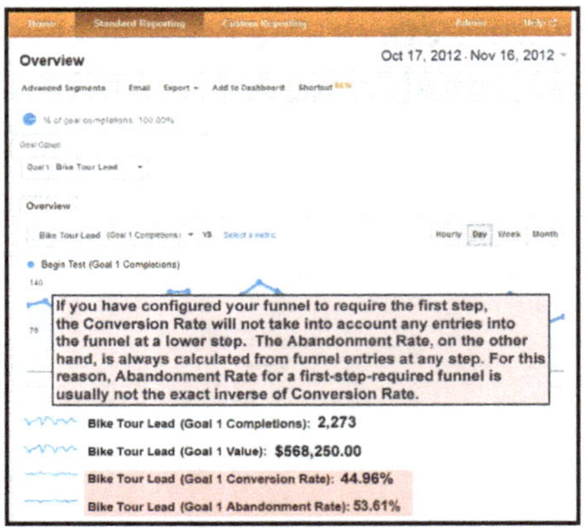


## No Advanced Segments in the Funnel Visualization Report

Because visitor segmentation is so fundamental to effective Web analytics, the biggest drawback of the Funnel Visualization report is perhaps the unavailability of built-in and custom Advanced Segments.

Let's say that you're paying $500USD monthly for a banner ad on www.newengland-vacations.com to generate clickthroughs to www.nebiketours.com. Within your Google Analytics profile, you could define an Advanced Segment based on traffic from www.newenglandvacations.com and then apply that segment to most other reports to view data exclusively for traffic originating from that one website.

Inconveniently, Advanced Segments are not available in the Funnel Visualization report.

## For Advanced Segmentation, Create Filtered Profiles

As an alternative or a supplement to Advanced Segments, you could easily create a separate profile and filter it for traffic originating only from www.newenglandvacations.com. After setting up your goal and funnel in that profile, you'd be able to view the Funnel Visualization report and the Funnel Conversion Rate for that one traffic source.

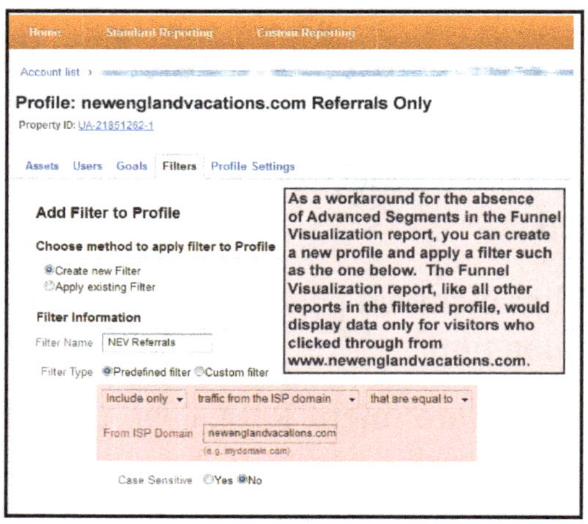


You can set up additional filtered profiles for any traffic segment for which you wish to view the Funnel Visualization report. You can create up to 50 profiles within each Google Analytics account, so there is normally no reason to hesitate in generating as many profiles as you need for visitor segmentation in Funnel Visualizations or for any other reporting purposes.

## Advanced Segments are Available in the Goal Flow Report

Another option for viewing funnel data is the Goal Flow report, which is in some ways similar to the Funnel Visualization. Goal Flow is somewhat more flexible and detailed and does allow Advanced Segments, but it does not calculate a single funnel conversion rate metric and generally requires a bit more interpretation.

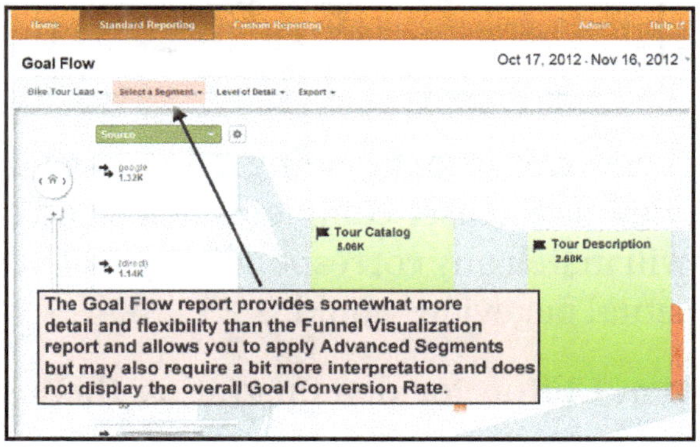


## View the Reverse Goal Path Report for Additional Funnel Ideas

If the Reverse Goal Path report indicates that many visitors are reaching your goal page through a path that you did not anticipate, you can set up a corresponding funnel and begin formally monitoring Funnel Conversion Rate and step-to-step drop-off for that path.

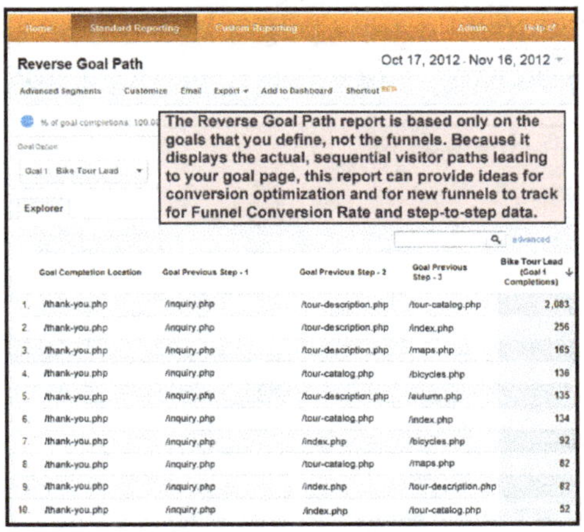


## Use Virtual Pageviews to Create a Funnel for a Single Form

By representing a single form as a funnel, you can isolate drop-off to specific form fields, but how can you track individual fields when each funnel step in Google Analytics corresponds to a separate pageview?

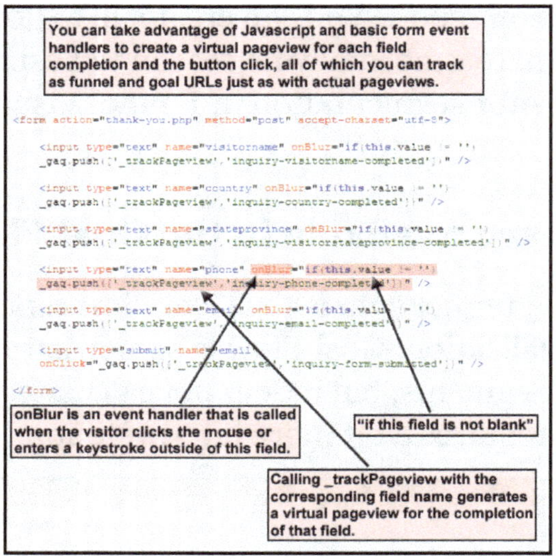


The answer is virtual pageviews. Without loading a new page into the browser, you can generate a "virtual" pageview as the user completes fields and clicks the submit button. These virtual pageviews will match any corresponding goal URL or funnel step that you have defined, just as an actual pageview would.

Thanks once more to Brian Clifton for demonstrating this useful technique to track forms as funnels.

## Use Virtual Pageviews When the Page URL doesn't Change

Many websites now take advantage of Ajax technology, which allows Web browsers to communicate with Web servers in the background and update the page without loading a new URL. This creates a smoother user experience, as it avoids the flicker that usually occurs when the browser requests a new page, but it also poses a greater challenge to Google Analytics pageview tracking since the URL does not change.

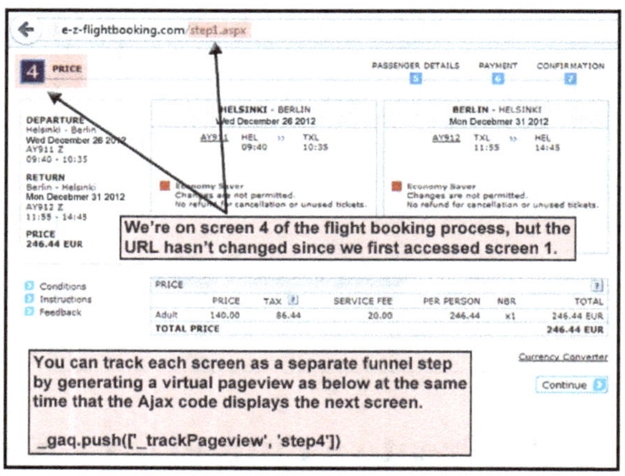


Similar to the approach detailed above for tracking a single form as a funnel, you can take advantage of virtual pageviews to track a multiscreen conversion process in which the page URL doesn't change.

### Goals and Funnels are not Retroactive, So Don't Delay

Keep in mind that Google Analytics does not calculate goal completion retroactively, so make sure to set up your goals and funnels as early as possible in your implementation process. Equipped with your funnel reports and some specialized funnel know-how, you can immediately begin to isolate problems in key website processes, create better end-user experiences, and significantly optimize your website's conversion performance.

## Uplift Modelling

Predictive models typically estimate the likelihood of future events, such as whether it will rain tomorrow or which customers are most likely to "churn" by cancelling their phone contract. In the case of the weather, we do not expect to change it; we just want to know how to adapt. However, the goal for most use cases is to be more proactive; we want to understand what action to take to change the outcome in a favorable way. In these cases prescriptive, not just predictive, analytics is required. The return on investment comes directly from knowing the impact of alternative treatments. By knowing the impact of each treatment, resources can be targeted where they will be most effective and withheld where they will have negligible effect or worse, have a negative effect. This great objective of data science, to intelligently drive day-to-day business decisions based on data, is the purview of uplift modeling.

### Predictive Models vs. Prescriptive Uplift Models

| Use Case | Targeted Outcome | Treatment |
|---|---|---|
| Phone Customer | Not Churn | *Offer upgrade* |
| Patient | Recover | *Treat* |
| Voter | Vote | *Message* |
| Donor | Donate | *Solicit* |
| Prospect | Join | *Invite* |
| Candidate | Accept Offer | *Pay Moving Bonus* |
| Inmate | Not Relapse | *Coach* |
| PSTD Veteran | Not self-harm | *Counsel* |
| Gas Well | Not Shut-in | *Insulate* |
| Retail Customer | Buy | *Offer sale* |

There are many applications of predictive modeling where the outcome is predicted as advice only to a human decision maker, and no action is directly taken automatically from the model result. An example is workload prioritization. For example, in the telecom industry we can predict which customers are most likely to churn (cancel their contracts). In healthcare we can predict which patients are most likely to recover. For universities or charitable organizations, we can predict which prospective benefactors are most likely to donate.

## Uplift Model Examples

Sometimes this is sufficient. For example, if the outcome of our weather prediction is that it is likely to rain, we take an umbrella. Since we can't change the weather we can only be better prepared for it.

But where we can, we aim to influence the outcome one way or another. Will a live agent offering the phone customer a contract upgrade decrease their likelihood to churn? Will soliciting a fund raising prospect with a flyer in the mail improve their chances of making a donation? Will offering a moving bonus increases the likelihood that a desirable candidate will accept our employment offer? The most common example where uplift modeling has taken hold is in retail marketing where the goal is to predict not the likelihood of a customer buying, but what can be done to increase the likelihood of them making a purchase.

## Uplift is Not Directly Measurable

Uplift modeling is also known as incremental modeling, treatment effects modeling, true lift modeling, or net modeling. Uplift is the increase in likelihood of the outcome with the treatment as compared to the outcome without the treatment. We can't observe this difference, or causal effect, directly, but must infer it from an experiment.

The salient knowledge sought is the impact of the treatment, not the estimate of the outcome. For instance, would you rather spend campaign dollars trying to persuade your most loyal supporters (those with the highest probability of "buying"), or on the voters who will be swayed the most by an additional engagement? Simply predicting the expected outcome is not sufficient to optimize your use of money and resources.

It is very helpful to visualize a 2×2 matrix, as shown in figure, with four categories of people (say) to be classified, as: (a) Persuadable, (b) Sure Thing, (c) Do-Not-Disturb, and (d) Lost Cause as shown in figure below.

| **Response if Treated** | N | **Do-Not-Disturb** *c* | **Lost Cause** *d* |
|---|---|---|---|
| | Y | Sure Thing *b* | Persuadable *a* |
| | | Y | N |
| | | **Response if not treated** | |

## Uplift Model Matrix

To promote a desired response we target the "a" population – those who are Persuadable.

For all others, the treatment is wasteful or, for the Do-Not-Disturbs, it is actually counterproductive. Contacting the Do-Not-Disturbs may result in the customers acting in the exact opposite way that was intended – it can be perilous to "wake a sleeping dog".

Uplift modeling's objective is to find persuadable. Of course, uplift modeling can apply to any modeled outcome, human or not, such as the effect of fertilizer on crop yields or sending email messages in political campaigns. Again, where traditional predictive modeling focuses on the outcome, uplift modeling focuses on the effectiveness of the treatment. Then, you can target resources on the cases that are likely to be positively impacted by the treatment.

## Estimating Uplift

Consider a telecom example of trying to prevent customer churn as shown in figure. The treatment is to offer an upgrade to a customer who is a potential churner. To perform uplift analysis, we conduct an experiment with 400 randomly selected test accounts to whom we offer a free upgrade, and a control group of 1600 accounts that receive no offer. (It is common to have a larger control group as it is less expensive).

| *2,000 Potential Churners* | |
|---|---|
| Offer free upgrade | No offer |
| 400 random test accounts | 1,600 control accounts |
| 8 churns | 160 churns |
| 392 non-churns | 1,440 non-churns |
| $R_T$: 2% churn | $R_C$: 10% churn |
| U: Offer had -8% uplift | |
| Churn Odds Ratio: 5.4 | |
| Odds Ratio 99% CL: 2.12 to 14.00 | |
| Uplift 99% CL \| $R_C$=10%: -5.0% to -9.2% | |

## Telecom Uplift Model Example

In this experiment, we record 8 churns in the group that received an offer, and 160 churns in the group that did not receive an offer. This means that there is a 2% churn in the experimental group (RT) and a 10% churn in the control group (RC). The offer has a -8% uplift (U):

$$\text{Overall Uplift } U = RT - RC = 2\% - 10\% = -8\%$$

The uplift in this case is negative because we are trying to avoid the target behavior rather than promote it.

For Uplift to be actionable in practice, we also need to know the treatment effect for each individual person uniquely, in addition to the general population. For example, someone's previous volume of online shopping may indicate that they are more persuadable to click on a particular advertisement than others in their same demographic group. Thus, we want to model how the attributes of a case impact the treatment uplift of that case. The way such a model is created in practice is as follows:

- Predict the outcome with the treatment applied (RTi in the telecom example).
- Predict the outcome without the treatment applied (RCi in the telecom example).
- Calculate the difference in the rates as the uplift (Ui=RTi-RCi).
- Compute the upper and lower 95% confidence limits on Ui.

Once these values are calculated, individuals can be allocated to the four quadrants of the treatment effect matrix using these rules:

- If the confidence limits of the Incremental Uplift (Ui) includes zero, the treatment effect can be thought of as unknown and not significant. Regardless of treatment, the Sure Things have high outcome likelihood and the Lost Causes have a low outcome likelihood.
- If the Incremental Uplift (Ui) is significantly greater than zero, the predicted outcome increases because of the treatment. These are the Persuadables if the outcome is positive.
- When the Incremental Uplift (Ui) is significantly less than zero, the predicted outcome is less likely because of the treatment. Traditionally, these are called the Do-Not-Disturbs.

Remember, of course, that this is a modeled estimate of a, b, c, and d, and not every persuadable individual will actually be persuaded by the treatment.

## Achieving a Return on Marketing Investment

In business it is always important to understand the return on investment for taking a course of action (applying a treatment). Uplift modeling enables you to estimate the expected return on treatment by summing the Incremental Uplift of those persuadable by treatment, which is the overall estimated treatment effect. Consider this retail targeting example where a purchase propensity model output was used to generate a campaign direct mailing list. As shown in figure the traditional predictive model was very accurate.

| Model Score Decile | Response Rate | Lift |
|---|---|---|
| 1 | 28.1% | 3.4 |
| 2 | 17.3% | 2.1 |
| 3 | 9.6% | 1.2 |
| 4 | 8.4% | 1 |
| 5 | 4.8% | 0.6 |
| 6 | 3.9% | 0.5 |
| 7 | 3.3% | 0.4 |
| 8 | 3.4% | 0.4 |
| 9 | 3.5% | 0.4 |
| 10 | 0.1% | 0 |
| Total | **8.2%** | |

## Retail Targeting Uplift Model Example

There, the response rate of the highest decile (the top ten percent as defined by the model score) is 281 times that of the bottom decile—a huge relative lift. The third column shows the lift of each decile over the base response rate of 8.2%, so the top three deciles are seen to have greater than average propensity to buy.

It is natural, at first, to use the predictive model directly, and want to promote the product to those predicted to be most likely to buy. Doing this, they mailed the promotion to (that is, treated) randomly selected persons in the first four deciles. They became the test group; and the rest, the control group, received no mailings. The top table in figure below compares the response rates for the two groups, and we see that the treatment was not helpful.

| Model Score Decile | Test Group Response Rate | Control Group Response Rate | Incremental Response Rate |
|---|---|---|---|
| 1 | 26.99% | 27.90% | -0.91% |
| 2 | 20.34% | 20.90% | -0.56% |
| 3 | 10.70% | 10.04% | 0.66% |
| 4 | 8.90% | 7.52% | 1.38% |
| Deciles 1-4 | **16.73%** | **16.59%** | **0.14%** |

| Uplift Model Score Decile | Test Group Response Rate | Control Group Response Rate | Incremental Response Rate |
|---|---|---|---|
| 1 | 18.80% | 12.90% | 5.90% |
| 2 | 7.80% | 5.40% | 2.40% |
| 3 | 6.90% | 4.50% | 2.50% |
| 4 | 4.30% | 3.60% | 0.70% |
| Deciles 1-4 | **9.45%** | **6.60%** | **2.88%** |

Top table shows retail targeting model results using a predictive model. The bottom table shows the Uplift model results.

In some cases, the control group bought more often, and overall, the response rate in the test group was only 0.14% higher. This is undoubtedly because many of those whom the model predicted were likely to buy were "sure things" and were going to buy anyway. The promotion didn't effect any change worthy of its cost.

However, if we take the predictive model scores, and do the further work necessary to create an uplift model we can then rank prospects by their uplift score, and put each person in deciles by that score. Now, treating the top four uplift model deciles, as shown in the bottom table of figure, reveals an incremental response rate improvement of 2.88%. This return on marketing investment is 20 times better.

### Benefits of Uplift Analytics

Uplift analysis models the effect of treatment, rather than the outcome directly. If we know how likely something is already, and how likely we are going to be able to change it with a treatment, we can classify prospects as either "sure things", "persuadables", "lost causes", or "do not disturbs". This is extremely valuable as a way to get the most out of ones analytics investment.

## Win–Loss Analytics

Successful Win-Loss research programs are built around a well-tailored research tool that collects crucial information from decision makers and influencers who are involved in the sales decision process. The overall goal of the research is to determine what factors are used as decision criteria in selecting a company for a project. Win-Loss research not only provides a valuable source of competitive intelligence, it also sheds light on the internal working of a company's sales processes and cycles. Win-Loss research can:

- Improve individual and company-wide competitive win ratios.
- Establish clear benchmarks for understanding performance.
- Increase the number of successful sales per employee.
- Build a successful sales organization that is always improving.
- Discover the reasons behind lost opportunities.
- Increase your competitive advantage.
- Enhance your understanding of competitors.

Unlike pricing research, Win-Loss research goes further, delving into the decision process of clients, client service issues, and the effective handling of proposals. The end result is a tool that can provide actionable information on competitors and a specific market.

## Methodology

Many clients ask which methodology is more appropriate: qualitative (in the form of in-depth interviews) or quantitative? A qualitative approach is best for the client who is just beginning the Win-Loss research process. The qualitative methodology allows for more investigation into what factors are actually at play in the sales selection process.

The quantitative approach is then employed once the dynamics of the market and sales process are understood and can be classified into standard metrics used over time.

In terms of quantitative data collection, much of this research is conducted via the telephone. In most cases this means sales representatives calling the client or prospect and enquiring as to why the company did (or did not) win the business. Many companies see this as a cost-effective way to learn more about the sales process and sales cycle. While telephone interviewing is a valid data collection methodology, having sales representatives making the calls is fraught with peril.

The second data collection methodology is face-to-face interviewing. For many companies with Win-Loss research programs in place, this is the preferred method because of the ability to interact with the client, read their body language, and probe for more in-depth responses to questions. Face-to-face interviewing is often used in sales situations where the product or service is expensive and/or complicated and technical.

Finally, online interviewing is also a well-recognized data collection methodology. It provides a timely and cost-effective means of collecting a large number of interviews. And, while a company may be limited in its ability to fully probe on open-ended questions, online interviewing works very well when the audience is technical.

## Critical Factors

Regardless of the data collection methodology chosen, creating the right survey instrument is critical. After all, if the right questions are not asked, in the right way, the data may be skewed or simply not informative or actionable.

The interview should last no more than 30 minutes in person, and no more than 15 minutes on the telephone or online. It is unreasonable to assume today's professionals can devote more than 30 minutes to a survey. Some key areas to focus on:

The buying process—evaluation and selection criteria:

- Decision drivers.
- Multiple influencers and decision chain.
- Product/Service features and functionality.

- External influences on the decision process.
- Branding/Marketing issues.
- Commercial issues—pricing, contracts, etc.

Many companies that conduct Win-Loss research fall into the trap of using their employees to perform the research. Clients and prospects, however, are unlikely to be candid with the sales representative they've been dealing with for some time and who have failed to meet their expectations. It is also unlikely that the sales representatives will be candid in passing along information that may highlight their weaknesses or be viewed in an unfavorable light.

Many clients have found it virtually impossible to get unbiased, factual information without the help of an outside agency. Many clients have reported that in-house researchers have found buyers unwilling to reveal their real decision criteria for fear of offending the sales representative, or having the representative re-engage them in the sales process. In short, data collected in this manner may not be accurate, thus compromising the decision-making process on critical issues.

Conducting this type of research and analysis in-house can lead to a series of problems. A comparison of in-house versus third-party research reveals the following differences:

| Category | Third Party | In-House |
|---|---|---|
| Performing Win-Loss Research | Experts in data collection and analysis of Win-Loss data | Tend to think of the research as just conducting a series of interviews |
| Resources | Trained, experienced, and dedicated staff working on the project | Will do the research projects when time and resources permit |
| Methodology | Various methodologies available—specific to the target audience and market | Often limited to telephone interviewing only |
| Data Analysis | Experienced analysts use statistical software and techniques to analyze data | Data is often analyzed in Excel and only in topline form |
| Report Creation | Ability to publish first class reports designed to meet the clients' specific needs | Reports are often topline only, with little depth or reporting in subgroups |
| Presentation of Results | Senior researchers analyze data and prepare an executive summary | Data is often presented to executives in raw form |
| Success of Research | Very high—most customers repeat and expand their projects based on having received actionable and relevant information | Often moderate or low—the project tends to cost more in time and resources than expected and is deemed not worth the cost |

## Reporting

Win-Loss research reports are usually composed of two types: Individual Performance Reports and Macro Trend Reports.

The Individual Performance Report (IPR) is designed to provide in-depth information on a particular sales opportunity. This report provides insight into how well the sales organization performed on a specific proposal opportunity; in particular, how well they understood the needs of the client and how well the product or service was received by the client/prospect.

This report also provides information on how well the competition performed in the sales process, how it positioned itself in the sales opportunity, and what the prospect saw as its strengths or weaknesses. Ultimately the IPR provides insight into why each prospect is selected in a specific sales opportunity.

The Macro Trend Report (MTR) is designed to present data on a quarterly basis and provides an overview of all the sales opportunities in a specific quarter. Its primary focus is on the business trends appearing in your market, which include:

- The perceived positioning and pricing of the competition.
- Emerging competitors in the market.
- Strengths and weaknesses of your product or service offerings.

## Advanced Analytics

Sample sizes in Win-Loss research often vary widely according to the price of the product or service (the higher the costs, the fewer "buyers" there normally are). Where there is enough samples, additional analysis can be conducted.

In addition to standard analytic procedures, Win-Loss research normally employs several multivariate analytical techniques to better understand the motivation and decision-making process of your clients.

Derived importance analysis is a statistical technique designed to understand the underlying factors that drive the decision process. For example, in most stated importance questions price normally rises to the surface as one of if not the most important factor in the selection criteria. Derived importance analysis digs deeper to understand what factors actually drive the decision-making process.

Factor analysis is another technique used to better understand how clients view the marketplace in regard to brand attributes and perceptions. This technique groups brands with their associated attributes and displays them in a graphic format known as a perceptual map.

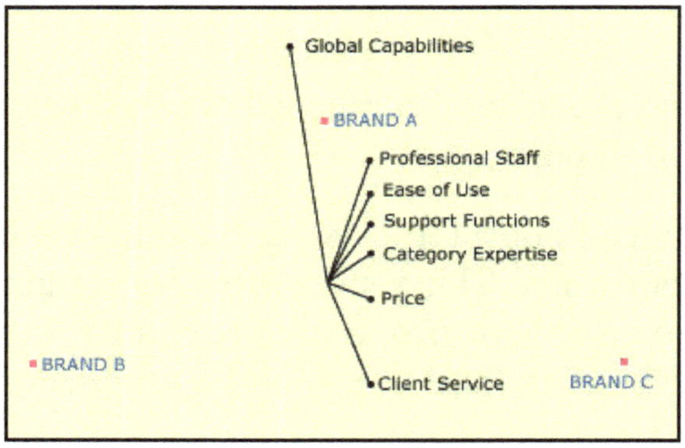


As the above example indicates, the map identifies the distinguishing characteristics of a brand and those of its competitors, and provides information on which factors are seen as "cost of entry" by the client. This analysis allows for better tailoring of proposals so that they highlight a client's strengths, while also exploiting the weaknesses of competitors.

In addition to these techniques, there is an entire suite of advanced analytical tools specifically designed to give in-depth information on the performance in the sales cycle and the performance of competitors. These additional techniques include: regression analysis, discriminant modeling, cluster analysis, and conjoint modeling.

In conclusion,A Win-Loss analysis will reveal the risks and opportunities associated with sales strategies, competitors' strategies, and target markets. A marketer can learn about the marketplace in a way that transcends simply knowing about one's customers.

A Win-Loss analysis will also reveal the varied buying habits, challenges, and adoption rates of customers' competitors' customers, and mutual prospects. Just remember some guidelines to follow:

Use professional researchers who are skilled in developing and implementing a comprehensive and unbiased research plan.

Select a good mix of win and loss situations to research—a mix that provides a representative sample of recent business activity. This is critical in order to ensure that you are gaining the most insight from the target markets/clients that matter most.

Develop a comprehensive research instrument that will serve as a framework for producing insightful, timely, and actionable information.

By obtaining reliable and unbiased feedback from recent sales opportunities, sales representatives can refine their techniques, learn how to effectively target a client's needs, and make appropriate presentations that put their companies and products in the best possible light. A Win-Loss research program provides empirical, yet pragmatic, information to drive business, products, and marketing decisions toward an improved competitive advantage.

## References


- Six-styles-of-customer-analytics, smarter with gartner: gartner.com, Retrieved 20 July 2020
- Understanding-business-performance-management: cornerstoneondemand.com, Retrieved 10 April 2020
- Business-performance-management-systems: yash.com, Retrieved 10 May 2020
- Customer-analytics-1456: techopedia.com, Retrieved 30 March 2020
- Uplift-modeling-making-predictive-models-actionable-8578: predictiveanalyticsworld.com, Retrieved 08 April 2020
- 5-essential-steps-to-mastering-customer-intelligence: qualtrics.com, Retrieved 13 July 2020
- What-is-customer-intelligence: visioncritical.com, Retrieved 20 March 2020

# Permissions

All chapters in this book are published with permission under the Creative Commons Attribution Share Alike License or equivalent. Every chapter published in this book has been scrutinized by our experts. Their significance has been extensively debated. The topics covered herein carry significant information for a comprehensive understanding. They may even be implemented as practical applications or may be referred to as a beginning point for further studies.

We would like to thank the editorial team for lending their expertise to make the book truly unique. They have played a crucial role in the development of this book. Without their invaluable contributions this book wouldn't have been possible. They have made vital efforts to compile up to date information on the varied aspects of this subject to make this book a valuable addition to the collection of many professionals and students.

This book was conceptualized with the vision of imparting up-to-date and integrated information in this field. To ensure the same, a matchless editorial board was set up. Every individual on the board went through rigorous rounds of assessment to prove their worth. After which they invested a large part of their time researching and compiling the most relevant data for our readers.

The editorial board has been involved in producing this book since its inception. They have spent rigorous hours researching and exploring the diverse topics which have resulted in the successful publishing of this book. They have passed on their knowledge of decades through this book. To expedite this challenging task, the publisher supported the team at every step. A small team of assistant editors was also appointed to further simplify the editing procedure and attain best results for the readers.

Apart from the editorial board, the designing team has also invested a significant amount of their time in understanding the subject and creating the most relevant covers. They scrutinized every image to scout for the most suitable representation of the subject and create an appropriate cover for the book.

The publishing team has been an ardent support to the editorial, designing and production team. Their endless efforts to recruit the best for this project, has resulted in the accomplishment of this book. They are a veteran in the field of academics and their pool of knowledge is as vast as their experience in printing. Their expertise and guidance has proved useful at every step. Their uncompromising quality standards have made this book an exceptional effort. Their encouragement from time to time has been an inspiration for everyone.

The publisher and the editorial board hope that this book will prove to be a valuable piece of knowledge for students, practitioners and scholars across the globe.

# Index